After Cloven Tongues of Fire

Also by David A. Hollinger

Morris R. Cohen and the Scientific Ideal (1975)

In the American Province (1985)

Postethnic America: Beyond Multiculturalism (1995, 2000, and 2006)

Science, Jews, and Secular Culture (1996)

Reappraising Oppenheimer (co-edited with Cathryn Carson, 2005)

Cosmopolitanism and Solidarity (2006)

The Humanities and the Dynamics of Inclusion since World War II (edited, 2006)

The American Intellectual Tradition (co-edited with Charles Capper, 6th edition, 2011)

After Cloven Tongues of Fire

PROTESTANT LIBERALISM IN MODERN
AMERICAN HISTORY

David A. Hollinger

PRINCETON UNIVERSITY PRESS

PRINCETON AND OXFORD

Library of Congress Cataloging-in-Publication Data

Hollinger, David A.
  After Cloven Tongues of Fire : Protestant Liberalism in Modern American History /
    David A. Hollinger.
    pages cm
  Includes index.
  ISBN 978-0-691-15842-6
1. United States—Church history—20th century. 2. Liberalism (Religion)—United States.
3. Liberalism (Religion)—Protestant churches. I. Title.
BR525.H63 2013
280´.40973–dc23

                    2012046644

British Library Cataloging-in-Publication Data is available

This book has been composed in New Baskerville Standard

Printed on acid-free paper. ∞

Printed in the United States of America

10 9 8 7 6 5 4 3 2 1

For Carol J. Clover

My Most Regular and Helpful Interlocutor on All Things Protestant

Contents

Preface

"MY FATHER REFERRED TO METHODISTS as Baptists who could read," wrote Norman Maclean. Any Methodist who heard Maclean's Presbyterian father say this might have responded with what Methodists often declare about Presbyterian condescension: Presbyterians are Methodists with money. Baptists, long skilled in the politics of competitive humility, often allow that they walk more humbly in the Lord than the more status conscious Methodists and Presbyterians.

Light-hearted but with an edge, such banter can remind us of differences in class and culture within the broad, multidenominational Protestant community of faith that until fairly recently enjoyed cultural hegemony in the United States. The extent of that community's influence is easily forgotten in an era when not one of the nine justices on the Supreme Court of the United States was born into a Protestant family, although one is an Episcopalian convert. This simple fact about the United States in the twenty-first century illustrates how much the ethnoreligious demography of the nation had changed in the previous five decades. Prior to 1960, if you were in charge of something big and had opportunities to influence the direction of the society, chances are you grew up in a white Protestant milieu. And most likely you were affiliated, at least nominally, with one of the "mainline" churches, of which Methodists, Congregationalists, Presbyterians, Episcopalians, Northern Baptists, and Disciples of Christ were prominent, along with several Lutheran and Reformed bodies and a smattering of smaller confessions.

The election of a Catholic President in 1960 and the rise during the same era of Jews—secular as well as religious—and of Catholics to cultural leadership changed American life, as did the massive immigration from the 1970s onward of many peoples from non-Protestant countries in Asia and Latin America. But at the time John F. Kennedy was elected, all branches of the federal government and most state and local governments were under the comfortable supervision of men and women who shared a religious ancestry. The same was true of the overwhelming majority of the leading universities, foundations, and cultural institutions. A handful of Jews and Catholics had served on the Supreme Court and elsewhere in national leadership; it is easy to list other exceptions to the rule famously enunciated by President Franklin D. Roosevelt in 1942 when he remarked, "You know this is a Protestant country, and the Catholics and Jews are here under sufferance." But this extraordinary hyperbole did point toward a truth of sorts, and that so magnanimous and diversity-accepting a leader as Roosevelt felt comfortable voicing it in the presence of the Jewish Henry Morgenthau and the Catholic Leo Crowley is a sign of how much the United States had to change before its Supreme Court could consist exclusively of six Catholics and three people of Jewish descent. I remind us of these social transformations not to celebrate them, and certainly not to lament them, but to alert us to some basic dynamics of American history that can be lost from view if we forget the cultural authority long exercised by men and women whose religious home was in one or another of the classic American Protestant denominations.

This book is about the struggles of Protestant liberalizers to achieve a satisfactory relation with the increasingly secular culture of the North Atlantic West and the increasingly diverse population of a nation endowed with a godless constitution that enabled religious pluralism. People like Maclean's father and his Montana neighbors described in *A River Runs Through It* were important to these struggles because the voluntary nature of American Protantism required its leaders to persuade the masses in the church pews of the soundness of what these leaders were doing at the peril of losing the community they were trying to lead. Hence the history of American Protestantism displays an especially vivid example of the tension between cosmopolitan elites and provincial masses: educated leaders try to move the faithful in directions apparently dictated by the shifting circumstances of history, while the constituency perceives global issues through local lenses and worries that the leadership is being seduced by a treacherous modernity being articulated in places like New York City and the capitals of Europe.

"Too worldly" was a common complaint against the cosmopolitan liberals of every American generation of Protestants, especially those who, from the late nineteenth century onward, developed the "social gospel" and sought to build equitable human communities expected to endure. It is this liberalizing dynamic that I flag with the phrase, "After Cloven Tongues of Fire." As I explain at greater length in chapter 2, which like the entire volume carries that title, the key word is "after."

If the spiritual solidarity of all humankind could be achieved in fleeting, ecstatic moments like the one recorded in the biblical story of Pentecost (Acts 2:1–11), when the faithful of diverse tribes heard each other testify "with cloven tongues of fire" as if each spoke in the other's language, what comes next? What does one do in the world, in the prosaic routines of daily life, to act on this vision of human community inspired by the Jesus of Nazareth? Not all Christians pushed that question. Some preferred to remain focused vertically, one might say, on the individual believer's relation to the Divine. But liberalizing Protestants, in their horizontal worldliness, often did push that question. Hence they became great organizers, institution builders, and social reformers, searching for ways to enact what they understood to be Christian ideals within worldly affiliations and through their instrumentality.

The studies collected in this volume also address quarrels and uncertainties about religious belief itself and its relation to secular inquiry, especially science. William James, who figures prominently in these pages, was not much interested in institutions and reform projects. But no birthright Protestant in all American history agonized more eloquently and with more notice than James did about the fate of religion in an epoch of rapid and commanding scientific advance. And no one had a sharper sense than he of the difference between charismatic, mystical experiences and the worldly business of deciding what ideas and practices were true and right.

The liberalizers invite our attention because they played a greater role in American history than is commonly recognized. What did they do?

The liberalizers enabled countless Americans born into deeply Protestant environments to entertain sympathetically a vast range of ideas and practices that they might not have otherwise felt so comfortable engaging. They were great bridge builders. The Protestantism these liberalizers developed, maintained, and critically revised from generation to generation served as a halfway house to post-Protestant secularism for many Americans, but for others it served as a viable, enduring spiritual home consistent with cultural modernity, and remains so to this day. Persons who are now preoccupied with the survival of Christianity are sometimes rueful that the United States is a less thoroughly Christian country than it was in Franklin Roosevelt's day, even though it remains by far the most Christianity-affirming society in the industrialized North Atlantic West. Some of these "Christian survivalists," as I like to call people who evaluate historical developments according to their having advanced or retarded what they take to be the interests of the Christian project, are pleased with the flourishing of the evangelical styles of religion and eager to see the Religious Right exercise more influence over public affairs. But other Christian survivalists lament the relative decline in recent decades of the mainline, ecumenical churches, and worry that this decline might have been prevented if the liberalizers had done some things differently. I will not try to resolve that debate about what might be in the best interests of Christianity, but I do want to insist that if the nation rather than the community of faith is one's referent point, the liberalizers have been anything but a passive, defeated element. They created a succession of institutional and intellectual middle grounds on which Americans of Protestant origin could stand while processing and deciding how to act upon a never-ending sequence of challenges to orthodoxy. What has come to be called liberalism in politics and in the debates over social and cultural issues owes what triumphs it has enjoyed to many forces in American life, one of which is the success of the Protestant liberalizers in pushing their constituents in those directions. In the long run the liberalizers did lose the institutional control of Protestantism they once had, but in return they furthered the causes in the national arena to which they were the most deeply committed.

Chapter 2 explicitly makes this argument with reference to the period since World War II. In that chapter I hold that the mainline, ecumenical churches powerfully advanced in the national arena a set of classically "progressive" causes to which they had become devoted by the 1960s, when amid multiple crises these churches lost many of their children to a post-Protestant secularism and yielded much of the symbolic capital of Christianity to their evangelical rivals, who then invested that capital in right-wing political initiatives. Chapter 3 sets forth the World War II context for the events analyzed in chapter 2, while chapter 1 sketches the larger, world-historical drama of the accommodation of Protestant Christianity and the Enlightenment as it was played out on the highly conspicuous American site over several centuries. Chapters 4, 5, and 6 address the secular-religious divide as negotiated by William James and his science-engaged contemporaries of the late nineteenth and early twentieth centuries, reminding us that James's scientific loyalties made it exceedingly difficult for him to affirm anything religious even while he repeatedly presented himself as a champion of the Protestant beliefs of his neighbors and then bequeathed a secular legacy that was composed in a decidedly Protestant key. Chapter 7 explores issues in American Jewish history that run parallel in some respects to the issues in Protestant history that define this volume, and calls attention to the subversive effect on Protestant hegemony exercised by the activities of a substantial population of well-educated and economically prosperous non-Christians. Chapter 8 describes the personal setting in which I came to write about these topics. Chapter 9 tries to bring clarity to the often frustrating debates over the role of religion in higher education, and defends a balance between critical distance and empathic appreciation. Chapter 10 urges a more robust, public debate in our own time about the religious ideas that political figures invoke but rarely are called upon to defend. An epilogue uses the particular case of Reinhold Niebuhr to explore some of the complexities of what we call, for lack of a better term, "secularization."

Like other writers on these topics, I use a number of labels that make sense in context, but perhaps invite clarification here. The term "evangelical" had been used by most Protestant denominations to refer to themselves from the early nineteenth century onward, following the expansion of church membership during what we call "the Second Great Awakening." But with the founding in 1942 of the National Association of Evangelicals (NAE), this term came to be more narrowly associated with all of the groups who opposed the Federal Council of Churches (the FCC, which after 1950 became the National Council of Churches, or NCC), a decidedly ecumenical—in the classic sense of trying to unite many confessions in common enterprises and to minimize their particularity—organization that the liberalizers had established in 1908. The prime movers in the new NAE were fundamentalist veterans of the storied fundamentalist-modernist conflicts of the 1920s, but by the 1940s these scripture-centered activists were joined by a variety of Pentecostal and holiness groups that were not as text-oriented as the fundamentalists, and that had not been centrally involved in the quarrels of the 1920s. What united this new, highly organized evangelical alliance was what its leaders saw as an orthodox alternative to the liberalizers who had effective control of all of the major, standard denominations and the principle cross-denominational organizations. "Liberal" was a term increasingly often applied to these then-triumphant leaders of the churches that were often called "mainline" because of the social power they had achieved. The term "modernist" lost the currency it had during the 1920s and 1930s, when it had flagged the strongly pro-science perspective that the liberalizers of that era defended against the anti-evolution, anti–Higher Criticism parties that were known as "fundamentalist." But "ecumenical" has emerged as the least confusing term to identify the liberal side in the division that has rent American Protestantism from the 1940s through the early twenty-first century. The liberalizing Protestants of that era put more and more energy into transdenominational projects and shifted the emphasis of their foreign missions from conversion to social service, welcoming syncretistic religions into the Body of Christ. Their emblematic enterprise was the World Council of Churches (WCC), the founding of which in 1948 was largely a result of their labors. The ecumenical leadership accepted into the pluralistic Protestant community of faith a greater variety of theologies and practices than the more orthodox evangelicals did, and endorsed a number of socially progressive causes that struck their NAE rivals as the substitution of social activism for true religion. "Ecumenical" and "evangelical" are more specific than "liberal" and "conservative," and more commodious than "modernist" and "fundamentalist," and thus work reasonably well to denote the post-1940s

After Cloven Tongues of Fire

CHAPTER 1

The Accommodation of Protestant Christianity with the Enlightenment: An Old Drama Still Being Enacted

Commissioned for a special issue of Daedalus *on "American Narratives," this essay outlines a theme in American history so grand that it has sometimes been forgotten while scholars diligently pursue narrowly defined research topics. A common complaint about historians of the late twentieth century was that in their professional caution they were reluctant to address "big ideas," even ideas that frame debates about the basic character of the nation and the principles that should guide its public affairs. The accommodation of Protestant Christianity with the Enlightenment is certainly one of the biggest and oldest of all such ideas and is one that, I remind us here, continues to structure the culture and politics of the nation even as visible in presidential campaigns well into the twenty-first century. Many historians have addressed this idea, including Henry F. May, whose influence on my thinking about the history of the United States I am glad to have here another opportunity to acknowledge.*

I identify two closely related dynamics that propelled and gave structure to the process of accommodation. A succession of scientific developments, including the Darwinian revolution in natural history and the archaeological and linguistic study of how the Bible came to be written, caused Protestant intellectuals to reformulate the inherited faith in terms better able to meet modern standards of cognitive plausibility. In the meantime, the demographic transformation of a society of largely British and Protestant stock into one that included many Catholics, Jews, and other non-Protestants from throughout Europe and beyond brought pressure upon inherited assumptions. Proximity to other orthodoxies raised doubts about one's own and produced a greater willingness to entertain new ideas consistent with the ostensibly global community of secular inquiry. I invoke the writings of philosopher Charles Peirce to illustrate how the dynamic of demographic diversification worked in tandem with the advancement of science to generate liberalized versions of Christianity.

Protestant liberalism is the central presence in this entire, sprawling drama. Sometimes neglected in our own era's preoccupation with the political prominence of culturally and theologically conservative evangelicals, Protestant lib-

eralism is in fact a huge reality in American history, and is indeed a creation of the accommodation with the Enlightenment. In the jagged, stuttering course of this accommodation, one generation after another of the most educated of Protestant intellectuals struggled not only to define and proclaim their religion but also to mobilize national, secular institutions as well as denominational fellowships in the service of that revised, ostensibly cosmopolitan faith. Along the way these liberals were routinely accused by their orthodox rivals of having become essentially secular. Hence they and their critics enacted yet again the classic contention within religious communities over what is "authentic" and what is a "corruption." Do the orthodox cling to doctrines that had been pasted onto the essential faith at a particular historical moment, and now mistake these anachronisms for the substance rather than surface of the faith? Do the liberals chase after the worldly fashions of the moment, untrue to the still-valid faith of the fathers? Such charges and countercharges are the standard stuff of Christian history and also of the history of the United States, the population of which remains today the most Christianity-affirming of any national population in the North Atlantic West.

This essay invokes as a truism the idea that Christianity itself was a prominent influence upon the Enlightenment as the latter developed in the seventeenth and eighteenth centuries. I now wish I had underscored the point more vividly, which I hereby do. Some readers, properly concerned that the Enlightenment is sometimes treated as autochthonous rather than a historic product of many classical and Christian discourses, worry that secular scholars rush too quickly past the religious matrices out of which Locke, Gibbon, Franklin and other Enlightenment thinkers developed their ideas.

This essay was originally published in Daedalus *CXLI (Winter 2012), 76–88. Its last few pages overlap with the essay that follows it in the pages of this volume, focusing on the period since World War II.*

IN HIS "LETTER FROM BIRMINGHAM JAIL," Martin Luther King Jr. invoked the Pilgrims landing at Plymouth Rock and Jefferson writing the Declaration of Independence. In that 1963 meditation on American national destiny, fashioned as a weapon in the black struggle for civil rights, King repeatedly mobilized the sanctions of both Protestant Christianity and the Enlightenment.[1] Like the great majority of Americans of his and every generation, King believed that these two massive inventories of ideals and practices work together well enough. But not everyone who has shared this basic conviction understands the relation between the two in quite the same terms. And there are others who have depicted the relation as one of deep tension, even hostility. Protestant Christianity, the Enlightenment, and a host of claims and counterclaims about how the two interact with one another are deeply constitutive of American history. We often speak about "the religious" and "the secular," or about "the heart" and "the head," but American life as actually lived beneath these abstractions has been much more particular and demands scrutiny in its historical density.

The United States, whatever else it may have been in its entire history as a subject of narration, has been a major site for the engagement of Protestant Christianity with the Enlightenment. This engagement was—and continues to be—a world-historical event, or at least one of the defining experiences of the North Atlantic West and its global cultural extensions from the eighteenth century to the present. Still, the United States has been a uniquely conspicuous arena for this engagement in part because of the sheer demographic preponderance of Protestants, especially dissenting Protestants from Great Britain, during the formative years of the society and long thereafter. Relatively recent social transformations can easily blind contemporaries to how overwhelmingly Northern European Protestant in origin the educated and empowered classes of the United States have traditionally been. The upward mobility of Catholic and Jewish populations since World War II and the massive immigration following the Hart-Cellar Act of 1965—producing millions of non-Protestant Americans from Asia, Latin America, and the former Soviet lands—have given the leadership of American society a novel look. To be sure, there have long been large numbers of non-Protestants in the population at large, but before 1960, if you held a major leadership position and had real opportunities to influence the direction of society, you most likely grew up in a white Protestant milieu. The example of King is a reminder, moreover, that the substantial population of African Americans has long been, and remains, largely Protestant.

In the United States, the engagement of Protestant Christianity with the Enlightenment most often took the form of "accommodation." The bulk of the men and women in control of American institutions—educational, political, and social—have sought to retain the cultural capital of the Reformation while diversifying their investments in a variety of opportunities and challenges, many of which came to them under the sign of the Enlightenment. The legacy of the Enlightenment in much of Europe, by contrast, played out in the rejection of, or indifference to, the Christianity to which the Enlightenment was largely a dialectical response, even while state churches remained fixtures of the established order. In the United States, too, there were people who rejected Protestant Christianity. But here the legacy of the Enlightenment most often appeared in the liberalization of doctrine and biblical interpretation and in the denominational system's functioning as an expanse of voluntary associations providing vital solidarities midway between the nation, on the one hand, and the family and local community, on the other.

The sharper church-state separation in the United States liberated religiously defined affiliations to serve as intermediate solidarities, a role such affiliations could less easily perform in settings where religious authority was associated with state power. Hence in addition to orthodox, evangelical Protestants who have been more suspicious of the critical spirit of the Enlightenment, American life has included a formidable population of "liberal" or "ecumenical" Protestants building and maintaining religiously defined communities even as they absorbed and participated in many aspects of modern civilization that more conservative Protestants held at a distance. As late as the mid-1960s, membership in the classic "mainstream liberal" denominations—Methodist, Presbyterian, Episcopalian, and so on—reached an all-time high. Because educated, middle-class Americans maintained Protestant affiliations well into the twentieth century, the Enlightenment was extensively engaged within, rather than merely beyond, the churches. Had the educated middle class moved further from Protestantism, the cultural capital of the Reformation would not have been preserved and renewed to the degree that made it an object of struggle for so long.

The intensity of the Enlightenment-Protestant relationship in America resulted also from the discomforts created by the very church-state separation that encouraged the flourishing of religious affiliations. The United States is the only major nation in the world that still operates under an eighteenth-century constitution, one that, anomalously in the governance cultures of even that century, makes no mention of God. The U.S. federal government is a peculiarly Enlightenment-grounded entity, and for that reason has inspired many attempts to inject Christianity into it, or to insist that God has been there, unacknowledged, all along.[2]

The role of liberal religion in American history is too often missed by observers who consider the consequences of the Enlightenment only outside religion and recognize religion only when found in its most obscurantist forms.[3] The fundamentalists who rejected evolution and the historical study of the Bible and have lobbied for God to be written into the Constitution receive extensive attention in our textbooks, but the banner of Protestant Christianity has also been flown by defenders of Darwin and the Higher Criticism and by critics of the idea of a "Christian America." Quarrels within American Protestantism revolve around the feeling among more orthodox, evangelical parties that mainstream liberals are actually secularists in disguise, as well as the feeling among ecumenical parties that their evangelical co-religionists are sinking the true Christian faith with an albatross of anachronistic dogmas and alliances forged with reactionary political forces. These quarrels, shaped in part by the campaign for a "reasonable Christianity" waged by Unitarians early in the nineteenth century, continue to the present day, sharply distinguishing the United States from the historically Protestant countries of Europe. The Netherlands, the United Kingdom, and the Scandinavian nations have long been among the most de-Christianized in the world. The United States really is different. Accordingly, the copious literature on "secularization" often treats the United States as a special case.[4]

Never was the United States a more special case than it is today. Indeed, contemporary American conditions invite renewed attention to the historic accommodation of Protestant Christianity with the Enlightenment. An increasingly prominent feature of public life is the affirmation of religion in general and of Protestant Christianity in particular. Republican candidates for office especially have been loquacious in expressing their faith and firm in declaring its relevance to secular governance. Michele Bachmann, Mike Huckabee, Sarah Palin, Richard Perry, Mitt Romney, and Rick Santorum are among the most visible examples.[5] Leaders of the Democratic Party, too, including President Barack Obama, have proclaimed their faith and have contributed to an atmosphere in which the constitutional principle of church-state separation is widely held to have been interpreted too strictly.

The Enlightenment-derived arguments of John Rawls and Jürgen Habermas, which maintain that debates over public policy should be confined to the sphere of "public reason," are routinely criticized as naïve and doctrinaire. We are awash with confident denunciations of "the secularization thesis" (usually construed as the claim that the world becomes less religious as it becomes industrialized) and with earnest pleas to listen empathically to the testimonies—heavily Protestant in orientation—of religious yearning and experience now prevalent in popular culture. The writings of the "new atheists" revive the rationalist-naturalist critiques of religion that had largely gone into remission during the decades when religion was widely understood to have been privatized and hence less in need of refutation by skeptics. Affirmations of a secular orientation less strident than those of the new atheists provoke extensive attention, moreover, because debates about the nation and its future are so much more religion-saturated that at any time since the 1950s. In a country that has now elected a president from a member of a notoriously stigmatized ethnoracial group, atheism remains more anathema than blackness: almost half of all voters are still comfortable telling pollsters that they would never support an atheist for president. Observers disagree whether American piety has religious depth or is a largely symbolic structure controlled by worldly interests; either way, religious formations are indisputably part of the life of the United States today.[6]

In this contemporary setting, it is all the more important to understand how the accommodation of Protestant Christianity with the Enlightenment has taken place and how the dynamics of this accommodation continue to affect the public culture of the United States. Two processes have driven the accommodation, growing increasingly interconnected over time. One is "cognitive demystification," or the critical assessment of truth claims in light of scientific knowledge. In this classic dynamic of "science and religion" discourse, the specific content of religious belief is reformulated to take account of what geologists, biologists, physicists, astronomers, historians, and other naturalistically grounded communities persuade religious leaders is true about the world. Normally, the religious doctrines rejected in this process are said to have been inessential to begin with. They are cast aside as mere projections of historically particular aspects of past cultures, which can be replaced by formulations that reflect the true essentials of the faith and vindicate yet again the compatibility of faith with knowledge. Sometimes, however, cognitive demystification pushes people toward nonbelief.

The second process, "demographic diversification," involves intimate contact with people of different backgrounds who display contrasting opinions and assumptions and thereby stimulate doubt that the ways of one's own tribe are indeed authorized by divine authority and viable, if not imperative, for other tribes, too. The dynamic here is also classical: cosmopolitanism—a great Enlightenment ideal—challenging provincial faiths. Wider experiences, either through foreign travel or, more often, through contact with immigrants, change the context for deciding what is good and true. Living in proximity to people who do not take Protestant Christianity for granted could be unsettling. Here again, the standard response is to liberalize, to treat inherited doctrines as sufficiently flexible to enable one to abide by them while coexisting "pluralistically," or even cooperating, with people who do not accept those doctrines. Sometimes, however, awareness of the range of human possibilities results in abandoning the faith of the natal community altogether.

Philosopher Charles Peirce understood how easily the two processes can be linked. In "The Fixation of Belief," Peirce argued that all efforts to stabilize belief will ultimately fail unless you adopt beliefs that can withstand exposure to the world at large. When you encounter other people who hold very different opinions from your own, and who can present striking evidence to support those opinions, it is harder to be sure that you are right. Your own experience and that of those around you may yield a particular set of certainties, but if another group of people moves into the neighborhood and obliges you to confront their foreign experience and the truth claims apparently vindicated by that experience, your old certainties become less so. Can you keep the rest of the world away from your own tribe? Perhaps, but it is not easy. Peirce made this argument in 1877, while defending the superiority of science in the specific context of the Darwinian controversy. He understood science to entail the taking of all relevant evidence into account, wherever it came from, and truth to be what all the world's inquirers could agree on if all their testimonies could be assimilated. He perceived modernity as an experience of difference in which hiding out with one's own kind was not likely to work. In this way, he integrated the Enlightenment's cosmopolitanism with its critical spirit.[7]

Hence demographic diversification and cognitive demystification can have their own force, but also reinforce one another; and they can even overlap. When Westerners brought modern medicine into locales where it was new, indigenous belief systems were put under stress by the Westerners and their novel and often highly effective means of interpreting and treating disease. When the 1893 Chicago World Parliament of Religions made Americans aware of the sophistication of many non-Christian religions and of the ways in which myths assumed to be peculiarly Christian had ready analogues in other faiths, confidence in the uniqueness and supreme value of Christianity required a bit more energy to maintain.[8] When Jewish intellectuals in the middle decades of the twentieth century advanced secular perspectives in a variety of academic disciplines and other arenas of culture, a common Protestant culture was more difficult to sustain. Cognitive demystification can proceed within a tribe, but commerce with neighboring tribes can diminish the predictable resistance to it.

Cognitive demystification operated most aggressively in the nineteenth century, especially in relation to the Darwinian revolution in natural history. Virtually all Americans who gave any thought to the relation of science to religion prior to the Darwinian controversy believed that reason and revelation, rightly understood, reinforced one another. Bacon and Luther, it had often been said in the years just before Darwin, were twins in the advancement of modern life. In the context of this deeply entrenched understanding of the symbiotic nature of the Protestant Reformation and the Scientific Revolution, the religious implications of natural selection were debated in the United States with more intensity, and for a longer period of time, than in the other countries of the North Atlantic West. Although some discussants concluded, then or much later, that Darwinian science was fatal to Christianity, the overwhelming majority of American commentators were "reconcilers." The copious discourse of the late nineteenth century sought mainly to establish that science and religion were not in conflict after all, no matter what the freethinking philosophers of Europe asserted. Even Andrew Dickson White, author of the monumental 1896 work *A History of the Warfare of Science with Theology in Christendom*, insisted that the only warfare attendant upon the advance of science was caused by the mistaken efforts of theologians to go beyond their proper sphere. Christianity itself, allowed the stolid Episcopalian president of Cornell University, was just as sound as ever. The persistence of strong creationist constituencies right down to the present shows that the greatest single instance of cognitive demystification remains contested in the United States. At the other extreme, the fact that biologists are the most atheistic of all American groups today reminds us that the Darwinian revolution has helped lead many people outside the faith. But the larger truth is that accommodation with evolution rather than rejection of it or of Christianity has been the rule for Americans who are born into Protestant communities.[9]

Many other examples of the process of accommodation in the face of cognitive demystification could be cited, including the adjustments compelled by the historical study of the Bible. But because this process and its prominent examples are well known, I will simply flag it with this supremely important instance and move on to the less-extensively discussed second process, demographic diversification, which emerged most strikingly in the twentieth century.

Demographic diversification began with some highly pertinent agents of change functioning at a geographical distance. The sympathetic study of foreign cultures by anthropologists promoted the "cultural relativism" associated above all with Margaret Mead and Ruth Benedict. This movement explicitly and relentlessly questioned the certainties of the home culture by juxtaposing them with often romanticized images of distant communities of humans.[10] Another factor was the gradual effect American Protestant missionaries had on the communities that had sent them abroad. Returning home with positive readings of foreign peoples and with jarring suggestions for changes in American churches and the surrounding society, missionaries and their children, exemplified by the writer Pearl Buck, often were potent liberalizers. But the chief agent of change, which I focus on here, was immigration compounded by upward class mobility.

The prodigious increase of Catholic and Jewish immigration starting in the 1880s positioned Protestant Christianity even more firmly on the defensive. Certainly, Protestants well before the Civil War had felt sufficiently threatened by Catholic migration from Ireland, and to some extent from Germany, to discriminate systematically against Catholics and thereby keep "popish" corruptions from disrupting their religious confidence and their control of American institutions. Public schools in many parts of the country became more secular in order to neutralize the charge that these schools were de facto Protestant institutions (which to a large extent they had been, as Catholics correctly discerned).[11] But well into the twentieth century, two circumstances rendered the numerous Catholics more of a political problem for Anglo-Protestant hegemonists than a religious one for believers: the extensive system of Catholic schools kept the bulk of the Catholic population something of a thing apart in local communities, and the relatively weak class position of most Catholics until after World War II diminished the frequency with which their ideas circulated in the national media and academia. A few Protestants converted to Catholicism, but the vast majority of Protestants of all persuasions felt so superior to Catholics that the latter's opinions and practices rarely called their own into question. Demographic diversification was held at a certain distance.

Yet only temporarily. The situation changed rapidly in the early 1960s with the election of John F. Kennedy as president and the dramatic liberalization of Catholic doctrine by Pope John XXIII's Vatican II Council. These developments turned Catholics into more serious interlocutors. Catholics became sufficiently intimate neighbors to compel the sympathetic attention that helped "provincialize" American Protestantism, pushing Protestant leaders to renounce the proprietary relationship to the American nation that had so long been a foundation for their own authority. To be sure, the most theologically and politically conservative elements within Protestantism continued to espouse the idea that the United States was a Protestant nation. But in the view of the mainstream leadership, as voiced by *The Christian Century*, Kennedy's inauguration marked "the end of Protestantism as a national religion" and the fuller acceptance of the secularity of a nation grounded in the Enlightenment.[12]

In the meantime, the much smaller population of immigrant Jews and their descendants presented a sharper challenge to Protestant epistemic and social confidence. Enthusiastically immersed in public schools and seeking full participation in American institutions of virtually all sorts, the highly literate and upwardly mobile Jewish population of the post-1880 migration was concentrated in the nation's cultural capital, New York City. Jews were harder to dismiss as bearers of ideas and practices at odds with the Protestant heritage. Their witness was so compelling that it eventually forced the development of the concept of "the Judeo-Christian tradition." But long before that phrase caught on in the 1950s, Jewish intellectuals had begun to converse with John Dewey, Oliver Wendell Holmes Jr., Randolph Bourne, Hutchins Hapgood, and other products of American Protestant culture who were already stretching its boundaries in secular directions (in the context of many episodes of cognitive demystification) and were eager to explore the diversity Jews embodied.

Unlike the Catholic population, moreover, many Jews were resoundingly secular in their orientation and carried not an alien religion but rather the most radically Enlightenment-generated strains of European thought, including Marxist and Freudian understandings of religion itself. Secular Jews were also leaders in the exploration of modernist movements in the arts that contested the more rationalist elements in the legacy of the Enlightenment while offering precious little support to the Protestant orthodoxy against which the Enlightenment was so largely defined. As non-Christians, the Jewish intellectuals were more foreign than the Catholics, yet, paradoxically, their high degree of secularism created a common foundation with liberalizing Protestants, many of whom continued to see Catholics as superstitious dupes of a medieval establishment in Rome. Especially in literature, the arts, and social criticism, Jewish intellectuals joined ecumenical Protestants and ex-Protestants in national leadership during the middle decades of the twentieth century. Two antiprovincial revolts, one against the constraints of traditional Jewish life and another against the constraints of traditional American Protestant life, reinforced each other and accelerated the cosmopolitan aspirations of both.[13]

The role of Jewish Americans in the process of demographic diversification increased when the barriers against their inclusion in academia collapsed after World War II. The teaching and public discussion of philosophy, literature, history, sociology, and political science had remained an Anglo-Protestant reserve long after resistance to Jews had diminished in medicine, law, engineering, and natural science. The leading secular academic humanists and social scientists of the prewar generation, exemplified by lapsed Congregationalist John Dewey, had been of Protestant origin. The postwar change was rapid and extensive. By the end of the 1960s, the Carnegie Foundation reported that self-identifying Jews, while constituting only about 3 percent of the national population, accounted for 36 percent of sociologists, 22 percent of historians, and 20 percent of philosophers at the seventeen most prestigious universities. Later in the twentieth century, the increase of female and black faculty brought a different sort of demographic diversification, one that discredited sexist and racist traditions rather than religious biases. But there was also another difference: the addition of women and African Americans to the humanities and social sciences was often justified by the need for the special perspectives they could bring to scholarship and teaching. This was decidedly not the case with Jews. No one declared that there was a need for "a Jewish perspective." It was instead the epistemic universalism of the Enlightenment that defined intellectually the coming of Jews into American academia. Hence that episode stands as a peculiarly vivid case of the overlap between demographic diversification and cognitive de-mystification: the Jewish academics, like their counterparts in literature and the arts, were living examples of how life's deepest challenges could be addressed beyond the frame provided by Protestant Christianity.[14]

All these developments presented a striking challenge to Americans with institutionalized responsibility for the preservation and critical revision of Protestantism during the second half of the twentieth century. One of the most portentous phases of the entire multicentury accommodation of Protestant Christianity with the Enlightenment, broadly construed, was the crisis experienced by the old "Protestant Establishment" during and after the 1960s. The theologically and politically liberal leaders of the National Council of Churches and its most important denomina-tional affiliates (the United Methodists, the United Church of Christ, the Northern Presbyterians, the Northern Baptists, the Episcopalians, the Disciples of Christ, and several Lutheran bodies) were caught in the ferocious cross fire of national controversies over all the classic issues of the period, especially civil rights, Vietnam, empire, feminism, abor-tion, and sexual orientation. As ecumenical Protestant leaders tried to mobilize their constituencies on the leftward side of these issues, they were simultaneously attacked by evangelicals for selling out religion to social activism and abandoned by many of their own youth for moving too slowly. Membership in the historically mainstream denominations declined rapidly in the late 1960s and 1970s, while evangelicals, who maintained a strong public following, moved aggressively into national political leadership during the 1970s and 1980s.

This religious crisis revolved around a particular outlook the ecumen-ical leadership brought to the conflicts of that era. A cosmopolitan and rationalist perspective, it was inspired by the demographic diversifica-tion that liberal Protestants observed in their social environment and by the cognitive demystification of their cosmos that modern science had achieved. Self-consciously "modern," this viewpoint included an in-creasingly generous opinion of foreign peoples and their inherited reli-gions, a revulsion toward the persistence of antiblack racism in their own country, a recognition that the American nation was as much the possession of non-Protestants as of Protestants, a positive response to secular psychology and sociology, and a growing receptivity to theologies that rejected or downplayed the role of supernatural power. The accommodations the ecumenical Protestant leadership made with secular liberalism generated countermeasures from fundamentalist, Pentecostal, and holiness Protestants. These conservatives, deeply resenting the authority exercised by the mainstream liberals partly as a result of the latter's generally strong class position, established a formidable array of counterinstitutions. The National Association of Evangelicals was founded in 1942, Fuller Theological Seminary in 1947, and *Christianity Today* in 1956. In the 1960s, evangelicals were able to offer the public a credible, highly visible alternative to the style of Protestantism promoted by the National Council of Churches, the Union Theological Seminary, and *The Christian Century*. By 1965, when the liberal theologian Harvey Cox concluded his best-selling *The Secular City* with the injunction to stop talking about God and focus simply on "liberating the captives," evangelicals had provided religious cover for Protestants dubious about the captive-liberating, diversity-welcoming, supernaturalism-questioning projects of the ecumenists.[15]

In a fateful dialectic, enterprising, media-savvy evangelical leaders espoused a series of perspectives that remained popular with the white public during the turmoil of the 1960s and early 1970s, just as the ecumenical leadership more firmly renounced these views. The idea of a "Christian America" is a prominent example, though there were many more such cases. While the ecumenical leadership, deciding that its missionary project was culturally imperialist, diminished its size and turned from preaching to social services, evangelicals took up and pursued with a vengeance the traditional missionary function of preaching the gospel. When the ecumenical leadership finally backed away from the traditional assumption that the heterosexual, nuclear, patriarchal family is God's will, evangelical leaders seized the idea, called it "family values," and ran with it to great success. Evangelicals remained largely aloof from the civil rights movement—often declaring racism to be an individual sin rather than a civic evil to be diminished by state power—while ecumenical leaders widened the gap between themselves and their rank-and-file church members by strongly supporting the activities of Martin Luther King Jr. and numerous kindred initiatives, including the Freedom Summer operation launched in 1964 to register blacks to vote. The departure of civil rights issues from the agenda of American politics eliminated a barrier to the Religious Right's national credibility, facilitating their triumphs in the 1980s: evangelicals gained more power during the Reagan years by merely acquiescing to civil rights measures that many of them had opposed, treating them now as a *fait accompli*.

Ecumenists engaged in extensive, probing discussions of the antisuper-
naturalist writings of the most radical of their theologians. The buzz in
the seminaries, *Time* reported in 1965, was that "it is no longer possible
to think about or believe in a transcendent God who acts in human
history. . . . Christianity will have to survive, if at all, without him." Evangelicals stood fast for traditional understandings of the Bible and made
it clear that God really was in charge of things. These certainties played
well in the average church pew.[16]

The accommodating ecumenical Protestants, having absorbed much
of modernity, found their social base diminishing while Protestantism
was increasingly associated with people who had resisted these accommodations. Ecumenists' approval of contraception and a role for sex
other than reproduction had a marked effect on birth rate differentials
between the two Protestant parties: during the baby boom, Presbyterian
women had an average of 1.6 children, while evangelical women had an
average of 2.4, a birth rate considerably higher than even for Catholic
women during that era. Ecumenical leaders encouraged their youth to
explore the wider world of which evangelical leaders counseled their
own youth to be suspicious. They also accepted perspectives on women
and the family that reduced their capacity to reproduce themselves at
precisely the same time they took positions on empire, race, sex, abortion, and divinity that diminished their ability to recruit new members
from the Seventh Day Adventist and Church of the Nazarene, ranks that
in earlier generations provided many converts to the more respectable
Methodist and Episcopalian faiths. Evangelicals, by contrast, had more
children and kept them.

What happened to ecumenical Protestantism during the 1960s crisis and
its aftermath can be instructively compared to what happened simultaneously to the Democratic Party in national politics. "We have lost the South
for a generation," President Lyndon Johnson is widely quoted as having said in 1964 when the Democratic Party aligned itself with the cause
of civil rights for African Americans. The manner in which ecumenists
risked their hold on American Protestantism is similar to the way the
Democratic leadership imperiled its hold on the South, and with similar
consequences. At issue in the control of American Protestantism was not
only race—the crucial issue for the Democrats—but also imperialism,
feminism, abortion, and sexuality, in addition to critical perspectives on
supernaturalism. Ecumenical leaders were not as aware as the president
was of the risks they were taking, nor were they as blunt in the moments
when the truth dawned on them. But they, like Johnson, believed that
the time had come to redirect the institutions and populations they were
trying to lead, and they behaved accordingly. They encouraged secu-

lar alliances that blurred the boundaries of their faith community and risked the gradual loss of their children to post-Protestant persuasions. Just as Democrats lost most of the South to the Republican party, so, too, did ecumenists yield more and more of the cultural capital of the Reformation to the evangelicals.

But Protestantism is not America. Neither is the South. The Democrats did well enough in the national arena by paying the price of turning the states of the Old Confederacy over to white Republicans. The ecumenists, even while they lost the leadership of Protestantism, advanced many of the goals of secular liberalism that they had embraced. The United States today, even with the prominence of politically conservative evangelical Protestants, looks much more like the country ecumenical leaders of the 1960s hoped it would become than the one their evangelical rivals sought to create. Sociologist N. J. Demerath III has put this point hyperbolically: the ecumenical Protestants scored a "cultural victory" while experiencing "organizational defeat." They campaigned for "individualism, freedom, pluralism, tolerance, democracy, and intellectual inquiry," Demerath observes—exactly the Enlightenment values that gained rather than lost ground in American public culture in the second half of the twentieth century.[17] These values were not peculiar to ecumenical Protestants, but their emphatic espousal demonstrated an accommodation with secular liberalism, especially as instantiated in specific causes such as civil rights, feminism, and the critical reassessment of inherited religious doctrine.

To treat the ecumenical Protestant saga of the last half-century as a culmination of the accommodation of Protestant Christianity with the Enlightenment, as I do here, invites several qualifications. It will not do to suppose that the evangelical Protestants, who in my telling of the story are primarily resisters to modernity, experienced neither transformations within their own ranks nor internal diversification. An excellent guide to disagreements within American evangelical Protestantism is historian Mark Noll's well-titled *The Scandal of the Evangelical Mind*, which characterizes the fundamentalist movement of the twentieth century as "an intellectual disaster." But I believe it is fair to say that many of the loudest voices in the evangelical conversation today, exemplified by Nancy Pearcey's *Total Truth: Liberating Christianity from Its Cultural Captivity*, make Noll look like no less impassioned a defender of the Enlightenment than Harvey Cox. It is all a matter of degree and emphasis.[18]

Neither will it do to imagine that every novelty prompted by cognitive demystification and demographic diversification amounts to a triumph of the Enlightenment narrowly construed as a set of naturalistic and rationalist dispositions. The Enlightenment as a presence in modern history certainly was just that; indeed, much of its legacy can be traced to the power of those dispositions to explain human experience and diminish suspicion of the alternatives to Protestant orthodoxy confronted in the process of demographic diversification. But the Enlightenment provided more than an outlook to accommodate increasing diversity. It functioned as an almost infinite series of stepping-stones to many ideas and practices that eighteenth-century intellectuals never contemplated. The world that American Protestants and their progeny eventually made their own, in cooperation with Americans who had no Protestant past whatsoever, is a vast expanse encompassing dispersed elements of culture from throughout the globe. The Enlightenment was destined to be a great provider of stepping-stones for European-derived American Protestants because the Enlightenment was largely a product of European Christian self-scrutiny in the first place.

Finally, we are left with the mystery of where a given historical formation such as "ecumenical Protestantism"—or even "the Enlightenment" itself—is best considered an agent and where it is best considered a vehicle. The heavily Christian foundations of modern science and of the Enlightenment are now widely acknowledged. And the Christianity of Paul the Apostle was itself as much a collection of historical results as of causes. It is easy to say that Protestants who most fully accommodate secular liberalism have turned their institutions into vehicles for agencies outside Christianity, but the trajectories that flowed into ecumenical Protestantism and helped make it what it became were not, in themselves, autochthonous: those forces were complex results of earlier conditions, like strong winds that had picked up many diverse materials from the various territories through which they had blown.

The accommodation of Protestant Christianity with the Enlightenment will find a place among American narratives so long as there are Americans whose formation was significantly Protestant and who owe a large part of their understanding of human reason to the seventeenth- and eighteenth-century savants who inspired Benjamin Franklin and Thomas Jefferson. If you think that time is passing, look around you.

Notes

1. Martin Luther King Jr., "Letter from Birmingham Jail," *The Christian Century*, June 12, 1963, 769–775.

2. There were strong movements to this effect in the middle of the nineteenth century, and they continued episodically in the twentieth. In 1947 and again in 1954, the National Association of Evangelicals attempted to amend the Constitution to include the following passage, introduced into the U.S. Senate

(where it died in committee) by Vermont Republican Senator Ralph Flanders: "This nation devoutly recognizes the authority and law of Jesus Christ, Savior and Ruler of nations, through whom we are bestowed the blessings of Almighty God"; see "The Congress: Hunting Time," *Time*, May 24, 1954, 23.

3. The heavily religious character of the Enlightenment as it flourished even in late-eighteenth- and early-nineteenth-century America is emphasized in what remains after more than three decades the standard account of its topic, Henry F. May, *The Enlightenment in America* (New York: Oxford University Press, 1976). The range and vitality of liberal theological endeavors throughout the nineteenth and twentieth centuries have been documented and analyzed in the massive work of Gary Dorrien, *The Making of American Liberal Theology*, 3 vols. (Louisville, KY: Westminster John Knox Press, 2006).

4. Prominent examples from recent years include Steve Bruce, *God Is Dead: Secularization in the West* (Malden, MA: Blackwell Publishers, 2002); Pippa Norris and Ronald Englehart, eds., *Sacred and Secular: Religion and Politics Worldwide* (New York: Cambridge University Press, 2004); David Scott and Charles Hirschkind, eds., *Powers of the Secular Modern: Talal Asad and His Interlocutors* (Stanford, CA: Stanford University Press, 2006); and Callum G. Brown and Michael Snape, eds., *Secularisation in the Christian World: Essays in Honour of Hugh McLeod* (Surrey, UK: Ashgate, 2010).

5. For an unusually probing exploration of this feature of American politics, see Ryan Lizza, "Leap of Faith," *The New Yorker*, August 15 and 22, 2011, 54–63.

6. Three excellent collections of original academic essays exploring these current engagements are Craig Calhoun, Mark Juergensmeyer, and Jonathan Van Antwerpen, eds., *Rethinking Secularism* (New York: Oxford University Press, 2011); George Levine, ed., *The Joy of Secularism: 11 Essays for How We Live Now* (Princeton, NJ: Princeton University Press, 2011); and Ira Katznelson and Gareth Stedman Jones, eds., *Religion and the Political Imagination* (New York: Cambridge University Press, 2011). See also the most searching and comprehensive recent contribution to the sociology of religion in the United States, Robert Putnam and David Campbell, *American Grace: How Religion Divides and Unites Us* (New York: Simon & Schuster, 2010).

7. Charles Peirce, "The Fixation of Belief," *Popular Science Monthly* 12 (November 1877): 1–15.

8. An influential study of this pivotal episode in demographic diversification at a geographic distance is Grant Wacker, "A Plural World: The Protestant Awakening to World Religions," in *Between the Times: The Travail of the Protestant Establishment in America, 1900–1960*, ed. William Hutchison (New York: Cambridge University Press, 1989), 253–277.

9. Andrew Dickson White, *A History of the Warfare of Science with Theology in Christendom* (New York: D. Appleton, 1896). Among the many excellent studies of the religious aspects of the Darwinian controversy, two have been especially influential: James R. Moore, *The Post-Darwinian Controversies: A Study of the Protestant Struggle to Come to Terms with Darwin in Great Britain and America, 1870–1900* (New York: Cambridge University Press, 1979); and Jon H. Roberts, *Darwinism and the Divine in America: Protestant Intellectuals and Organic Evolution, 1859–1900* (Madison: University of Wisconsin Press, 1988). The standard work on the per-

sistence of creationist ideas is Ronald L. Numbers, *The Creationists: From Scientific Creationism to Intelligent Design* (Cambridge, MA: Harvard University Press, 2006). For the religious views of biologists, see Benjamin Beit-Hallahmi, "Atheists: A Psychological Profile," in *The Cambridge Companion to Atheism*, ed. Michael Martin (New York: Cambridge University Press, 2007), 312. Biologists challenging a literal reading of the Bible remain in difficulty even today in some Protestant colleges; see, for example, http://m.insidehighered.com/layout/set/popup/news/2011/08/15/a_professor_s_departure_raises_questions_about_freedom_of_scholarship_at_calvin_college.

10. A recent, exhaustive treatment of this movement is found in John S. Gilkeson, *Anthropologists and the Rediscovery of America, 1886–1965* (New York: Cambridge University Press, 2010).

11. Fresh light on the Protestant-Catholic relationship in the middle decades of the nineteenth century is cast by Jon Gjerde, *Catholicism and the Shaping of 19th Century America* (New York: Cambridge University Press, 2012).

12. Martin Marty, "Protestantism Enters Third Phase," *The Christian Century*, January 18, 1961, 72.

13. I have discussed the coming together of these two antiprovincial revolts in "Ethnic Diversity, Cosmopolitanism, and the Emergence of the American Liberal Intelligentsia," *American Quarterly* 27 (1975): 133–151. A recent and highly original contribution to the study of these developments is Daniel Greene, *The Jewish Origins of Cultural Pluralism: The Menorah Association and American Diversity* (Bloomington: Indiana University Press, 2011).

14. For an extended treatment with attendant documentation of the developments summarized in this paragraph, see David A. Hollinger, *Science, Jews, and Secular Culture: Studies in Mid-Twentieth Century American Intellectual History* (Princeton, NJ: Princeton University Press, 1996), esp. chap. 2, "Jewish Intellectuals and the De-Christianization of American Public Culture in the Twentieth Century."

15. Harvey Cox, *The Secular City: Secularization and Urbanization in Theological Perspective* (New York: Macmillan, 1965), 268.

16. "Theology: The God Is Dead Movement," *Time*, October 22, 1965. For a fuller account with attendant documentation of the developments mentioned in this paragraph and those following, see chapter 2 in this volume.

17. N. J. Demerath III, "Cultural Victory and Organizational Defeat in the Paradoxical Decline of Liberal Protestantism," *Journal for the Scientific Study of Religion* 34 (1995): 458–469, esp. 458–460.

18. Mark Noll, *The Scandal of the Evangelical Mind* (Grand Rapids, MI: W.B. Eerdmans, 1994); Nancy Pearcey, *Total Truth: Liberating Christianity from Its Cultural Captivity* (Wheaton, IL: Crossway Books, 2004).

CHAPTER 2

After Cloven Tongues of Fire: Ecumenical Protestantism and the Modern American Encounter with Diversity

Why did the "mainline" Protestant churches experience a dramatic loss of numbers from the mid-1960s through the early twenty-first century, while the evangelical churches grew? This is only one of several questions I address in this essay, but it is the one that has generated the most interest. I want to summarize my answer to that question here as plainly as I can.

I argue that the evangelicals triumphed in the numbers game by continuing to espouse several ideas about race, gender, sexuality, nationality, and divinity that remained popular with the white public when these same ideas were abandoned by leaders of the mainline, ecumenical churches as no longer defensible. Some of the rank-and-file Methodists, Presbyterians, and Episcopalians who were uncomfortable with the progressive character of ecumenical leadership migrated to the evangelical churches. But this church-switching, much heralded in the popular press, has been shown by social science research to be a relatively small factor. Much more important was a demographic change driven by this shift in ecumenical attitudes. The ecumenists supported an expanded role for women, approved a role for sex other than procreation, and encouraged the use of contraceptives. These steps away from tradition resulted in a substantial loss of reproductive power relative to evangelicals, whose leadership was much slower to move in these directions. Evangelical women birthed many more children than did ecumenical women. Demographic changes are sometimes cited as if they were autonomous forces in history, but they rarely are, and certainly were not in this case. Differential birth rates do not develop in cultural vacuums.

The progressive stances the ecumenical churches took on social and political issues had another crucial consequence. These stances made it more difficult to recruit members from what had traditionally been a huge foundation for their own growth: the more conservative, evangelical communities. In earlier times, upwardly mobile members of the Seventh Day Adventists, Church of the Nazarene, and other evangelical denominations swelled the "mainline" churches by "moving up" to them. The more the ecumenical leadership stretched to meet the conditions of a diverse society and to address its inequalities, the less attractive their churches were to those Americans, especially in the Protestant-intensive South and rural Midwest, who were glad for ways to remain Christian without accepting the social obligations imposed on the faithful by ecumenical leaders.

In the meantime, many of the children of the ecumenists, even if agreeing with the ecumenical leadership's abandonment of ideas increasingly seen as racist, sexist, imperialist, homophobic, unscientific, and excessively nationalistic, did not affiliate with their ancestral church or with any other church. Often these young people found secular vehicles for the liberal values they had learned from the elders. These elders had encouraged ecumenical youth to explore the diversity of a world they knew was not going to disappear, rather than to hide from it. Simultaneously, the evangelicals warned against the perils of a diverse modernity and preached "home truths." Thus evangelicals not only had a lot more children; they kept most of the ones they had. Thereby the evangelical communities produced the formidable cultural and social foundation for the Religious Right.

Yet the major question I address in this essay is much broader. What was the historical significance of ecumenical Protestantism for U.S. history since World War II? I argue that it facilitated an engagement with many aspects of a diverse modernity that millions of Americans would not have achieved without the support and guidance of the ecumenical churches. Much of the influence of Protestant liberalism is now visible outside the churches, and for that reason has often been missed by scholars who focus on church membership. It is hyperbolic to claim that the ecumenists won the United States while yielding much of the symbolic capital of Christianity to the evangelicals, but there is something to it. The vision for American society espoused by the ecumenical leaders of the early 1960s has been frustrated in many ways, but much of their antiracist, antisexist, antihomophobic, anti-imperialist, nationalism-suspecting, supernaturalism-resisting program has been accepted by vast segments of the American public. In the meantime, the goals that the evangelical leaders of the early 1960s advanced with the most conviction have been increasingly on the defensive outside the Republican party and have been replaced in the hearts of many younger evangelicals with pluralistic attitudes that owe much to the ecumenical tradition. The point is not that Protestant liberalism changed American life by itself—on the contrary, this essay explicitly acknowledges the power of other, parallel forces—but that for many Americans born into an ecumenical Protestant milieu, that milieu propelled them in liberal directions that have affected their lives as "post-Protestants," understood as people who have been shaped by a Protestantism that they no longer espouse.

A clear understanding of the place of Protestantism in modern American history has been impeded by "Christian survivalism," a term I coined to denote a commitment to the survival of Christianity amid the influences that appear to be diminishing it in the North Atlantic West. This essay laments that the study of American Protestantism since World War II has been heavily influenced by a Christian survivalist agenda, according to which the significance of this or that religious event is measured not according to its function in the society as a whole but rather by what role it plays in the strengthening or weakening of Christianity, however defined. From a Christian survivalist point of view, insofar as Protestant liberalism has become a halfway house to secularism, that is a mark against Prot-

estant liberalism. But I wrote this essay in a historicist spirit, resisting teleological judgment and treating religious solidarities as contingent entities that come and go, serving sometimes as vehicles as well as agents.

*I allude to Reinhold Niebuhr's refusal to meet with Billy Graham at the time of Graham's New York rally of 1957, but some of Niebuhr's defenders, including his daughter, Elisabeth Sifton, have cautioned me that this story may be apocryphal. Yet Graham himself reports it in his own autobiography (*Just as I Am *[New York, 1997], 301), and the most thorough student of the Graham-Niebuhr relationship accepts the story as true and even reports that Niebuhr refused "to grant an interview despite pressure from Union Seminary's board of trustees" (Andrew Finstuen, "The Prophet and the Evangelist: The Public 'Conversation' of Reinhold Niebuhr and Billy Graham,"* Books and Culture, *August/September 2006, 8–9, 37–42). As Finstuen and other scholars have established, however, Niebuhr was divided about how to deal with Graham, and his private correspondence with Graham's often angry supporters was considerably more generous about the great evangelist than he was in print.*

This essay was originally published in Journal of American History *XCVIII (June 2011), 21–48. For an example of the discussion it generated among today's leaders of ecumenical Protestantism, see Amy Frykholm, "Culture Changers: David Hollinger on What the Mainline Achieved,"* The Christian Century, *July 11, 2012, 26–28.*

THE LIFE OF HUMAN BEINGS TODAY "is cast in a multicultural context," wrote the great comparativist Wilfred Cantwell Smith in 1960. "Every community on earth is becoming a minority in a complexity of diverse groups," he continued. In this "age of minorities," no particular "we" can any longer credibly claim superiority to any "they." The most defensible solidarity is now "humanity itself," insisted Smith, who then identified Christians, capitalists, communists, and Muslims as prominent minorities slow to recognize their true status. It was especially important, he asserted, to get the truth across to white people and "Westerners" who "seem almost incapable of adjusting themselves to a new world" in which they, too, are minorities. For Smith, the recognition of the diversity of the human species and the diminution of inequalities within it were intimately bound up with one another.[1]

These ideas resonate well with the multicultural initiatives of the 1990s and even more resoundingly with the whites-are-a-minority exclamations of the 2000s. That these observations were offered with such urgency in 1960 in the pages of *The Christian Century* and by one of the period's most respected ecumenical Protestants can flag for us the role that ecumenical Protestants played in diminishing Anglo-Protestant prejudice and embracing the varieties of humankind. Recognizing this role can lead us, in turn, to an understanding of the dialectical process by which ecumenical Protestants lost their numbers and their influence in public affairs while evangelical Protestants increased theirs. Politically and theologically conservative evangelicals flourished while continuing to espouse popular ideas about the nation and the world that were criticized and abandoned by liberalizing, diversity-accepting ecumenists. Appreciating the significance of this Protestant dialectic, within which the two great rivals for control of the symbolic capital of Christianity defined themselves in terms of each other, can yield a more comprehensive and accurate account of the place in modern American history of the so-called Protestant Establishment.[2] We now have an extensive and increasingly helpful literature on evangelical Protestantism in the twentieth century, but studies of ecumenical Protestantism remain fewer in number, narrower in scope, and lower in professional visibility.

I refer to "ecumenical" Protestantism because this label has proven to be the least confusing way to distinguish the family of Protestants of which I speak from the fundamentalist, Pentecostal, holiness, and other conservative persuasions within American Protestantism that came to be described collectively as "evangelical," even though the latter term had earlier denoted a much greater range of Protestant orientations. This distinction between ecumenical and evangelical Protestants hardened during the 1940s and after as a result of the discomfort felt especially by fundamentalists with how far the "mainstream liberals" had pushed their program of cooperation across denominational lines and of alliances with non-Protestant, non-Christian, and eventually secular parties. Indeed, it was opposition to this program that most united the fundamentalists with other conservative Protestants, enabling all of them to form the commodious religious expanse known since the 1940s as "Evangelical Protestantism."[3] While the ecumenists increasingly defined themselves through a sympathetic exploration of wider worlds, the evangelicals consolidated "home truths" and sought to spread them throughout the globe.

The ecumenical Protestant encounter with diversity was built, in a fashion, on the ancient myth of Pentecost. Members of every tribe and nation addressed each other with "cloven tongues of fire," according to the second chapter of Acts, hearing each other as if all were speaking in the hearer's own language. "Parthians, and Medes, and Elamites, and the dwellers in Mesopotamia, and in Judaea, and Cappadocia, in Pontus, and Asia, Phrygia, and Pamphylia, in Egypt, and in the parts of Libya about Cyrene, and strangers of Rome, Jews and proselytes, Cretes and Arabians, we do hear them speak in our tongues the wonderful works of God," as the testimony is recorded in the Authorized (King James) Version of the Bible that was still widely used until the mid-twentieth century.[4] For the particular subset of evangelicals called Pentecostals, with whom this scripture is the most identified, what mattered was the spiritual intensity of the moment, the re-creation of the immediate experience of unity among the varieties of humankind. Fellowship across various divisions was to be achieved though a charismatic engagement with the gospel in which everyone could share. For ecumenists, however, the big issue was what happens next.

After the cloven tongues of fire have shown the possibility for a species-wide solidarity, how can that solidarity be institutionalized? Beyond mystical moments, how can one diminish social divisions in the long run, in the course of earthly life day after day? The ecumenists were more institution builders than revivalists, more devoted to creating and maintaining communities than to facilitating a close emotional relationship with the divine, and more frankly concerned with social welfare than with the state of the individual soul. Evangelicals could be institution builders, too, but the solidarities that the evangelicals sought to institutionalize were more particularistic. The ecumenical Protestants of twentieth-century America were preoccupied with mobilizing massive constituencies to address social evils. They wanted to reformulate the gospel of the New Testament in terms sufficiently broad to enable people of many cultures and social stations to appreciate its value, if not actually to embrace it. Among their favorite scriptural warrants was one from Paul the Apostle's letter to the Galatians: "Ye are all one in Christ Jesus," for in him "there is neither Jew nor Greek, there is neither bond nor free, there is neither male nor female." They sought to overcome the curse of Babel not in fleeting moments of ecstasy but in the prosaic routines of daily life.[5]

Surely, we are now tempted to protest, the doings of all those white Presbyterians, Baptists, Methodists, Congregationalists, Lutherans, and Episcopalians could not have mattered that much. In response to this intuition, it helps to remember that ecumenical Protestantism was anything but marginal to American life during the decades of the mid-twentieth century. The population of the United States remained, after all, overwhelmingly white and Protestant. Membership numbers in the major, classical denominations were at an all-time high. Persons at least nominally affiliated with these denominations controlled all branches of the federal government and most of the business world, as well as the nation's chief cultural and educational institutions, and countless state and local institutions. If you were in charge of something big before 1960, chances are you grew up in a white Protestant milieu. Until the 1970s, moreover, the public face of Protestantism itself remained that of the politically and theologically liberal ecumenists of the National Council of Churches (NCC) and its pre-1950 predecessor, the Federal Council of Churches (FCC). Only later did the more conservative Protestants of the National Association of Evangelicals (NAE)—an organization founded in 1942 in explicit opposition to the ecumenists—gain the public standing it enjoys today. The evangelicals gradually became the dominant public face of Protestantism, partly because these evangelicals continued for many decades to espouse a number of diversity-resisting perspectives that remained popular with the white public even as these perspectives were being renounced by self-interrogating ecumenist intellectuals such as Wilfred Cantwell Smith.

This mood of self-interrogation demands emphasis. One of the most neglected features of twentieth-century American history is the intensity and range of the self-critique carried out by the intellectual leadership of mainstream liberal Protestantism during the 1940s, 1950s, and 1960s. The critical revision of inherited traditions was no monopoly of such people, to be sure, but they made a great production of attacking the ethnocentrism and sectarianism they professed to find all around them, including in their own churches. While evangelical leaders were trying to foster collective pride and were protesting against the patronizing and dismissive remarks often made about evangelicals by elite religious and secular intellectuals, many ecumenical leaders were giving themselves hell. When historians treat the growth of evangelicalism in a religious vacuum—attending to social structural, political, and popular cultural conditions but neglecting the religious—they miss the historical process by which religious liberals abandoned a series of diversity-resisting ideas and practices that the liberals had concluded were mistaken, only to find these same ideas and practices serving as a vital foundation for the growth in the public standing of evangelicalism.

Among the most important of these popular diversity-resisting perspectives was the claim that Christians, especially Protestants, had a proprietary relationship to the American nation that could be easily exercised despite the constitutional separation of church and state. The notion of a "Christian America" remained popular in evangelical circles long after the ecumenical leadership put itself at risk by renouncing this crucial foundation for its own authority in public affairs. In 1947 and again in 1954 the National Association of Evangelicals actually mounted campaigns to amend the Constitution to include reference to Jesus of Nazareth and his God. "This nation devoutly recognizes the authority and law of Jesus Christ, Savior and Ruler of nations, through whom are bestowed the blessings of Almighty God," began the text of this proposed constitutional amendment as the Republican senator Ralph E. Flanders introduced it in the Senate, where it died in committee, partly because most ecumenical Protestant leaders refused to support it.[6]

The self-interrogative mood of the ecumenists in relation to the disputed notion of a "Christian America" was well documented by one of the editors of *The Christian Century* in 1961. Martin Marty asked that the inauguration of the Catholic John F. Kennedy as president be treated as "the end of Protestantism as a national religion and its advent as the distinctive faith of a creative minority." The acceptance of Catholics as full partners in the nation was in itself a striking step. The Protestant establishment had long been vocally, if not vehemently anti-Catholic. Indeed, the ecumenical movement was intensified in the 1940s and 1950s by fear that Protestant disunity and Catholic unity would lead to a Catholic takeover of the country. This suspicion was rendered credible by the slowness of the Catholic hierarchy to accept the wisdom of the pluralistic attitude toward religion that the ecumenists and their Jewish allies espoused and that was later put in place by Vatican II and by the great American Jesuit politician and theorist John Courtney Murray. At issue for Marty in 1961 was not only the long-awaited acceptance of Catholics into full and equal partnership as Americans. He also explicitly recognized "Jewish and secular" voices as genuinely constituent parts of the diversity of American life.[7] The notion of a Protestant nation was being renounced, and so too was the notion of a Christian nation, and even of a religious nation.

Marty's outlook was far from that of evangelicals at the time. This point requires underscoring because in later decades evangelicals joined forces ecumenically with many Catholic and Jewish organizations in opposition to abortion, in support of Israel, and in other common causes. In the context of this recent history, the positions taken by evangelical leaders in the 1950s and 1960s are easily lost from view. Even after Kennedy had won over the bulk of the ecumenical leaders with his famous church-state separation speech before several hundred ministers in Houston in September 1960, the NAE expressed alarm that with the election of a Catholic, the United States "will no longer be recognized as a Protestant nation in the eyes of the world." The NAE did not formally endorse Richard M. Nixon's presidential candidacy, but there was no doubt where the organization stood. Its national office actually coordinated special election-targeted prayers in evangelical churches throughout the country to be offered on every Sunday prior to the November election. In the meantime one of the most popular Protestant clergymen in the country, the theologically liberal Norman Vincent Peale, registered his distance from the ecumenical leadership by refusing to join them in this crucial step away from the defense of Protestant nationhood and siding instead with evangelicals. For this Peale was vigorously attacked by the theologian Reinhold Niebuhr and other ecumenical leaders and was never forgiven by them.[8]

Disagreements between ecumenists and evangelicals about the place of Christianity in America paralleled disagreements about the relation of Christianity to human rights globally. While ecumenists were proud of having played a role in advancing a human rights agenda within the United Nations (UN) and had no trouble recognizing that the diversity of the UN's constituencies made predicating human rights on a narrowly Christian foundation inappropriate, evangelicals castigated the UN's Universal Declaration of Human Rights because, in the words of the *Christianity Today* editor Carl F. H. Henry in 1957, the declaration "incorporates no references to a supernatural Creator, nor does it anywhere assert that God endows mankind with specific rights" and "duties."[9]

Marty speculated that withdrawal from the traditional idea of a Christian nation and from a picture of the entire human species as virtually Protestant might enable Protestants to find in their new modesty a measure of self-respect based on a confident and accurate understanding of their situation in the world. Marty worried, however, that the "orgies of public scourging and self-examination" had taken "the Protestant principle of self-criticism" to "almost masochistic extremes."[10] These spasms of self-flagellation were far from over, and they constitute a portentous episode in the history of Protestantism in the United States.

Collective self-criticism soon accelerated, became more strident, and spread across a greater expanse of issues. Two books of 1964 illustrate the intensity and direction of this episode and the centrality to it of the challenge of recognizing and accepting diversity. One is William Stringfellow's *My People Is the Enemy: An Autobiographical Polemic.* Stringfellow was an Episcopal layman who had spent seven years living amid poverty in Harlem while serving as a lawyer to indigent black people. His book excoriated American churches for not responding more aggressively to the evils of racism and for not accepting black people more fully. "The churches of white society in America have largely forfeited any claim to leadership" in diminishing these evils, Stringfellow complained, while offering page after page of searing testimony of how a truly Christian approach, as he understood it, would engage a color-defined population still not incorporated as fully American. Stringfellow, a close associate of the radical Catholic activist Daniel Berrigan, was a vivid and controversial presence in the 1960s. He attracted the attention of the great German theologian Karl Barth, who declared that Stringfellow was one of the most engaging of the Americans Barth had met during a visit to the United States in 1962.[11]

The second book, *The Unpopular Missionary*, was written by Ralph E. Dodge, a senior Methodist missionary to Angola and Rhodesia. The book pushed with novel passion and urgency the long-standing complaint of liberal missionary theorists that missions had been too closely connected to colonialism and had tried to impose on indigenous peoples denominational distinctions that made no sense abroad. By failing to turn more control and resources over to the indigenous churches of Africa, India, and other mission fields, Dodge warned, American and European missionary projects were doomed to go the way of colonial governments: out for good, and for the same reasons. Those back home who continued to want the Baptist, Lutheran, and Methodist churches abroad to operate on the same traditional principles that applied in Pennsylvania and Indiana were projecting onto the larger, diverse world their own parochial sectarianism. The basic problem, Dodge explained, was that the missionary project was still too slow and tepid in accepting indigenous peoples as "*human beings*" and as "full brothers in Jesus Christ" on their own terms—not as copies of Christians in Memphis and Minneapolis. The church "must reject categorically all attitudes and practices of racial superiority."[12]

Stringfellow's exploration of domestic American racism and Dodge's commentary on missionary colonialism sharpened themes in ecumenical Protestant self-critique that were already well established by the early 1960s. Other voices pushed that self-critique in directions that were more novel, that distinguished the ecumenical discourse yet more starkly from evangelical discourse, and that embraced even more omnivorously the diversity of the world beyond white Protestantism. Two additional books of the same historical moment can represent these more radical voices that questioned even the foundations that were left unchallenged by Stringfellow and Dodge.

Honest to God was written in England by the Anglican bishop John A. T. Robinson but gained enormous notoriety in the United States from the moment of its publication in 1963. The book attacked as hopelessly anachronistic the ideas about God and Jesus that were common among Christians, mocking the supernaturalism that "suggests that Jesus was really God almighty walking about on earth, dressed up as a man . . . taking part in a charade." Although much of Robinson's message was already incorporated into the discourse of liberal seminaries as a result of the calls for "demythologized" and "religionless" Christianity made somewhat cryptically by the German theologians Rudolph Bultman and Dietrich Bonhoeffer, his breakaway best seller popularized as never before the strivings of a theological elite to update Christian teachings in relation to contemporary culture and modern notions of cognitive plausibility. For a prominent cleric to characterize as downright dishonest the sincere God talk to which the average churchgoer was accustomed served to expose as never before the gap between the people in the pew, on the one hand, and the increasingly cosmopolitan church leadership on the other.[13]

Robinson and his champions were quick to insist that the Christian faith was just as true as it ever was, once properly understood. Still, many of Robinson's colleagues condemned the book as dangerously misleading because of its sensational vocabulary. This debate was ostensibly intramural to believers, but it undoubtedly diminished the credibility of the specific beliefs that Robinson attacked (for example, the notion of a God "out there") more than it enhanced the credibility of the beliefs he defended (for example, God is our "ground of being").[14] Taking to a new extreme a classical impulse in ecumenical Protestantism to engage the world rather than to withdraw from it, Robinson dramatically legitimized the diverse world of contemporary culture as an arena for sympathetic engagement, no longer a domain to be held at a biblically warranted distance. Indeed, prior to writing *Honest to God*, Robinson was best known for having testified in court against the sexually repressive censorship of D. H. Lawrence's *Lady Chatterley's Lover* (1928). Robinson made the generic ideal of honesty, rather than any specifically Christian doctrine, the touchstone for his testimony, and he blurred the line between what most people thought Christianity was and the rest of modern life.

A young Baptist minister, Harvey Cox, who was then at Andover-Newton Theological Seminary but would soon join the Harvard University Divinity School, blurred this line more purposively in 1965 in *The Secular City*. Cox's manifesto proposed a politically engaged religion organized around human responsibility for the destiny of a world that many Christians wrongly assumed to be in God's hands. The book soon sold more than one million copies. Cox celebrated "secularization" as a liberation from "all supernatural myths and sacred symbols." While insisting that God was no less present throughout secular domains than within what traditionalists called "religion," Cox concluded iconoclastically that the very name of God was so misleading that it might be well to stop mentioning God until our worldly experience gives us a new vocabulary. "Like Moses," he wrote in the book's concluding sentence, let us be "confident that we will be granted a new name by events of the future," but for now "we must simply take up the work of liberating the captives."[15]

Central to Cox's contrast of religion and the new secular field for spiritual strivings was the inability of the provincial Christian to deal with the wider world that the theologians had come to master, and which they had an obligation to explain to the faithful. "Secularization" took place "only when the cosmopolitan confrontations of city living exposed the relativity of the myths and traditions" once thought to be "unquestionable." Convinced of the virtues of "heterogeneity" and "the color and character lent by diversity," Cox pressed the case for "pluralism and tolerance" throughout the world, but especially in the United States, where the recent "emancipation of Catholics, Jews, and others" from "an enforced Protestant cultural religion" bode well for further diversification. Cox himself soon gravitated toward "liberation theology," while countless symposia on *The Secular City* wondered just where else this book's line of analysis might lead.[16]

Might it lead outside the faith, to a post-Protestant or post-Christian orientation, influenced by the Protestant tradition but defined by elements of the secular world? Ecumenical leaders had been railing against secularism throughout the 1940s and 1950s, advancing a more genuinely ecumenical Christianity as the only viable alternative to an increasingly secular world. Cox created such a stir because he broke so decisively and bluntly with this deeply entrenched practice. Moreover, *The Secular City* appeared in 1965, right in the middle of the civil rights era, when vehicles other than the church presented themselves as more rapid and maneuverable means of advancing causes to which the ecumenical leadership was committed. In that same year the Mississippi Catholic writer Walker Percy lamented that it was not the Christian who most often did what needed to be done from the white side of the color line; this contribution was instead made most conspicuously by "the liberal humanist." The people who actually "taught the ignorant, fed the hungry," and "went to jail with the imprisoned," observed Percy, were "more likely than not" to be "Sarah Lawrence sociology majors, agnostic Jewish social workers like Mickey Schwerner, campus existentialists," and others sent from "the Berkeley-Cambridge axis."[17]

To be sure, the National Council of Churches had been among the sponsors of Freedom Summer in 1964, and there had been a small but steady stream of northern liberal clerics and laypersons in Martin Luther King Jr.'s demonstrations. Percy underestimated the role of ecumenical Protestants in the civil rights movement. But in the mid-1960s if one were looking for ways to "liberate the captives," as Cox had called on Christians to do, and if one was now authorized to apply oneself to this task without any God talk, one could quickly find secular organizations such as the Congress of Racial Equality and the Student Nonviolent Coordinating Committee that were trying to do just that. The secular liberators of the Berkeley-Cambridge axis were not encumbered, moreover, as were the National Council of Churches and its denominational affiliates, by a reluctant rank and file who paid the bills and who sometimes listened to the complaints of increasingly vocal evangelicals to the effect that the ecumenical elite was selling out true religion for social activism.

The expanding gap between the leadership and the churchgoing laity of the mainstream denominations demands closer attention here because this gap, as it widened during the crisis of the 1960s, became the demographic and doctrinal matrix for two closely connected developments that reshaped American politics and culture from the 1960s through the 1990s: (1) the rise to political prominence of conservative-leaning evangelical Protestantism and (2) the loss by the old Protestant establishment to secular enterprises of some of the energies that had made it a formidable presence in American life. The center could not hold. That it could hold was a complacent assumption of ecumenical leaders that rendered them more comfortable with rigorous self-interrogation yet slow to see what now seem, in the perspective of history, to be the risks to their institutional standing this self-interrogation entailed.[18]

The gap was defined by the leadership's increasing engagement with national and international issues that were of less interest to rank-and-file churchgoers whose concerns were centered on their own congregations. The classic local-cosmopolitan tension between pulpit and pew, between seminary and congregation, had long been a standard feature of Protestant life. This tension had been displayed in the fundamentalist-modernist controversies of the 1920s and in the foreign missions debates of the 1930s when liberals advocated social service in place of the older goal of religious conversion.[19] By 1940, however, several generations of missionary activity had populated the governing boards of many denominations and of many interdenominational service organizations such as the Young Men's Christian Association (YMCA) and Young Women's Christian Association (YWCA) with internationally conscious men and women convinced that denominational distinctions were being rendered increasingly anachronistic by cross-cultural contact. Meeting the challenge of a culturally diverse world demanded greater unity and a focus on essentials. Hence an energetic but decidedly top-down movement pushed not only for greater cooperation between denominations at home but for a world organization that would unite American Protestants with those of Europe, Asia, Africa, and Latin America. The establishment of a World Council of Churches, originally planned for the late 1930s, was delayed by World War II, but in 1948 the World Council became a reality. It was dominated by Americans who then campaigned earnestly through publications, sermons, and study conferences to educate their own constituencies on the need to supplement a local perspective with a global one.

In the meantime, American entry into World War II generated a new and concentrated effort to outline what church leaders described as a Christian basis for a just, equitable, and peaceful future for the United States and the entire world. Inspired by the magnitude of transformations attendant upon World War II, including decolonization abroad and the domestic exposure of the contradiction between racial discrimination and war aims, the heirs of the Social Gospel agreed on a program of political action that focused on the United Nations and on the diminution of racial and economic inequalities within the United States.

This ambitious program was developed and adopted by "study conferences" of several hundred church leaders convened by the Federal Council of Churches in 1942 and 1945 with the support of nearly every prominent figure in the Protestant establishment of that era, including John Foster Dulles, who was the chief mover behind both of these conclaves. Many of these leaders were, like the majority of churchgoers, Republicans. But the resolutions of these wartime conferences were substantially to the left of the standard Republican outlook of that period and even further to the left of the Jim Crow–sustaining bulwark of the Democrats. These resolutions called for the self-government of all colonized peoples, insisted that the United States could not play a productive role abroad until racial discrimination was ended within American borders, advocated experimentation with noncapitalist forms of economic organization, envisaged some form of "world government" as the only viable antidote to the evils of nationalism, and endorsed the basic principles that President Franklin D. Roosevelt enunciated as an "economic bill of rights" during his 1944 State of the Union message.[20]

These assembled bishops, seminary presidents, church officials, and famous preachers did not agree on everything. Some of them, most conspicuously Dulles, soon pulled away from the political orientation that was put in place at these 1940s conclaves. But the Federal Council of Churches and the officials of its affiliated denominational bodies, along with *The Christian Century* (the house organ of the Protestant establishment), entered the postwar world publically committed to causes that were understood in contemporary American politics as liberal, if not radical. *Time* characterized the resolutions of the assembled church leaders at the 1942 conference as "sensational" in their degree of radicalism.[21]

Acting on the momentum of the two wartime conclaves, the FCC in 1946 officially declared racial segregation to be "a violation of the Gospel of love and human brotherhood," and called on its affiliates to work toward "a non-segregated society" as well as "a non-segregated church." In that same year the national YWCA implemented the desegregation of its local chapters. Those steps, while properly seen by historians as landmarks in the movement of churches toward a more actively antiracist posture that would be achieved by civil rights organizers in the coming years, did virtually nothing to integrate local congregations.[22] Individual black clergy, including Benjamin E. Mays, Howard Thurman, and Channing H. Tobias became increasingly prominent in the national ecumenical leadership, but blacks were almost nonexistent in local mainstream churches throughout the United States.

Hence it would be a mistake to exaggerate what these ecumenical Protestants actually accomplished in diminishing white racism. Yet it would also be a mistake to ignore what they did. In the 1940s even modest gestures distinguished the FCC from most other groups of empowered white Americans. The huge study conferences of 1942 and 1945 were held in integrated Ohio cities only after council officials had tried and failed to get assurances from hotel owner associations in Detroit and other cities that their black delegates would not be obliged to stay in segregated hotels. Very few national organizations remotely similar in size to the FCC were then refusing to convene in cities where their black participants would be humiliated. This step was not taken at the Organization of American Historians—then known as the Mississippi Valley Historical Association—until 1951, when Merle Curti refused to deliver his presidential address at the 1952 annual meeting unless that meeting was moved out of New Orleans.[23]

Moreover, the leadership of ecumenical Protestantism was sufficiently linked with civil rights advocacy to lead President Harry S. Truman to appoint one of its most vocal activists, Dorothy Tilly, to the commission that produced *To Secure These Rights* in 1948. Tilly was then serving as chair of the Women's Division of the Board of Missions of the Methodist Church. She was one of only two women appointed to this presidential commission. In addition, some affiliated groups did engage in direct action. The ecumenically saturated Fellowship of Reconciliation joined with the Congress of Racial Equality in 1947 to place interracial groups of travelers on Greyhound and Trailways buses in the Atlantic South. This "Journey of Reconciliation" prefigured the freedom rides of 1961 and, in the words of the historian Joseph Kip Kosek, "marked a watershed in the development of a sophisticated form of Christian non-violence deployed on behalf of racial equality."[24]

The integrationist agenda of the Protestant establishment in the 1940s was more talk than action, but some of the talk approached eloquence. Especially important in this respect were the essays and editorials in *The Christian Century*, which was the most prominent national magazine to protest against the internment of Japanese Americans as a racist violation of American constitutional principles. Further, there issued from the Methodist and Congregationalist seminaries of the period a series of forceful, analytically ambitious antiracist treatises. Among these were Edmund D. Soper's *Racism: A World Issue* and Buell G. Gallagher's *Color and Conscience: The Irrepressible Conflict*, two of the most searching and extensively developed critiques of racism written by any institutionally prominent white American at any time prior to the 1960s. Gallagher was the chief organizer of an interracial church in Berkeley, California, and was an unsuccessful candidate for Congress in 1948. He came within one percentage point of winning and probably would have entered Congress had he not allowed the Progressive party presidential candidate Henry Wallace to speak at a rally in his support. Gallagher, anticipating a style later practiced more sharply by William Stringfellow, castigated his fellow churchmen for failing to develop measures to combat Jim Crow remotely as forceful as those implemented by the Communist party.[25]

Gallagher's respectful reference to the communists can remind us that the ecumenists whose story I am telling in this essay were far from alone in engaging diversity and trying to diminish group-specific inequality. Prominent among the other agents of change were three that are extensively studied: the organized pursuit of civil rights by church-centered African Americans, the propagation of cultural relativism by social-scientific intellectuals, and the egalitarianism of the most radical of the labor unions, including those with strong Communist party leadership. Many of the relevant movements were decidedly secular in orientation and had a heavily Jewish demographic base. The significance of these well-recognized movements need not be diminished to register the role of ecumenical Protestantism. I am less concerned about measuring the relative influence of these movements than explaining the role that diversity issues played in American Protestantism and showing how the ecumenical leadership's willingness to take chances on these issues with its constituency created space for the eventual triumph of the religious Right in the public affairs of the United States.

Hence it is crucial to understand that the various initiatives of the ecumenists I have mentioned—all of which seem so mild from today's perspective—carried the ecumenical leadership quite far out in front of the average Methodist or Presbyterian. Just how far did not become evident until the 1960s, when social-scientific surveys as well as daily experience in the denominational trenches concerning civil rights, feminism, sex, and the Vietnam War made the gap impossible to miss. The crisis of the 1960s was more severe because church leaders did not see it coming. They underestimated the width and depth of the gap between themselves and their constituents.[26]

Two conditions of the 1940s and 1950s had obscured the gap. One condition was the sheer increase in members. New sanctuaries and "Christian education" units were financed and built in suburbs all over the country. Churches of all kinds were popular community institutions among the parents of baby boomers, especially in an atmosphere when religion was widely praised in contrast to "godless communism." Whatever reservations the expanding population of the faithful had about the policies advanced by their preachers and administrators, these policies did not prevent the mainstream churches from flourishing. Yet the membership boom was deceptive. It did not quite keep up with the growth rate of the national population. It proved to be an anomaly in the long-term decline, visible in the 1920s and 1930s, of the relative place of mainstream churches in American society as whole. All religious organizations grew in the twenty years after World War II. The ecumenists failed to place their own prosperity in proper demographic perspective.

A second condition fostering complacency was the Protestant establishment's high standing in Washington, DC, and in the national media. This status followed, in large part, from the strong class position of the segment of society found in the mainstream churches. Harry Emerson Fosdick's "National Radio Pulpit" dominated Sunday morning broadcasting because the Federal Communications Commission deferred to the Federal Council of Churches and later the National Council of Churches. *Time* and other national magazines paid close attention to officials of the Federal Council of Churches, and after 1950 to that organization's enlarged successor, the National Council of Churches. Presidents Harry S. Truman and Dwight D. Eisenhower showered ecumenical leaders with respect. Reinhold Niebuhr enjoyed close relations with the State Department during the decade following the end of World War II. The patriarch of Protestant missions and of the YMCA, John R. Mott, was awarded the Nobel Peace Prize in 1946. Ecumenical leaders were thrilled with their apparent impact on the formation of the United Nations. At the San Francisco organizing conference of 1945 they managed to get accepted four of the nine amendments they offered to the United Nations charter, including a historic one calling for a declaration of human rights.[27] "How much do we have to worry if the people in the pew are a bit slow to catch up with us," ecumenical leaders had some reason to say to themselves, "when all these signs of our success are visible?"

Yet from the late 1940s onward the Protestant establishment was subject to increasingly pointed and well-organized attacks from the political Right—especially from evangelicals. By the time the civil rights movement, feminism, the sexual revolution, and the crisis over the Vietnam War forced ecumenical leaders to confront the magnitude of the gap between them and their rank-and-file laity, evangelicals had created a formidable set of rival institutions and public postures that undercut the claims of the ecumenists to speak for American Protestantism and provided religious cover for Protestants who were unmoved by the call of religious liberals for greater attention to social justice. The 1947 and 1954 campaigns of the National Association of Evangelicals to put Jesus of Nazareth in the Constitution of the United States and that organization's 1960 opposition to the very idea of a Catholic president were only small parts of this extensive evangelical mobilization. Evangelicals were not, contrary to a popular impression, politically quiescent until galvanized into political action by the legalization of abortion in 1973 by *Roe v. Wade*.[28]

Evangelicals mobilized against the United Nations and were hostile toward ecumenicals for their support of the organization. When Congress was considering a 1947 resolution to strengthen the United Nations, the NAE demanded instead that Congress resolve to "support and strengthen missionary endeavors throughout the world." A vibrant world Christianity, not compromise and accommodation with diversity, was the answer to the globe's problems. Carl McIntire, a New Jersey radio preacher with a large national following, declared the National Council of Churches to be "an ally of Russia." In 1953 McIntire distributed a pamphlet titled *Bishop Oxnam, Prophet of Marx*, aimed at G. Bromley Oxnam, the president of both the National Council of Churches and of the World Council of Churches. As a result of such accusations, Oxnam testified before the House Un-American Activities Committee (HUAC) to defend himself against charges of having communist sympathies. Just prior to Oxnam's hearing, the NAE, despite its ambivalence toward McIntire's florid and demagogic style, passed a resolution supporting government investigations into the loyalty of church officials.[29]

Even within the denominational bodies identified with ecumenical outlooks, programs of egalitarian outreach were subject to severe attacks. The Methodist Federation for Social Action, a national body led by Bishop Francis J. McConnell and Dean Walter J. Muelder of Boston University School of Theology, was condemned in a widely circulated 1951 pamphlet, *Is There a Pink Fringe in the Methodist Church?*, produced by the Texas-based Committee for the Preservation of Methodism. The tract described the social action organization as claiming to be Christian but actually serving as "a propaganda vehicle for spreading socialistic and communist ideas." The pamphlet authors offered as evidence for this charge a list that showed the range of their complaints and of the centrality of diversity issues to those complaints. The allegedly nefarious activities of the social action Methodists included calls for the repeal of the Chinese Exclusion Act and for the diplomatic recognition of the People's Republic of China, a resolution asking for "a stronger Civil Rights section of the Department of Justice," a statement favoring an end to "economic, political, and military support of colonial regimes," and a declaration of commitment to "social-economic planning to develop a society without class or group discriminations and privileges." The pamphlet listed dozens of Federation leaders by name and by local affiliation, including several bishops and prominent professors of theology.[30]

Among the Presbyterians, the most prominent target was the Princeton Theological Seminary president John A. Mackay, perhaps the most influential Presbyterian in the world besides John Foster Dulles.[31] Mackay's early 1950s advocacy of the diplomatic recognition of the People's Republic of China considerably fattened his file as kept by the House Un-American Activities Committee, a copy of which was secretly passed to the fundamentalist firebrand L. Nelson Bell, who was eager for ammunition to use against Mackay.

Bell and his son-in-law Billy Graham were major forces behind the 1956 launching of *Christianity Today*, the magazine designed to counter *The Christian Century*. The new magazine was financed by the Sun Oil Company magnate J. Howard Pew after the National Council of Churches repeatedly refused his demands that it repudiate its liberal political positions. *Christianity Today*'s founding editor, Carl F. H. Henry, proved to be a relentless scourge of the ecumenists. In 1959 he attributed "Communist affiliations" to 105 of the 237 clergy recently assembled by the National Council of Churches to address foreign policy issues. J. Edgar Hoover's warnings about communist subversion appeared regularly in *Christianity Today*.[32]

Bell was also representative of the large segment of white southern Protestantism that was ambivalent, if not hostile, toward the 1954 U.S. Supreme Court ruling in *Brown v. Board of Education*. Immediately after the decision, Bell publicly alluded to "those barriers of race which have been established by God" and declared his sympathy for individuals whom he described as among the finest Christians in the world, who believed that it is "unchristian" to force these barriers away. To be sure, Bell and Graham fought against the most entrenched segregationists of their milieu. Graham insisted that his own rallies be racially integrated. But the voices of Bell and Graham, like those of so many other evangelicals, routinely condemned racism only in its capacity as an individual sin, not in any capacity as a civic evil to be overcome by the actions of governmental authority. Even as late as 1963 Graham himself refused to support Martin Luther King Jr.'s March on Washington and declared civil rights demonstrations to be counterproductive.[33]

The Christian Century returned the hostile favors of *Christianity Today*. The pages of both magazines display the mutual annoyance that marked this often-bitter rivalry between the two major Protestant parties. A widely noted and emblematic episode in this ecumenical-evangelical quarrel was the refusal of Reinhold Niebuhr to even meet with Billy Graham at the time of Graham's enormously successful crusade in New York City in 1957. Niebuhr accused Graham of holding "obscurantist" views of religious doctrine and of playing to the most childlike emotions of the faithful. In the pages of *Life* magazine he wrote of Graham's pathetic narrowness of view: Graham cannot speak to anyone "who is aware of the continuing possibilities of good and evil in every advance of civilization, every discipline of culture, and every religious convention." While some ecumenical leaders counseled accommodation and tact, many others, such as Niebuhr and his Union Theological Seminary colleague John C. Bennett, were certain that Graham and his kind were beneath them, and they were not afraid to say so. Evangelicals did not appreciate being treated as ignorant country bumpkins by elite ecumenists.[34]

Yet the frequency and intensity of evangelical attacks on ecumenists for their liberal activism led the National Council of Churches to hold back. The most thorough historian of the civil rights activities of the council, James F. Findlay Jr., concludes that its leaders were intimidated throughout the 1950s and very early 1960s by these attacks. Only in 1963, the year *The Christian Century* published King's "Letter from the Birmingham Jail," did ecumenical leaders return to the level of antiracist engagement displayed in the 1940s.[35]

But 1963 proved to be late in the day. Shortly after the ecumenical leadership renewed and intensified its antiracist program, national conflicts over civil rights, feminism, sex, and the Vietnam War produced the crisis that ended the Protestant establishment, diminished the authority of all of its constituent denominational bodies, and paved the way for the triumph of the evangelicals. These escalating conflicts not only exposed the gap between the cosmopolitan leadership and the provincial churchgoers but also created a new challenge. While these church leaders were trying to bring the people in the pews up to speed, they were rapidly being left behind by the highly articulate minority who gravitated toward the Berkeley-Cambridge axis because they found churches too moderate and clunky in the task of "liberating the captives." The Protestant establishment was not going far enough.

But for some Protestants, the establishment was going too far. Those white Protestants who were less concerned about liberating the captives were able to find religious sanction in the increased credibility of evangelical claims to speak for American Christianity. Two decades of concerted effort by increasingly media-savvy evangelicals had placed before the public a face of Christianity that was very different from that displayed by the National Council of Churches and *The Christian Century*. In addition to establishing the National Association of Evangelicals and *Christianity Today*, the evangelicals created Fuller Theological Seminary in Pasadena, California, and developed an extensive network of radio and television ministries.[36] Upwardly mobile Seventh-Day Adventist and Church of the Nazarene congregants who had joined the more respectable Methodists and Presbyterians a generation earlier now had better reason to stay put; they now saw the churches of their nativity recognized as real on television and radio and in national politics. And one could now be comfortably and confidently Christian without taking on the social obligations that ecumenical leaders insisted were incumbent on any authentic Christian witness in the circumstances of the times.

Since the mid-1960s all of the mainline denominations have experienced a precipitous drop in membership numbers. Part of this decline followed from the diminished migration from denominational fellowships with lower social standing, which for many decades had been a source of membership strength for the mainline churches. Even so, the decline was much too rapid and extensive to be explained by the drying of this membership source. The Methodists, having reached an all-time high of 11.1 million members in 1964, were down 9 percent eleven years later, and by the early twenty-first century the Methodist numbers were down 28 percent. Episcopalian membership peaked at 2.3 million in 1967 and only eight years later had declined by nearly 9 percent. The United Presbyterians declined by 19 percent between 1965 (their peak year, at 3.3 million) and a decade later.[37] These denominations had grown between 1945 and the mid-1960s, but after 1965 they actually lost members in absolute numbers.

Why a decline of this scale at this time? Not because masses of believers switched from the liberal churches to the conservative ones, although some people did just that. The migration to evangelical churches was not large and was actually smaller than the modest migration to Roman Catholicism. Nor can the decline of ecumenical numbers and the rise of evangelical numbers be attributed to the latter's outsider status and the former's close association with established American institutions, as has been repeatedly suggested. In fact, the ecumenists prospered most when they were closely linked with other major American institutions during the 1950s, and they lost numbers when their leaders took positions that distanced them from popular understandings of "the American way of life." Evangelicals gained members and public standing exactly as their espousal of such patriotism distinguished them more and more sharply from the ecumenists. Billy Graham—not the seminarians at Union Theological Seminary, Harvard Divinity School, and Yale Divinity School—was a regular at the White House from the presidency of Richard M. Nixon through that of George W. Bush. By the 1980s it was the evangelicals rather than the ecumenists who so dominated the public space of the Air Force Academy as to generate litigation by nonevangelicals complaining of religious oppression. The part of the national order toward which the evangelicals can be properly called the most "oppositional" was the secular, heavily Jewish academic and literary intelligentsia that included voices sharply critical of what evangelicals saw as the traditional American way of life. Indeed, the ecumenists' accommodation with modern philosophy, science, and art was something the evangelicals held against ecumenists.[38]

What then, does explain the sudden and sharp decline in membership in the old mainstream churches? The central factor was the decision of the children of members not to become members themselves. Some of these young people adopted other religious affiliations, but the great majority of the departing youth did not affiliate religiously at all and in turn raised secular children who, like their 1960s-influenced parents, did not join any churches. The exodus of young people from the mainstream churches was the most massive in the early 1970s. This exodus did not persist at quite the same rate during the 1980s and after, but the significance of the nonretention of ecumenical children was heightened by another, more enduring condition: a differential birth rate. During the baby boom Presbyterian women produced an average of only 1.6 children, while evangelical women produced an average of 2.4—more even than Catholic women delivered during the same period. Women who were not members of any church produced even fewer children than the Presbyterian, Episcopalian, and United Church of Christ women. Educational level was the strongest predictor of fertility. Some evangelical women were as well educated as their ecumenical and secular counterparts, but most were not. Ecumenical women bore fewer children, and their churches contained fewer and fewer women of childbearing age. In 1957 only 36 percent of Lutherans were over the age of 50, yet by 1983 this figure had gone up to 45 percent. During those same twenty-six years, the percentage of Methodists over the age of 50 increased from 40 percent to 49 percent, and the percentage of Episcopalians over the age of 50 increased from 36 to 46. The evangelical triumph in the numbers game from the 1960s to the early twenty-first century was mostly a matter of birthrates coupled with the greater success of the more tightly boundaried, predominantly southern, evangelical communities in acculturating their children into ancestral religious practices. Evangelicals had more children and kept them.[39]

This demographic dynamic had obvious cultural foundations. The rapidity and extent to which ecumenical women took advantage of birth control technologies is consistent with their greater recognition of a role for sex beyond procreation, just as the propensity of ecumenical youth to leave the church was facilitated by their greater exposure to a diverse world and by the greater encouragement their elders gave them to explore it. Had the ecumenists been as conservative, they might have produced more children and had more success in keeping them in the religious fold. They might even have won more converts from the evangelical churches that provided a secure shelter for Protestants who were dubious about diversity-accepting, captive-liberating projects. The heavily evangelical population that Robert Wuthnow calls "exclusivist Christians" feels threatened, Wuthnow writes, by "Christian groups that appear to have lost their moral compass and become too eager to embrace diversity." The threat is often "cast in terms of homosexuality, promiscuous lifestyles, or relativistic values," any of which "may be loosely associated in people's minds with diversity." The standard response to this threat is to go "back to basics," which means "studying the Bible, returning to the supposed teachings of the early Christians or the Christian values of the nation's founders," and "finding security in the Ten Commandments."[40]

The political coordinates of the ecumenical-evangelical divide must be underscored in the context of the recent movement of several prominent evangelicals in more "progressive" directions on some economic and environmental issues. This highly publicized shift within evangelical Protestantism remains contested and is indeed a very recent phenomenon. During the pivotal 1960s, 1970s, and 1980s—and even after—the liberal-conservative political divide mapped quite easily onto the ecumenical-evangelical divide. Rank-and-file evangelicals were less extreme than the leaders of their institutions, just as rank-and-file ecumenists were less extreme than the leaders of theirs. The two great parties within American Protestantism were never monolithic, and they are not now; it will not do to suppose that everyone on one side or the other thinks and behaves identically. The overall pattern is clear, however. One sociological study after another has established substantial differences in outlook between the mass constituencies of the two rival leadership groups. Relative to evangelicals, ecumenicals have been more accepting of religious pluralism, more comfortable with church-state separation, more sympathetic to antiracist legislation and judicial rulings, more skeptical of American foreign policy, more supportive of abortion rights, more favorable toward the equal rights amendment, more concerned with civil liberties issues, more tolerant of nonmarital cohabitation, and more accepting of same-sex relationships.[41]

One major quarrel about same-sex relationships is a poignant illustration of the dynamics of the ecumenists' fateful crisis. This quarrel, involving the Methodist youth magazine *motive*, can also remind us that membership statistics tell only part of the story: relevant, too, were the decisions of elites and activists, especially in the younger generation. An arts-and-culture periodical that never had a circulation beyond 40,000, *motive*—which displayed its avant-garde self-conception by refusing to capitalize the first letter of its name—became "the virtual national magazine of the entire American student Christian movement" of the ecumenical churches, observes one historian. Its readership included many college and seminary faculty. William Stringfellow and Harvey Cox published in its pages. When the magazine's attacks on segregation annoyed Methodists in southern states, G. Bromley Oxnam himself stood down a group of southern ministers by slamming a stack of copies on a table and claiming to agree with every word in them. In 1965 *motive* was runner-up only to *Life* in the Columbia University School of Journalism's Magazine of the Year competition, and in 1966 *Time* praised *motive* as the literary equivalent of a "miniskirt at a church social."[42] Yet in 1972 *motive* abruptly ceased its thirty-one years of publication with two provocative and defiant issues celebrating gay and lesbian sexuality. The context in which the editors did this is revealing.

Methodist leaders found themselves barraged with criticism generated by a *motive* issue of 1969 on "women's liberation." As with so many of the period's efforts to liberate captives, *motive*'s radical feminist stance threatened to so alienate the churchgoing base of the ecumenical denominations that church officials, who like Oxnam had repeatedly expended their political credit to defend *motive* against conservative critics, felt obliged to call a halt. The Methodist leadership would continue to support *motive* only if its editors could find ways to cause less trouble for the church. The editors refused and proceeded in the diversity-affirming directions in which they were already headed, including serving as an unpublicized safe harbor for gay and lesbian Methodists. With what little money they had left after declaring their independence from the Methodists, the editors detonated their institutional suicide bomb.[43]

One of the central figures in this episode later described what the experience meant to her. "The more feminist I became . . . the more impatient I was with the phallocentricity of Christianity," wrote Charlotte Bunch, "and with the slowness of the institution to see how it oppressed women." When Bunch "came out as a lesbian" simultaneously with the demise of *motive*, she also left the Methodist church because she was "simply not willing to be affiliated with an institution that labeled me a sinner or denied me the right to enter the highest callings." The most influential and long-serving editor of *motive*, B. J. Stiles, remained an ordained Methodist minister but spent the rest of his career as a program officer and executive of secular nonprofit foundations, including those devoted to acquired immune deficiency syndrome (AIDS) prevention.[44]

While the editors of *motive* went their own postecclesiastical way, exemplifying the difficulties of the ecumenical leadership in holding on to its young, the National Council of Churches tried desperately to keep up with the times. The council was deeply shaken in 1969 when the black activist preacher James Forman interrupted a Sunday morning service in New York's Riverside Church to read aloud his "Black Manifesto," demanding 500 million dollars in reparations from the National Council of Churches and its affiliates to support programs of black economic development.[45] Ecumenical leaders managed to reject that specific demand but tried to compensate by taking more and more radical positions on other issues. Between 1972 and 1975 the council, beyond its adamant opposition to the Vietnam conflict, supported Palestinian independence from Israel, endorsed the resumption of normal relations with Cuba, put money and legal resources behind the United Farm Workers Union, rallied to the support of the American Indian Movement during the siege at Wounded Knee, and took sides with Soviet-backed African insurgents against Portuguese colonial regimes.

These steps failed to stem the youth exodus and they further alienated the council's churchgoing base. In the dozen years after 1975, the budget of the National Council of Churches declined by 53 percent. Between the late 1960s and the late 1980s, the size of its staff declined by 68 percent. Local congregations and denominational boards became increasingly wary of the council's leadership. Here, more immediately than in the decline of membership numbers, we see the consequences of the leadership-laity gap. Efforts to retain the confidence of the council's own denominational constituencies were constantly undercut by attacks from the evangelical Right, to which the national press paid increasing attention. In 1983 *Reader's Digest* and CBS News's *60 Minutes* gave a sympathetic ear to critics who said the National Council of Churches was in the pockets of minority group lobbyists, had "substituted revolution for religion," and was financing "Marxist-Leninist projects" throughout Africa, Asia, and Latin America with the money given by churchgoers who had no idea what the ecumenical elite was doing with their donations.[46] The problem for the politically active ecumenist leaders, often missed by scholars who focus only on membership statistics, was not just that their numbers were down but that many of the members they retained proved reluctant to support their programs.

In the meantime, the evangelicals continued to enact their part of the fateful dialectic by which the two major persuasions in American Protestantism pulled farther apart from each other. In the late 1970s and early 1980s the Nazarene leader James Dobson and others developed "family values" as a rallying cry for evangelicals who had previously been less engaged than the ecumenicals with debates over the nature of the ideal Christian family. But precisely at the time that the Christian Family Commissions of one ecumenical denomination after another pulled away from the old, uncritical assumption that the traditional, patriarchal, nuclear family was God's will, the evangelicals latched onto this idea and ran with it. As the historian Margaret Bendroth has explained, "evangelicals became pro-family" largely as a way of asserting their claims to leadership of the society as a whole, determined no longer to be "cultural outsiders." Just as the evangelicals took up the notion of a Christian America while it was being discarded by the ecumenicals and persisted in traditional missionary ideologies rejected as culturally imperialist by the ecumenicals, so too did the evangelicals exploit popular ideas about the family that ecumenical leaders found themselves unable any longer to defend.[47]

Moreover, exactly at the time the ecumenicals were dealing anxiously with the consequences of the risks they had taken during the civil rights era, the evangelicals, by merely acquiescing as a *fait accompli* in the expansions of civil rights that many of them had opposed, were thus able to gain credibility as a force in national politics from the very beginning of the Ronald Reagan era. The National Association of Evangelicals and a host of megachurch televangelists went from strength to strength. Jerry Falwell's Moral Majority became a force in the Republican party. *Christianity Today* surpassed and rapidly outdistanced *The Christian Century* in circulation. During his 1980 presidential campaign Reagan famously declared to a convention of evangelicals, "I endorse you," playing cleverly on that body's inability to endorse formally his candidacy while turning their applause into exactly such an endorsement. Three years later, as president, Reagan delivered his legendary "evil empire" speech to a meeting of the National Association of Evangelicals.[48]

What happened to ecumenical Protestantism during the crisis of the 1960s and its aftermath can be instructively compared to what happened simultaneously to the Democratic party in national politics. "We have lost the South for a generation," President Lyndon B. Johnson is widely quoted as having said on behalf of the Democratic party in 1964 when the Democrats aligned themselves with the cause of civil rights for African Americans. What ecumenical Protestant leaders did is not quite the same, but there is a parallel visible in the context of what historians of American religion often call Protestantism's "two-party system": a series of polarities going back to the seventeenth century, in which the modern split between the ecumenists and evangelicals is the most recent.[49]

Ecumenists put at risk their hold on American Protestantism in a manner similar to that by which the Democrats risked their hold on the South, and with similar consequences. At issue in the control of American Protestantism was not only race—the crucial issue for the Democrats—but also imperialism, feminism, abortion, and sexuality, in addition to the critical perspectives on supernaturalism popularized by thinkers such as Harvey Cox and John A. T. Robinson. Ecumenical leaders were not as aware as President Johnson apparently was of the risks they were taking, nor were they as blunt in the moments when the truth dawned on them. But they, like he, believed that the time had come to redirect the institutions and populations they were trying to lead and they behaved accordingly. Hence they abandoned to opportunistic evangelicals both the classical foreign missionary project and the powerful claim of a proprietary relation to the American nation. In pursuit of causes they believed to be inspired by God, the ecumenical leaders encouraged secular alliances that blurred the boundaries of their faith community and risked the gradual loss of their children to secular communities. The ecumenical leaders accommodated perspectives on women and the family that diminished their capacity to reproduce themselves exactly at the same time that they took positions on empire, race, sex, abortion, and divinity that diminished their ability to recruit as new members those Protestants who had been reared in an evangelical milieu and might otherwise find it congenial to become an Episcopalian. Just as the Democrats had lost most of the South to the Republican party, the ecumenists yielded more and more of the space of Protestantism to the evangelicals.

Further, just as Lyndon Johnson and the national Democrats could not contain Fannie Lou Hamer and the Mississippi Freedom Democrats in 1964, the ecumenical leaders could not contain the self-consciously progressive forces exemplified by the editors of *motive*. Even so, the domain of the Mississippi Freedom Democrats and their kind was ultimately the nation, not the South. Such radicals could return to their party after its need to placate white southerners was decisively diminished; indeed, they were obliged to do just that because in the absence of a new major party the only way for the Left to remain active in electoral politics was to make peace with the Democrats. But the captive-liberating and supernaturalism-rejecting projects of the editors of *motive* and their counterparts in all the mainstream denominations could be advanced without any kind of Protestantism whatsoever. The radical progeny of the ecumenists had less incentive to return to their party in the two-party system of Protestantism. So what if Protestantism fell increasingly into the hands of the other party, the evangelicals? That mattered only if one continued to believe that the Christian religion was ultimately the most viable foundation for the kind of society that ecumenical Protestant leaders had come to advocate by the 1960s.

That belief in the indispensability of Christianity, while regarded as a conceit by secular thinkers and adherents of other religions, had long sustained even the most liberal of ecumenical Protestants in their worldly activities and helps explain their complacency. Reinhold Niebuhr never tired of accusing secularists of failing to appreciate the special capacity of Christianity to interpret the world and to inform human conduct. Even Wilfred Cantwell Smith, for all his accommodation with diversity, held firmly to the faith that the Christian minority was still the best hope for humankind if only that uniquely endowed minority would reconstitute itself on the basis of modern experience. Harvey Cox's embrace of the secular world in the name of Christianity was enabled by his conviction that the entirety of the universe was peculiarly responsive to the same divine power that Cox believed had guided the ancient Hebrews and had provided, in Jesus of Nazareth, a prophet of unparalleled authority.

But this belief in the unique contribution of Christianity to the world lost its hold on many followers of Niebuhr, Smith, and Cox, who allied themselves intimately with secular agencies. Christianity became one of a number of useful vehicles for values that transcended that ancestral faith. For such people, Christianity of any variety became a strategic and personal option rather than a presumed imperative. To be sure, many Americans continued to believe in the unique ability of Christianity to speak to those needs. But just as a substantial portion of the missionaries found that the Hindus and Buddhists they encountered abroad were not quite so much in need of Christian conversion as once assumed, thousands of children of the old Protestant establishment found that Christianity was not so indispensible to the advancement of the values most energetically taught to them by their Methodist and Congregationalist tutors.[50]

But secular alliances were not new for ecumenical Protestants. The drift to post-Protestantism was more pronounced in the 1960s and after because the ethnoreligious demography of that era was so different from that of earlier episodes during which ecumenical Protestants allied themselves with secular forces. Catholics and Jews were much more visible in American civic life in the 1960s and after than they had been in the Progressive Era, when Walter Rauschenbusch's *Christianity and the Social Crisis* authorized in God's name support for many of the most radically egalitarian of that period's initiatives, or even than in the 1930s, when Reinhold Niebuhr's *Moral Man and Immoral Society* encouraged Christians to support violent measures as needed in class struggle. The leading secular intellectuals of the 1960s were less grounded in a Christian past than their predecessors. Jewish intellectuals were very heavily represented in the cultural leadership of the United States by the 1960s. Prominent examples included Daniel Bell, Hannah Arendt, Herbert Marcuse, Betty Friedan, Stanley Cavell, Noam Chomsky, Lionel Trilling, Erik Erikson, Susan Sontag, Thomas Kuhn, Ayn Rand, J. Robert Oppenheimer, Nathan Glazer, Alfred Kazin, Paul Goodman, Milton Friedman, Richard Hofstadter, and Walter Kaufmann. Kaufmann was unusual because he explicitly criticized ecumenical Protestant thinking. In a 1958 book that was very popular on college campuses, *Critique of Religion and Philosophy*, Kaufmann went after Reinhold Niebuhr and Harry Emerson Fosdick by name for their mush-headed lack of logic and modern learning. Kaufmann found the ideas of evangelicals not even worth refutation, but many collegiate sons and daughters of mainstream Methodists and Presbyterians were part of the era's undergraduate engagement with Kaufmann that was propelled by his anthology of 1956, *Existentialism from Dostoevsky to Sartre*. This collection was one of the blockbuster campus books of the era. It summarily dismissed the religiously oriented existentialists—in contrast to the forthright atheists on whom Kaufmann focused respectful attention—as altogether marginal to the new and exciting existentialist movement.[51]

Neither during the Progressive Era nor in the 1930s did Protestants confront a cultural environment remotely as heavily populated with non-Christians as did their successors of the 1960s and after. The greatest secular philosopher of the first half of the twentieth century, John Dewey, had been, after all, a lapsed Congregationalist, and had actually engaged religious issues rather than ignored them as irrelevant to serious intellectual inquiry. Even the flaming freethinker H. L. Mencken had spoken casually of being part of "Christendom," a term that had become a quaint anachronism by the time analytic philosophy had swept Protestant-inflected metaphysics out the academic window and *Partisan Review* and *Commentary* had become central venues for the intelligentsia. And in the world beyond the North Atlantic West that the ecumenists engaged, non-Christians were much more empowered in the 1960s than they had been before and were in charge of many nation-states in Asia and Africa. The end of the European empires and the diminution of the missionary project shattered the Christian lenses through which even the most liberal of American Protestants had been looking at the non-European world.[52]

In this setting, countless individuals who inherited the tradition of ecumenical Protestantism put their energies into an imposing collection of secular agencies, including the human rights organizations that flourished during the 1970s and after. These post-Protestant endeavors are a major feature of modern American life, yet our recognition of them has been obscured by a survivalist bias, by which I mean a preference for if not a commitment to the survival of Christianity in general and of the institutions of ecumenical Protestantism in particular. From a survivalist point of view, the key questions about ecumenical Protestantism are, first, whether it has been able to perpetuate itself on its own terms, and second, whether it has advanced the Christian project effectively or contributed to the actual weakening of that project. These questions dominate the scholarly and popular literature and reflect the religion-protecting outlook of the Lilly Endowment, which has funded most of the scholarship on the destiny of ecumenical Protestantism. The ecumenical leadership's "tolerance of diversity and openness," write Wade Clark Roof and William McKinney, "tended to erode loyalty" to the inherited religious order and ultimately "spawned" many secularists among its own progeny. Mainline Protestantism's "emphasis on inclusiveness and diversity" made it function rather like a "sieve," as Roof and another of his collaborators put it.[53]

This figure of speech is typical of commentators who treat the decline of ecumenical Protestantism's standing as something to be lamented and who suggest that if only ecumenists had more vigorously accultur-ated their youth and maintained tighter organizational discipline things might have turned out more favorably for the churches. This survivalist perspective misses a reality to which this essay draws attention: the his-toric function of self-interrogating ecumenical Protestantism as an en-vironment in which many Americans found themselves able to engage sympathetically a panorama of ethnoracial, sexual, religious, and cul-tural varieties of humankind. These varieties potentially threatened to destabilize inherited practices and beliefs, but ecumenical Protestantism provided a community and an orientation that facilitated these engage-ments for people who might otherwise have avoided them. The lead-ership of ecumenical Protestantism, as it engaged the diversity of the modern world, enabled its community of faith to serve, among its other roles, as a commodious halfway house to what for lack of a better term we can call post-Protestant secularism.

To recognize the historic function of ecumenical Protestantism as a halfway house, if not actually a slippery slope to secularism, is in no way invidious unless one approaches history as a Christian survivalist. Reli-gious affiliations, like other solidarities, are contingent entities, gener-ated, sustained, transformed, diminished, and destroyed by the changing circumstances of history. Those circumstances still render ecumenical Protestantism a vibrant and vital home for many persons. A genuinely historicist approach to the history of religion will not teleologically imply that those committed to that faith today are headed for history's dustbin. On the contrary, historicism demands that we address every human phe-nomenon in its local and global contexts, and be as respectful as we can of the honest decisions people make in those settings and refrain from thinking we know the future.

Once this historic function of ecumenical Protestantism is noninvidi-ously recognized, however, it becomes possible to see that ecumenical Protestantism actually advanced some of its central goals even while its organizational hegemony disappeared. The diversity-preoccupied as-pects of public American life today look much more like what the edi-tors of *The Christian Century* in 1960 hoped it would look like than what the editors of *Christianity Today* were then projecting as an ideal future. Ecumenical leaders may have lost American Protestantism, argues N. J. Demerath III, but they won the United States. The ecumenists cam-paigned for "individualism, freedom, pluralism, tolerance, democracy, and intellectual inquiry," observes Demerath, exactly the liberal values that gained rather than lost ground in the public culture of the United States in the second half of the twentieth century.[54] These values were not peculiar to ecumenical Protestants, but the latter's emphatic espousal of these values enacted ecumenical Protestantism's accommodation with secular liberalism. These values served as key justifications for many of the transformations of the 1960s, and have been invoked since that time in countless specific contexts as the United States has confronted massive immigration from non-European lands and has sought to find ways to do justice to the descendants of its enslaved and conquered peoples.

What Demerath calls "the cultural victory" of ecumenical Protestantism is easily exaggerated, but so, too, is that of the Democrats: American politics as a whole is massively influenced even today by the conservative Republicans of the states of the old Confederacy. Despite the election of Barack Obama as president in 2008—a development consistent with what the ecumenists of old hoped to see—it takes little scrutiny to identify features of American life in the 2010s that bear no resemblance to the vision articulated in the study conferences of the World War II years or in the 1960s pronouncements of the National Council of Churches. Certainly, the great authority exercised today by politically conservative evangelical Protestants in the U.S. Senate and House of Representatives bespeaks no victory for Reinhold Niebuhr and G. Bromley Oxnam. Yet one domain in which Demerath's hyperbole has impressive credibility is religion itself.

Two sociologists report that young adults of virtually all varieties of faith now talk "like classical liberal Protestants." Included in this company, insist Christian Smith and Patricia Snell, are religious Jews, Catholics, mainstream Protestants, African American Protestants, and white evangelicals. Smith and Snell declare that "Harry Emerson Fosdick would be proud" to hear today's religious chatter because even the white evangelicals—grandchildren of the people who so resented Fosdick's dominance of the airwaves of the 1940s—were now "paraphrasing passages from the classical liberal Protestant theologians, of whom they have no doubt actually never heard." Smith and Snell invoke H. Richard Niebuhr's famous 1937 parody of the antidoctrinal drift of the ecumenicals as producing a "God without wrath," men and women "without sin," a kingdom "without judgment," and a "Christ without a cross," but they observe that the bulk of today's religiously affiliated Americans appear to be quite happy with the faith that Reinhold Niebuhr's less well-known brother had mocked as vacant and bland. The liberal ideas developed by seminary theologians at Andover-Newton, Union, and Harvard have trickled down at last.[55]

Not all of those ideas, however. The commitment to diminish inequality that mattered so much to Wilfred Cantwell Smith and so many other ecumenists of old is not so abundant in the cheerful tolerance and diversity talk discovered almost everywhere by today's sociologists. If younger rank-and-file evangelicals have adopted many of the ecumenists' perspectives on religion as such, why are liberal political opinions still so decidedly a minority in evangelical circles? Our era's most distinguished political sociologist, Robert Putnam, and his collaborator, David Campbell, believe they have the answer to this question. They argue that political opinions are exercising more and more control over decisions about religious affiliation. There are fewer and fewer political liberals in any church and fewer and fewer political conservatives outside the churches. The popular association of religion with right-wing politics as consolidated during the Reagan era by evangelical entrepreneurs was highly successful but appears to have diminished the appeal of religion for anyone who is not comfortable with such a politics.[56] Religion has always had a political matrix, but in the twenty-first-century United States it may be in the process of becoming more epiphenomenal. As religious pluralism reigns and as doctrinally based distinctions between Protestant persuasions diminish, political distinctions become more powerful determinants of religious affiliation rather than demonstrable results of such affiliations. Is this secularization by stealth? Is the most ostensibly religious society in the industrialized North Atlantic West becoming more functionally secular even as the vast majority of its inhabitants declare themselves to be religious?

However we assess the contemporary scene and however we may speculate about the future, certain historical realities ought to be clear. The evangelicals gained the upper hand in the struggle for control of Protestantism just as the Republicans gained the upper hand in the struggle for the political control of the South. In both cases, the triumph was facilitated by the decisions and actions of the rival party. This analogy, like any, can be carried too far, but just as the nation got something in return for the loss of the South to the Republican party, so, too, did the nation obtain something in return for the loss of Protestantism to the evangelicals: the United States got a more widely dispersed and institutionally enacted acceptance of ethnoracial, sexual, religious, and cultural diversity. This sympathetic engagement with diversity that has become so visible and celebrated a feature of the public life of the United States is the product of many agencies, but prominent among them are the egalitarian impulses and the capacities for self-interrogation that ecumenical Protestants brought to the great American encounter with diversity during the middle and late decades of the twentieth century. Those impulses and capacities generated a cascade of liberalizing consequences extending well beyond the diminishing domain of the mainstream churches, running through the lives and careers of countless post-Protestant Americans distributed across a wide expanse of secular space. Our narrative of modern American religious history will be deficient so long as we suppose that ecumenical Protestantism declined because it had less to offer the United States than did its evangelical rival. Much of what ecumenical

Protestantism offered now lies beyond the churches, and hence we have been slow to see it.

A compelling emblem for this ongoing process is a decision made by the YMCA in 2010. In view of "the vibrancy and diversity of the organization," it dropped the word "Christian" from its label. Henceforth, it was to be known simply as "The Y." To be sure, in small print, the organization's materials declare that its "mission is to put Christian principles into practice," but here an organization that began in the nineteenth century as fervently evangelical and then in the twentieth century became increasingly ecumenical and egalitarian has, in the twenty-first century, proclaimed itself to be virtually secular and in the name of diversity.[57]

Notes

For critical readings of a draft, I thank Jon Butler, Paul S. Boyer, James Campbell, Joan Heifetz Hollinger, R. Laurence Moore, Ronald Numbers, Dana Robert, Molly Worthen, and especially Carol J. Clover, to whom I am also indebted for twenty years of illuminating conversations about the issues addressed in this essay. Daniel Immerwahr has been an exceptionally resourceful research assistant and has influenced the shape of this essay in many helpful ways.

1. Wilfred Cantwell Smith, "Christianity's Third Great Challenge," *The Christian Century*, April 27, 1960, p. 505. On Wilfred Cantwell Smith as a comparativist, see Talal Asad, "Reading a Modern Classic: W. C. Smith's 'The Meaning and End of Religion,'" *History of Religions*, 40 (Feb. 2001), 205–22.

2. On the concept of "Protestant Establishment," see William R. Hutchison, ed., *Between the Times: The Travail of the Protestant Establishment in America, 1900–1960* (New York, 1989).

3. The best single book on fundamentalists in the 1930s and 1940s persuasively argues that leading veterans of the old fundamentalist movement of the 1910s and 1920s united and organized the new evangelical alliance. See Joel E. Carpenter, *Revive Us Again: The Reawakening of Fundamentalism* (New York, 1999). On the political mobilization of fundamentalists and other evangelicals from the 1920s to the present, see Daniel K. Williams, *God's Own Party: The Making of the Christian Right* (New York, 2010).

4. Acts 2:1–11. The universalist reading of this text characteristic of ecumenical Protestants of the middle decades of the twentieth century is exemplified by that era's standard reference work on biblical interpretation. See George A. Buttrick, *The Interpreter's Bible*, 12 vols. (New York, 1954), IX, 38–39.

5. On the difference between evangelical and ecumenical approaches to diversity, see Grant Wacker, "Second Thoughts on the Great Commission: Liberal Protestants and Foreign Missions, 1890–1940," in *Earthen Vessels: American Evangelicals and Foreign Missions, 1880–1980*, ed. Joel A. Carpenter and Wilbert R. Shenk (Grand Rapids, 1990), 281–300, esp. 297–300. Harold Ockenga explains

the relation between the fundamentalist tradition and the broader evangelical persuasion that he was leading. Ockenga was the central figure in the creation of all three of the major evangelical institutions of the period: the National Association of Evangelicals, *Christianity Today*, and Fuller Theological Seminary. On the principles that informed institution building by American evangelicals of the mid-twentieth century, see Harold Ockenga, "Resurgent Evangelical Leadership," *Christianity Today*, Oct. 10, 1960, pp. 14–16. On Ockenga's career, see George Marsden, *Reforming Fundamentalism: Fuller Seminary and the New Evangelicalism* (Grand Rapids, 1995). Galatians 3:28.

6. On the notion of a "Christian America," see Jon Butler, *Awash in a Sea of Faith: Christianizing the American People* (Cambridge, MA, 1990). For an earlier study that shows a "Christian America" as a project to be achieved rather than a reality to be preserved, see Robert T. Handy, *A Christian America: Protestant Hopes and Historical Realities* (New York, 1971). "The Congress: Hunting Time," *Time*, May 24, 1954, p. 23.

7. Martin Marty, "Protestantism Enters Third Phase," *The Christian Century*, Jan. 18, 1961, p. 74. For a discerning study of the role of John Courtney Murray, see Patrick Allitt, "The Significance of John Courtney Murray," in *Catholic Polity and American Politics*, ed. Mary Segers (New Haven, 1990), 53–67.

8. Shaun Casey, *The Making of a Catholic President: Kennedy v. Nixon 1960* (New York, 2009), 184.

9. Carl F. H. Henry, "Human Rights in an Age of Tyranny," *Christianity Today*, Feb. 4, 1957, pp. 20–22. Cited in William Inboden, *Religion and American Foreign Policy, 1945–1960: The Soul of Containment* (New York, 2008), 86. On the ecumenical presence in the deliberations leading up to the Universal Declaration of Human Rights, see John S. Nurser, *For All Peoples and All Nations: The Ecumenical Church and Human Rights* (Washington, DC, 2004).

10. Marty, "Protestantism Enters Third Phase," 74.

11. William Stringfellow, *My People Is the Enemy: An Autobiographical Polemic* (New York, 1964), 133, 87.

12. Ralph E. Dodge, *The Unpopular Missionary* (Westwood, NJ, 1964), 30, 164. Emphasis in original. For another example of the struggle of ecumenical Protestants at this historical moment to reconfigure their missionary project, see Ronald K. Orchard, ed., *Witness in Six Continents: Records of the Meeting of the Commission on World Mission and Evangelism of the World Council of Churches Held in Mexico City, December 8th to 19th, 1963* (Edinburgh, 1964).

13. John A. T. Robinson, *Honest to God* (London, 1963), 66. For a selection of the earliest of critical responses to this book, see David L. Edwards, ed., *The Honest to God Debate: Some Reactions to the Book "Honest to God," with a New Chapter by Its Author, John A. T. Robinson, Bishop of Woolwich* (Louisville, 1963).

14. The notion that God was a "ground of being" had been popularized by the liberal émigré theologian Paul Tillich and was a flash point in the Protestant disputation during the midcentury decades. See Paul Tillich, *Shaking the Foundations* (London, 1949).

15. Harvey Cox, *The Secular City: Secularization and Urbanization in Theological Perspective* (New York, 1965), 2, 268.

16. Ibid., 1–3, 85, 99. For a compendium of the symposia and individual reviews published within a year of the book's appearance, see Daniel Callahan, ed., *The Secular City Debate* (New York, 1966). It is a mark of how far *The Secular City* took Cox from the theological tradition out of which he came that his work, one of the most widely circulated and extensively debated books ever written by a seminary professor, does not even find a marginal place in Gary Dorrien, *The Making of American Liberal Theology: Crisis, Irony, and Postmodernity, 1950–2005* (Louisville, 2006).

17. Walker Percy, *Signposts in a Strange Land* (New York, 1999), 329–30.

18. For an influential discussion of the gap between leadership and the churchgoing laity that emphasizes educational differences, see Robert Wuthnow, *The Restructuring of American Religion* (Princeton, 1988), 161–64. Although *The Restructuring of American Religion* is most often cited for its argument that denominational loyalties were largely replaced during the 1970s and 1980s by less organizationally specific loyalties to liberalism and conservatism, an underappreciated theme is Robert Wuthnow's emphasis on the function of higher education in moving Americans toward theological and political liberalism. A revealing example of the complacent, triumphalist perspective of ecumenical Protestant leadership in the 1940s and 1950s is Henry P. Van Dusen, *World Christianity: Yesterday, Today, Tomorrow* (New York, 1947). The president of Union Theological Seminary, Van Dusen was a sufficiently major figure in the United States to be featured on the cover of *Time* magazine on April 17, 1954, but his eclipse from history is now so complete that he does not even rate an entry in Wikipedia.

19. In many Protestant councils the debates over missions were more important than the disputes over evolution that have captured the interest of most historians who address the religious conflicts of the interwar decades. See William R. Hutchison, *Errand to the World: American Protestant Thought and Foreign Missions* (Chicago, 1987).

20. Among the other participants or supporters of study conferences were Reinhold Niebuhr, Harry Emerson Fosdick, A. J. Muste, John R. Mott, Henry Pitney Van Dusen, G. Bromley Oxnam, Georgia Harkness, Kenneth Scott Latourette, and Harvey S. Firestone. For a detailed account of the conferences and their resolutions, see chapter 3 in this volume.

21. "American Malvern," *Time*, March 16, 1942, pp. 44–45.

22. On the 1946 Federal Council of Churches pronouncement and its significance, see David W. Willis, "An Enduring Distance: Black Americans and the Establishment," in *Between the Times*, ed. Hutchison, 172. On the Young Women's Christian Association (YWCA), see Nancy Marie Robertson, *Christian Sisterhood, Race Relations, and the YWCA, 1906–1946* (Urbana, 2009).

23. Richard S. Kirkendall, "From the MVHA to the OAH, 1951–1981," in *The Organization of American Historians: The Writing and Teaching of American History*, ed. Richard S. Kirkendall (New York, 2011), 33.

24. On Dorothy Tilly's career, see Andrew M. Manis, " 'City Mothers': Dorothy Tilly, the Georgia Methodist Women, and Black Civil Rights," in *Before Brown: Civil Rights and White Backlash in the Modern South*, ed. Glenn Feldman (Tuscaloosa, 2004), 116–43. The standard account of "the journey of reconciliation"

is Raymond Arsenault, "'You Don't Have to Ride Jim Crow': CORE and the 1947 Journey of Reconciliation," in *Before Brown*, ed. Feldman, 21–67. Joseph Kip Kosek, *Acts of Conscience: Christian Nonviolence and Modern American Democracy* (New York, 2009), 204.

25. On the movement to defend Japanese Americans against incarceration, see Robert Shafer, "Cracks in the Consensus: Defending the Rights of Japanese Americans during World War II," *Radical History Review*, 72 (Fall 1998), 84–120. Edmund D. Soper, *Racism: A World Issue* (New York, 1947); Buell G. Gallagher, *Color and Conscience: The Irrepressible Conflict* (New York, 1946), 188.

26. On the radically different ideas about God, the Bible, the mission of churches, the role of the clergy, and race among the clergy and the laity in mainstream denominations, see Jeffrey K. Hadden, *The Gathering Storm in the Churches: A Sociologist Looks at the Widening Gap between Clergy and Laymen* (New York, 1969).

27. A judicious assessment of the slowness of the ecumenical leadership to appreciate their actual circumstances and to develop more coherent positions on church-state relations and other issues of the 1940s and 1950s is William McGuire King, "The Reform Establishment and the Ambiguities of Influence," in *Between the Times*, ed. Hutchison, 122–40. On the interaction between Protestant leaders and government officials, see Inboden, *Religion and American Foreign Policy, 1945–1960*. On the ecumenical Protestant impact on the United Nations, see Nurser, *For All Peoples and All Nations*.

28. *Roe v. Wade*, 410 U.S. 113 (1973).

29. Inboden, *Religion and American Foreign Policy, 1945–1960*, 57. On the condemnation of the Federal Council of Churches by the National Association of Evangelicals, see Williams, *God's Own Party*, 19. On Oxnam's difficulties with Carl McIntire and other evangelicals, see, for example, Mark Silk, "The Rise of the 'New Evangelicalism': Shock and Adjustment," in *Between the Times*, ed. Hutchison, 280. On Oxnam's difficulties with McIntire and on Oxnam's willingness to support what he saw as more judicious and well-targeted anticommunist investigations, see Robert Moats Miller, *Bishop G. Bromley Oxnam: Paladin of Liberal Protestantism* (Nashville, 1990), 528–34. For a detailed account of Oxnam's appearance before the House Un-American Activities Committee, see Ralph Lord Roy, *Communism and the Churches* (New York, 1960), 254–59. For a convincing defense of the claim that McIntire was a much more central figure in the political mobilization of evangelical Protestants than some historians have been willing to grant, see Markku Ruotsila, "Carl McIntire and the Anti-Communist Origins of the Religious Right," paper delivered at the annual meeting of the American Historical Association, Boston, Jan. 2011 (in David A. Hollinger's possession).

30. Committee for the Preservation of Methodism, *Is There a Pink Fringe in the Methodist Church?* (Houston, 1951), esp. unpaginated preface, pp. 4–7. This pamphlet apparently took its title from Stanley High, "Methodism's Pink Fringe," *Reader's Digest*, 56 (Feb. 1950), 134–38.

31. On the evangelical Right's assaults on John A. Mackay, see James H. Smylie, "Mackay and McCarthyism, 1953–1954," *Journal of Church and State*, 6 (Aug. 1964), 352–65.

32. Inboden, *Religion and American Foreign Policy*, 74, 82–83, 98; J. Edgar Hoover, "The Communist Menace: Red Goals and Christian Ideals," *Christianity*

Today, Oct. 10, 1960, pp. 3–5; J. Edgar Hoover, "Communist Propaganda and the Christian Pulpit, ibid., Oct. 14, 1960, p. 5; J. Edgar Hoover, "Soviet Rule or Christian Renewal?," ibid., Nov. 7, 1960, pp. 9–11.

33. *Brown v. Board of Education*, 347 U.S. 483 (1954). L. Nelson Bell, "Christian Race Relations Must Be Natural, Not Forced," *Southern Presbyterian Journal*, Aug. 17, 1955, p. 4. See also Julia Kirk Blackwelder, "Southern White Fundamentalists and the Civil Rights Movement," *Phylon*, 40 (Jan.–April 1979), 334–41. On the asymmetry of Billy Graham's call to end prejudice and his slowness to support the dismantling of Jim Crow, see Steven P. Miller, *Billy Graham and the Rise of the Republican South* (Philadelphia, 2009), 44. For an ambitious scholarly study of Graham that takes a more generous view, see Grant Wacker, "Billy Graham's America," *Church History*, 78 (Sept. 2009), 489–511.

34. For an overview of the rivalry between *Christianity Today* and *The Christian Century*, see Mark Toulouse, "*Christianity Today* and American Public Life: A Case Study," *Journal of Church and State*, 35 (Spring 1993), 241–84; and Mark Toulouse, "*The Christian Century* and American Public Life: The Crucial Years, 1956–1968," in *New Dimensions in American Religious History*, ed. Jay P. Dolan and James P. Wind (Grand Rapids, 1993), 44–82. Reinhold Niebuhr, "Differing Views on Billy Graham: A Theologian Says Evangelist Is Simplifying Views on Life," *Life*, July 1, 1957, p. 92. On the reaction of the ecumenical leadership to Graham, see Silk, "The Rise of the 'New Evangelicalism.'"

35. James F. Findlay Jr., *Church People in the Struggle: The National Council of Churches and the Black Freedom Movement, 1950–1970* (New York, 1993), esp. 28; Martin Luther King Jr., "Letter from the Birmingham Jail," *The Christian Century*, June 12, 1963, pp. 769–75.

36. On evangelical organizing in Southern California, see Daren Dochuk, *From Bible Belt to Sun Belt: Plain-Folk Religion, Grassroots Politics, and the Rise of Evangelical Conservatism* (New York, 2011). Dochuk provides vivid examples of the deep enmity with which some of the most energetic and influential evangelical preachers regarded ecumenical liberals and calls attention to the formidable link between the evangelical movement of Southern California and that of the states of the old Confederacy that produced so many westward migrants.

37. Dean R. Hoge, Benton Johnson, and Donald Luidens, *Vanishing Boundaries: The Religion of Mainline Protestant Baby Boomers* (Louisville, 1994), 2.

38. On the decline of ecumenical numbers and the rise of evangelical numbers, see Dean M. Kelley, *Why Conservative Churches Are Growing* (New York, 1972); and Wade Clark Roof and William McKinney, *American Mainline Religion: Its Changing Shape and Future* (New Brunswick, 1987), 20. Ray Suarez, *The Holy Vote: The Politics of Faith in America* (New York, 2006), 74–90. On the importance of Jews in the de-Christianization of the public life of the United States, see David A. Hollinger, *Science, Jews, and Secular Culture: Studies in MidTwentieth Century American Intellectual History* (Princeton, 1996); and chapter 7 in this volume.

39. Hoge, Johnson, and Luidens, *Vanishing Boundaries*, 7; C. Kirk Hadaway and Penny Long Marler, "Growth and Decline in the Mainline," in *Faith in America: Changes, Challenges, and New Directions*, ed. Charles Lippy (Westport, 2006), 5; Hoge, Johnson, and Luidens, *Vanishing Boundaries*, 73; Roof and McKinney, *American Mainline Religion*, 152, 161; Michael Hout, Andrew Greeley, and Me-

lissa J. Wilde, "The Demographic Imperative of Religious Change in the United States," *American Journal of Sociology*, 107 (Sept. 2001), 468–500.

40. Robert Wuthnow, *America and the Challenges of Religious Diversity* (Princeton, 2005), 184.

41. An important progressive voice within the evangelical leadership was Richard Cizik, chief lobbyist for the National Association of Evangelicals, who was forced to resign in 2009 after he spoke too approvingly of same-sex relationships and President Barack Obama. For an account of this event written from within evangelical circles, with quotations from Richard Land, Charles Colson, and other evangelical leaders, see Sarah Pulliam, "Richard Cizik Resigns from the National Association of Evangelicals," *Christianity Today*, Dec. 12, 2008, available at http://www.christianitytoday.com/ct/2008/decemberweb-only/150 -42.0.html. On ecumenicals' tolerance relative to evangelicals, see, for example, Lynn D. Nelson, "Disaffiliation, Desacralization, and Political Values," in *Falling from the Faith: Causes and Consequences of Religious Apostasy*, ed. David G. Bromley (Newbury Park, 1988), 122–39; Roof and McKinney, *American Mainline Religion*, 186–228; and Robert D. Putnam and David E. Campbell, *American Grace: How Religion Divides and Unites Us* (New York, 2010), 386.

42. Douglas Sloan, *Faith and Knowledge: Mainline Protestantism and American Higher Education* (Lexington, 1994), 83; "Methodists: A Jester for Wesleyans," *Time*, Oct. 21, 1966, p. 69.

43. Sloan, *Faith and Knowledge*, 165–66.

44. Charlotte Bunch, "Charlotte Bunch," in *Journeys That Opened Up the World: Women, Student Christian Movements, and Social Justice, 1955–1975*, ed. Sara Evans (New Brunswick, 2003), 139; B. J. Stiles to David A. Hollinger, e-mail, July 2, 2010 (in David A. Hollinger's possession).

45. On the "Black Manifesto" incident, see Findlay, *Church People in the Struggle*, 199–225; and Thomas J. Sugrue, *Sweet Land of Liberty: The Forgotten Struggle for Civil Rights in the North* (New York, 2008), 435–40.

46. Jill K. Gill, "The Politics of Ecumenical Disunity: The Troubled Marriage of Church World Service and the National Council of Churches," *Religion and American Culture*, 14 (July 2004), 189, 192.

47. Margaret Lamberts Bendroth, *Growing Up Protestant: Parents, Children, and Mainline Churches* (New Brunswick, 2002), esp. 135.

48. Ronald Reagan addressed the National Association of Evangelicals in Orlando, Florida, on March 8, 1983. See *Evil Empire Speech Memorial Foundation*, available at http://www.evilempirespeech.org. For a cogent analysis of the evangelical political mobilization that set the stage for the political triumphs of the Reagan era, see Paul Boyer, "The Evangelical Resurgence in 1970s American Protestantism," in *Rightward Bound: Making America Conservative in the 1970s*, ed. Bruce J. Schulman and Julian E. Zelizer (Cambridge, MA, 2008), 29–51.

49. Martin Marty, *Righteous Empire: The Protestant Experience in America* (New York, 1970), 177–87. On the political struggles of the ecumenical leadership during the 1940s and 1950s, see Martin Marty, *Modern American Religion*, vol. 3: *Under God Indivisible, 1941–1960* (Chicago, 1996).

50. On the ways ecumenical Protestantism served as an incubator for feminist and other radical and liberal careers beyond and within churches, see the

sixteen memoirs collected in Evans, ed., *Journeys That Opened Up the World.* On the transformation to a post-Protestant culture, see Amanda Porterfield, *The Transformation of American Religion: The Story of a Late Twentieth-Century Awakening* (New York, 2001), 6. On a Protestant deposit in the geological layering of secular American life, see Marty, *Righteous Empire,* 264.

51. Walter Rauschenbusch, *Christianity and the Social Crisis* (New York, 1907). Reinhold Niebuhr, *Moral Man and Immoral Society* (New York, 1932). On Niebuhr and *Moral Man and Immoral Society,* see Richard Wightman Fox, *Reinhold Niebuhr: A Biography* (Ithaca, 1996), 136–41, 161–66. Walter Kaufmann, *Critique of Religion and Philosophy* (New York, 1958), 287–303; Walter Kaufmann, ed., *Existentialism from Dostoevsky to Sartre* (New York, 1956), 50. Walter Kaufmann's centrality to the existentialist vogue of the postwar decades is documented in George Cotkin, *Existential America* (Baltimore, 2003), 147.

52. H. L. Mencken, *Prejudices,* 3 vols. (New York, 1922), III, 159.

53. For observations on the Lilly Endowment's protective approach to religion and its place in American life, see chapter 9 in this volume. Roof and McKinney, *American Mainline Religion,* 61–62, 242; Jackson W. Carroll and Wade Clark Roof, eds., *Beyond Establishment: Protestant Identity in a Post-Protestant Age* (Louisville, 1993), 352.

54. N. J. Demerath III, "Cultural Victory and Organizational Defeat in the Paradoxical Decline of Liberal Protestantism," *Journal for the Scientific Study of Religion,* 34 (March 1995), 458–69, esp. 458–60. See also Wade Clark Roof, *Spiritual Marketplace: Baby Boomers and the Remaking of American Religion* (Princeton, 1999), 309.

55. Christian Smith and Patricia Snell, *Souls in Transition: The Religious and Spiritual Lives of Emerging Adults* (New York, 2009), 288.

56. Putnam and Campbell, *American Grace,* 91–133, 370–71, 401.

57. For the Young Men's Christian Association's announcement of this change, see its news release of July 10, 2010, available at the YMCA website, http://www.ymca.net/news-releases/20100712-brand-new-day.html. For the resulting representation, see http://www.ymca.net/.

CHAPTER 3

The Realist–Pacifist Summit Meeting of March 1942 and the Political Reorientation of Ecumenical Protestantism in the United States

Deepening research on the history of American Protestantism in the twentieth century made me increasingly aware of the peculiar significance of 1942 as a historical moment at which the two major, religiously defined institutional forces of the entire period from World War II to the present were consolidated. Yet the scholarly literature, while attending to the founding of the National Association of Evangelicals (NAE) during that year, was largely oblivious to the simultaneous consolidation of the rival, ecumenical party into a relatively cohesive presence in American public life. Historians of "mainline" Protestantism devoted extensive attention to the war's having increased the credibility of the "Christian realist" Reinhold Niebuhr, whose 1930s attacks on pacifists appeared to be the salient foundation for the activities of the Federal Council of Churches (the FCC, in existence since 1908, and then renamed the National Council of Churches, or NCC, in 1950) and its denominational affiliates for some time afterward. Fair enough, but two important things were missing. First, I found little understanding of how the discredited pacifist faction, once the Japanese attack on Pearl Harbor rendered the conflict over American intervention in the war virtually moot, contributed to the leftist political orientation of the ecumenical Protestant leadership. Second, I found almost no analysis of the process by which the two factions came together, organizationally and doctrinally. I could not believe that the pacifists just disappeared into Niebuhr's shadow. I found that they did not.

Upon realizing that a large "study conference" of church leaders in March of 1942 was the crucial step in the merger of the pacifists with the realists, I wrote this essay to call attention to that conference's character as the "summit meeting" at which the two severely antagonistic groups of liberal Protestant leaders agreed upon an agenda for the postwar world. Although the theologian Niebuhr was a participant in the process, the central figure was the Presbyterian layman, John Foster Dulles, later to be Secretary of State under President Dwight D. Eisenhower. Dulles's background in "the Protestant Establishment" has been widely noted by historians of American foreign relations, but his authority within the domain of the churches invites more recognition that it has received. The archives of the Federal Council of Churches show how readily leaders of both the pacifist and realist factions were willing to follow Dulles, who worked through intermediaries more committed than he to achieving unity. The resolutions of this 1942 meeting, and those of a follow-up conference of 1945 that I also discuss here, are sharply etched artifacts of a World War II epoch when even self-styled "realists" were willing to endorse sweepingly egalitarian and universalist ideals that were then placed on the defensive during the Cold War. This essay also discusses the remarkably complacent—at least from today's perspective—confidence of ecumenical Protestant leaders that it was not so difficult to decide what a "Christian" public policy was, and that they—and they alone—were the people endowed with the authority to make this determination.

This essay was originally published in Church History *LXXIX (September 2010), 654–677.*

"I HOPE THAT THE MATTER OF THE AGREEMENT not to discuss the war can be satisfactorily clarified," Walter M. Horton wrote to the office of the Federal Council of Churches (FCC) in November of 1941, referring to a meeting of several hundred liberal Protestant leaders the FCC was planning for the following March. "I found some questioning about it" at a recent meeting of peace advocates, some of whom, Horton continued, expressed fear that if they went to the conference they would be obliged "to swear an oath not to say a word about the dominant reality on the horizon."[1] The distinguished Oberlin theologian worried that the question of "a just and durable peace" that was to be addressed at the "Delaware Conference"—so named on account of its being held on the Delaware, Ohio, campus of Ohio Wesleyan University—might not be effectively engaged because opponents of American entry into World War II were being asked to shut up in the presence of the self-styled "political realists" who were chiefly behind the conclave.

The Delaware Conference of March 3–5, 1942, invites the attention of historians because it was the first moment at which large numbers of Protestant leaders confronted each other face to face once their own country was actually at war.[2] It amounted to a summit meeting of the rival groups within the leadership of ecumenical Protestantism. These groups discovered on this occasion that they could work together in trying to diminish the power of several specific evils they agreed were inimical to "a just and durable peace": racism, imperialism, nationalism, and economic structures that perpetuated inequality. The sudden elimination, through American entry into the war, of the defining cause of the pacifist faction made that faction's considerable inventory of ideas and feelings about these other evils available for deployment within the realists' favorite framework: a world political body stronger than the League of Nations. Once the realist faction was released from the imperative to attack isolationists and other anti-interventionists, that faction's well-developed internationalism could be articulated in more direct and sustained relation to the deeply structured evils believed to make warfare more likely.

The realists in this family included President Henry Pitney Van Dusen of Union Theological Seminary, President John A. Mackay of Princeton Theological Seminary, and future Secretary of State John Foster Dulles, then known chiefly for his roles as a Presbyterian lay leader and as an out-of-office Republican expert on foreign affairs. The "agreement" to which Horton referred was an understanding promoted by the FCC that the conference should not be distracted by the well-worn but deeply felt disagreements between a peace-oriented group, for which *The Christian Century* was a leading voice, and a more interventionist group led by Union professor Reinhold Niebuhr, who early in 1941 had been instrumental in establishing a rival periodical, *Christianity and Crisis*, to counteract what Niebuhr took to be the persistently naïve political attitudes of the peace faction.[3] In 1940 the FCC had established the Commission for a Just and Durable Peace, chaired by Dulles and supported by Niebuhr, among many others, which was designed to map a Christian blueprint for the world once the Axis powers had been defeated. This body, which came to be known as the "Dulles Commission," generally took for granted that the United States would eventually join the war but in the meantime sought to establish a Protestant voice in debates about the postwar political order. The commission's Delaware Conference was a means toward that end.

No wonder Horton got a reassuring response by return mail from the FCC official in charge of the conference. Anyone who told you "that the mouths of the delegates would be sealed with respect to the war as such certainly is in a mental fog," declared Walter W. Van Kirk, who continued that people coming to Delaware "may say anything that is on their minds."[4] Van Kirk had good reason to be defensive and to overstate the case. Documents circulated within the commission's leadership marked "confidential" made explicit—and underscored—the plan that "the question of America's relation to the war will not be on the agenda."[5] The FCC had labored quietly to make sure that the commission and its crucial "Committee of Direction" included at least a few prominent figures in the pacifist camp. This Committee of Direction, on whose stationary the call to the Delaware Conference was issued, included pacifists Ernest Fremont Tittle, Albert Buckner Coe, Mary E. Wooley, and Georgia Harkness alongside such realist stalwarts as Van Dusen, Mackay, Dulles, and John C. Bennett.[6] When Van Kirk replied to Horton, he knew his job was to keep the pacifists on board for the big event in Ohio.

Van Kirk's job got much easier three weeks later when the Japanese attacked Pearl Harbor. With the United States in the war, the old pacifist–realist tussle lost some of its tension. The FCC had a better chance to redirect the conversation toward the new agenda of postwar planning. And it worked. The two antagonistic groups within the leadership of ecumenical Protestantism came together to establish a new political orientation, the character and consequences of which have been insufficiently recognized by historians still in the thrall of the "realism versus innocence" narrative of the religious history the 1940s and 1950s propagated at the time by Niebuhr himself and perpetuated by Niebuhr's countless, and often uncritical, admirers ever since.

This new alliance was not achieved without one last and dramatic skirmish. The dynamics of this clash attest to the "summit meeting" character of the conference, and also to the magnitude of the transformation the conference effected. Once the nearly four hundred delegates sent by twenty-seven Protestant denominations and nearly forty interdenominational organizations convened at Ohio Wesleyan, some of the pacifists insisted on what turned out to be a last stand. The early stages of the conference were divided into several "section" meetings, including one charged with clarifying "The Relation of the Church to a Just and Durable Peace" at which a move from the floor declared that "The Church as such is not at war"—a motion vociferously debated. Charles Clayton Morrison, editor of *The Christian Century* and one of the peace faction's most indefatigable voices, offered the portentous motion. In Niebuhr's absence at the conference, opposition was led by Mackay, a Scottish-born former missionary to Latin America whose position as the president of Princeton Theological Seminary made him one of the most influential Presbyterians in the world. The debate was later described by Van Dusen in *Christianity and Crisis* as the "single incident" that "somewhat marred the otherwise orderly and amicable progress" by which the Delaware Conference achieved "significant agreements." The motion actually passed in the section meeting by a vote of 64–58. Such strong support—four months after Pearl Harbor—for a resolution distancing the churches of the United States from their own government's military effort against the Axis powers indicates how formidable the pacifist persuasion remained within the ranks of the delegates. But when the report of this section was presented to the plenary session, this resolution was ruled out of order by the presiding officers, Dulles and FCC President Luther Weigle, on the grounds that the issue addressed by the motion was not relevant to the conference.[7]

Whatever grousing there was about this parliamentary ruling died down remarkably quickly. Within a month *The Christian Century* not only ran an enthusiastic editorial written by Morrison's protégé, Paul

Hutchinson, but also devoted a seven-page special feature to publishing the resolutions of the Delaware Conference in their entirety.[8] Soon thereafter the editors published and widely distributed a massive study booklet developing long lists of questions designed to facilitate the sympathetic discussion of the conference's resolutions in local churches and other organizations throughout the country.[9] The leaders of the peace faction had bought into the new agenda designed largely by Dulles but given a more critical edge (more about that later) by the input of the pacifist faction's own somewhat more left-leaning constituency. To be sure, Niebuhr and his comrades at *Christianity and Crisis* continued throughout the war to castigate pacifists for their lack of wholehearted support for the war effort, but Niebuhr's journal, no less than Morrison's, gave positive attention to the ongoing efforts of the FCC to direct discussions of the postwar world along the lines outlined at the Delaware Conference.[10] Scarcely a year after the conference, Niebuhr himself acknowledged that "The pronouncements on world problems by the Federal Council Commission on a Just and Durable Peace have become increasingly realistic and continue to stress America's responsibility to the world community."[11] So the old alignments did not disappear, but their relative importance diminished substantially.

Just what did the Delaware Conference agree upon and proclaim to the world? Which Protestant leaders, in addition to those named earlier, were present at the conference and/or helped to bring it about and to endow it with the character of a summit meeting? In what respects did the new political orientation established at the conference affect the destiny of ecumenical Protestantism? This essay is directed at these three questions.

What Was the Summit Meeting's Position on the Salient Issues?

The most striking features of the conference's message to Christendom when read today are two that were not very controversial at the time. One such feature was the repeatedly articulated presumption of a proprietary relationship between Protestant Christianity and the American nation. The leaders of ecumenical Protestantism in the 1940s took for granted that their churches had a unique role to play in guiding the United States—and the world—toward an ideal political order, and they displayed no doubt that Christian principles should be the foundation of such an order. They were certain, as they explicitly affirmed at the beginning of their resolutions, that "Christians and non-Christians can alike accept" these principles.[12] These confident men and women alluded often in their writings to the evils of secularism, but until the Cold War fostered the talk of "Godless Communism" that churchly Americans of all persuasions could easily exploit, this crowd displayed very little feeling that they needed to energetically contest, to say nothing of sympathetically consider, any ideas other than the ones they understood as Christian.

The second relatively noncontroversial feature that catches our attention today is the assumption that there was no great challenge in identifying what were the truly Christian principles. The leaders of ecumenical Protestantism had trouble taking seriously any construction of these principles put forth either by Catholics or by the more evangelical and fundamentalist segments of American Protestantism. It may be ironic that during same month of March 1942, the leaders of these "other" Protestants, who disdained the ecumenists as too liberal, were meeting in St. Louis to found the National Association of Evangelicals, which would eventually achieve a prominent place in American politics and today garners more press attention than the FCC's successor organization, the National Council of Churches. The "Protestant Establishment," as historians have come to call the ecumenical Protestant leadership of the first two-thirds of the twentieth century, did not doubt that it had the standing to speak for all of Christianity.

These two features of the Delaware Conference merely flag the distance between the 1940s and what the United States had become only a quarter-century later. More to the point of a more comprehensive interpretation of the event is an understanding of the positions the delegates took on issues that were alive at the time. Chief among these issues was the relation of national sovereignty to some kind of yet-to-be-created transnational political authority. "A world of irresponsible, competing and unrestrained national sovereignties, whether acting alone or in alliance or in coalitions, is a world of international anarchy," the conference declared. "The ultimate requirement" for a "just and durable peace" was "a duly constituted world government of delegated powers" complete with legislature, court, police, "and provision for world-wide economic sanctions."[13] It was in connection with this advocacy of "world government," as it was colloquially shortened, that ecumenical Protestants so closely followed the formation of the United Nations three years later.

In relation to this call for greater international organization, the conferees also called for an end to the colonial system. "Autonomy for all subject and colonial peoples" was to be realized, and in the interim "the task of colonial government" was to be taken away from colonial powers and "recognized as a common responsibility of mankind," with colonized people themselves assured "a voice in their government." Registering their sense that the process of decolonization was not likely to be achieved in one stroke, the delegates allowed that some colonized peoples might be "not yet capable of self-government," but they emphasized that the role of international authority was to substantially push forward the goal of "self-government" for all colonized populations. The conference repudiated the notions of racial hierarchy on which the colonial system was based, declaring that "no group of men is inherently superior or inferior to any other."[14]

The delegates applied this rejection of racialized thinking to the domestic American scene, too, and more controversially given the reality of Jim Crow. They clearly connected racism abroad and racism at home. "The securing of justice now for racial groups is essential if America is to make its full contribution in securing a just and durable peace," the conference resolved, while it acknowledged "with profound contrition the sin of racial discrimination." The United States "cannot safely be trusted with the making" of peace "so long as our attitudes and policies deny peoples of other races in our own or other lands the essential position of brothers." Citing recent, specific cases of antiblack rioting and lynching, the delegates demanded an end to "unequal treatment" of "American Negroes" in education, employment, working conditions, housing, transportation, the administration of justice, and voting. "We condemn all such inequalities and call upon our fellow Christians and fellow citizens to initiate and support" measures to achieve equality among "minority and cultural groups." More specifically, the conference called for action by the federal government to end "discrimination in industry and the public services against Negroes and persons of other racial and national origin," and it called, further, for the welcoming of Negroes and other racial minorities "into the membership, administrative personnel and fellowship of our churches, local and national."[15]

The conference's pronouncements on economic issues were less forthright, but did include the need for "experimentation with various forms of ownership and control, private, cooperative, and public." This was a definite nod toward the idea that the prevailing capitalist order needed to be altered in socialistic directions, but the delegates could not overcome their disagreements as to how this idea might be formulated more precisely. They offered a list of twelve recommendations for "special consideration and study," allowing that the conference "did not reach the same unanimity" on these recommendations as it did on the rest of its resolutions. These recommendations included what were described as a series of "rights," including the "right to employment of a kind that is consistent with human dignity and self-respect," and "the right to full-time educational opportunities" in youth and "economic security in retirement." Other recommendations in this list called for a revision of the tax system to promote a more equitable distribution of wealth, a greater role for labor in managing industry, and more effective "regulatory measures" that would control business cycles and protect against unemployment, "a universal system of money," and "a democratically controlled international bank" that would make capital available "in all parts of the world without the predatory or imperialistic aftermath so characteristic of large-scale private or governmental loans."[16]

Hence, the positions the delegates took on nationalism, empire, race, and the economy were understandably read as tilting toward the left-liberal, rather than the right-conservative side of American political discourse as constituted in 1942. *Time* magazine described the Delaware Conference as "sensational" in its collectivist economic ideas and in its "extreme internationalism," but allowed that it was not quite "as far to the left as its definitely pinko British counterpart, the now famous Malvern Conference."[17] Here, *Time* referred to a January 1941 meeting of British church leaders led by Archbishop of Canterbury William Temple that had indeed been an inspiration for the Delaware Conference: a suggestion that "an American 'Malvern' Conference be convened at the earliest possible moment" was "discussed at some length" at the initial meeting of the Dulles Commission's Committee of Direction on March 21, 1941.[18] *Time*'s characterization of the Delaware Conference as radically leftist reflected, of course, the magazine's political orientation, but *Time*'s summary account of the specific points agreed to at the conference was basically accurate. *Time* focused on the proposed migration of sovereignty from nation states to international authorities, but also represented, with accurate quotations, the conference's pronouncements on colonial peoples and American Negroes, on labor's role in industrial management, on economic "rights," and on the generally self-critical tone with reference to the United States.

Time also sensed that the number of distinguished and influential Americans who participated made the Delaware Conference highly unique:

> Among the 375 delegates who drafted the program were 15 bishops of five denominations, seven seminary heads (including Yale, Chicago, Princeton, Colgate-Rochester), eight college and university presidents (including Princeton's Harold W. Dodds), practically all the ranking officials of the Federal Council and a group of well-known laymen, including John R. Mott, Irving Fisher and Harvey S. Firestone Jr.[19]

Time's description of the conferees can turn us toward the second question I stated earlier, just who, among American Protestant leaders, was present at the conference and/or helped to bring it about and to endow it with the character of a summit meeting?

Who Made the New Progressive Consensus Happen, and How?

Since John R. Mott is no longer a household name, it is important to underscore his eminence in 1942. It made sense for *Time* to mention Mott, a figure so well-connected that he once in a single day paid social calls on the president of the United States (Coolidge) and two former presidents (Taft and Wilson).[20] Four years after the conference, Mott would win the Nobel Peace Prize for his several decades of leadership of the Young Men's Christian Association (YMCA) and a host of missionary organizations. Irving Fisher, the Yale economist and mathematician now most remembered as the founder of monetarist economic theory, was then known more for his energetic advocacy of peace, vegetarianism, and other progressive causes. Firestone's name is still recognized on account of the automobile tire company, but at the time of the conference, at which he was a delegate from the Episcopal Church, Firestone was one of a number of super wealthy men whose names appeared regularly in lists of supporters of church-sponsored causes.[21] Alfred Landon, the Republican presidential candidate in 1936, was registered as a delegate for the Methodist Church and was among the other immediately recognized public figures present at Delaware.

It is understandable that *Time* would focus on some of the more famous delegates and would remark upon the heavy representation of heads of seminaries, colleges, and denominational bodies. But the character of the Delaware Conference is best grasped through its organizational makeup and through the delegates' selection process. Notes kept by FCC General Secretaries Van Kirk and Bradford S. Abernethy during the late fall and early winter of 1941–1942, along with records of their correspondence, trace two sets of administrative actions that maximized the chances for a broad-based, high-stakes conference.

First, the FCC office invited the officials of each major denomination to select delegates. The number of delegates depended in part on the size of the denominational bodies affiliated with the FCC, resulting in heavy representation by Methodists, Congregationalists, Northern Baptists, and both Northern and Southern Presbyterians. Smaller but substantial delegations were also sent by the Episcopalians, the Unitarians, the Disciples of Christ, the Quakers, both the Dutch and the German Reformed, several Lutheran bodies, the Church of the Brethren, the Mennonites, the Salvation Army, the Moravians, and two historically black churches, the African Methodist Episcopal Zion and the Colored Methodist Episcopal. The FCC worked directly through denominational headquarters to ensure that each cooperating denomination had a stake in the conference and would send delegates capable of reflecting well on their own communion while interacting with other communions within the increasingly important FCC. Ecumenical conferences were not new, but this one had a distinctive and timely agenda. It was soon understood by all parties as the most important meeting of American church leaders in a generation. Prominent individuals writing to Van Kirk or Abernethy asking to be named delegates were sometimes referred back to their own denominational organizations with expressions of confidence that the applicant would, indeed, be chosen.[22]

A second set of administrative acts by Van Kirk and Abernethy, taken with counsel from Dulles, Mackay, and others on the commission's Committee of Direction, was the appointing of regionally based drafting committees charged with presenting the conference with written reports that could be the basis for discussion and enactment. There were four such committees, each assigned a specific cluster of issues (the exact terms of which shifted somewhat during the process, but were essentially social, political, economic, and ecclesiastical), based in Chicago, Philadelphia, New York, and Boston. Subcommittees in Tennessee and Ohio were also asked to offer suggestions. In each case the FCC office sought to mobilize each region's recognized lay and clerical elites, especially as connected with such institutions as missionary societies, magazines, women's groups, seminaries, and denominational boards. If a first choice was not available for a given slot, another prominent figure usually was. These drafting groups were closely controlled by the Committee of Direction and usually chaired by one of its members. The realist Mackay chaired the Philadelphia group. The pacifist Tittle, who was then the most popular Methodist preacher in the United States, chaired the Chicago committee (which included the volatile Morrison) and consulted with Dulles personally about his group's deliberations.[23]

The detailed operations of the New York regional committee in January and February of 1942 provide a telling instance of how the peace faction endowed the Delaware Conference with an edge more critical than it probably would have displayed in the absence of a vibrant contingent from that faction. The New York Committee was chaired by Leslie B. Moss, not a member of the Committee of Direction but who, as the Executive Secretary of the Committee on Foreign Relief Appeals in the Churches, was a bona fide presence in the Protestant Establishment. Another member of the New York group was A. J. Muste, the head of the Fellowship of Reconciliation and one of the most consistent and outspoken pacifists in all of American history. Muste first gained fame when he was dismissed by his Massachusetts congregation forthwith upon delivering a sermon opposing American involvement in World War I and was obliged to vacate his family from the parsonage that very afternoon. Muste was always "out there" and, at the end of his life, was an adamant opponent of the Vietnam War. But in this committee, Muste was not functioning as a pacifist. Moss assigned Muste the job of thinking through the position on "race" to recommend to the conference as a whole.

In that capacity, Muste wrote a four-paged, single-spaced memorandum labeled "tentative and confidential," concerning the failure of churches to "more thoroughly" eliminate the attitudes of superiority found especially among "white races toward Orientals and Negroes." Muste was enough of a diplomat to quote Dulles approvingly—twice— although not specifically on the racial question, on which Dulles was never loquacious. As it happened, this New York group's report formed the basis of the Delaware Conference's striking statements about racism in general and about Jim Crow discrimination in particular. This document—"Report of the Section on the Social Basis of a Just and Durable Peace"—when compared to the text adopted by the conference, shows minor editing, mostly rearranged paragraphs, but for the most part the New York group's language was adopted word for word by the conference. To be sure, a number of the realists of that era, as well as many of the pacifists, held antiracist views, but prior to the Delaware Conference their antiracism had taken a decidedly marginal place in a discourse dominated by issues of peace and war, and to a lesser extent by labor and management. The New York group thus generated what turned out to be some of the most liberal of the resolutions of the Delaware Conference. The group also included Channing Tobias, the only black member of the Committee of Direction, and two notably antiracist former missionaries, Luman J. Shafer and A. L. Warnshuis, but there is no doubt that Muste's influence was decisive.[24]

Beyond the orchestration of the drafting committees and the mobilization of denominationally defined constituencies, the FCC office did something else that made the Delaware Conference a landmark event. Van Kirk and Abernethy invited many local and national councils of churches and virtually all of the major cross-denominational organizations associated in any way with the ecumenical movement to send representatives, although not as voting delegates. The most important of these affiliated organizations were the Foreign Missions Conference, the United Council of Church Women, the YMCA, the Young Women's Christian Association (YWCA), the Student Volunteer Movement, and the Layman's Missionary Movement.[25]

The FCC achieved another organizational triumph by arranging for high-level State Department participation. Abernethy and Van Kirk had originally wanted Assistant Secretary of State Adolph Berle. When Berle was unavailable the State Department, after some private conversations arranged by Dulles, sent economist Leo Pasvolsky, a special assistant to Secretary of State Cordell Hull then assigned to the National Resources Planning Board. Pasvolsky was one of six plenary lecturers at the conference, along with Dulles himself, the Methodist Bishop Francis J. McConnell, and three carefully selected foreign leaders, Hu Shih (the Chinese ambassador to the United States), C. J. Hambro (the exiled president of the Norwegian parliament), and William Paton (a leading ecumenist from Britain).[26] But Pasvolsky's presence at the conference was more than symbolic.

Pasvolsky circulated a fifty-two-page document summarizing his agency's thinking about the postwar peace. That Pasvolsky was willing to do this (a decision presumably made with the approval of Hull himself) signals the seriousness with which the government was taking the Protestant Establishment. Moreover, Pasvolsky's document included what is in fact a draft of the key sections of President Roosevelt's legendary State of the Union Address of 1944, in which Roosevelt proposed his never-enacted "economic bill of rights." Historians have long understood that Roosevelt's speech, often hailed as his finest, was based on work done within the National Resources Planning Board. But here at Delaware the government's own representative was encouraging the Protestant Establishment to be thinking in line with the most radical trajectories of the New Deal concerning "rights" to "adequate food, clothing, shelter, and medical care" as well as to "education" and to "equality before the law."[27]

All of these actions by Abernethy, Van Kirk, and Dulles took place in the matrix of the commission for a Just and Durable Peace, an organization intended from the start to reach extensively into the ecumenical Protestant ranks but largely developed by the leaders of the realist persuasion who were simultaneously supporting Niebuhr's launching of *Christianity and Crisis*.[28] The commission itself rarely met and was mostly a list of names, but the smaller Committee of Direction that actually ran the enterprise quickly understood that success depended on mobilizing a broad base of support. The minutes of the committee's initial meeting of March 21, 1941, recorded the agreement that the commission's task was "difficult and delicate" because of "differences particularly" about possible American "participation in the war."[29] The first and apparently only meeting of the entire commission prior to the Delaware Conference was attended by fifty-three members, of whom Morrison was one. So, too, was Niebuhr.[30] The relatively weak representation of pacifists on the commission itself apparently mattered little given their stronger presence on the Committee of Direction and given the efforts of Van Kirk and others, as described earlier, to provide a big tent for the conference.

Hence, the "summit meeting" aspect of the conference was in part a product of the FCC's inability to proceed with a large-scale enterprise focused on world affairs without incorporating a pacifist element, the strength of which was then shown at Delaware in the measure of support given Morrison's motion even after Pearl Harbor. But this aspect was also a product of the contingencies of timing: had the conference been held three months earlier, or had the Japanese attack come three months later, there is no way of knowing how the assembled churchmen and churchwomen would have dealt with one another. Moreover, it is far from clear who, and how many, would have shown up. Since Abernethy did not even begin to impanel the strategically pivotal regional committees until December 10 (after the American declaration of war) and only some weeks later issued invitations to the various groups to send delegates, it is not clear how differently—or how similarly?—the entire process of organizing the conference would have proceeded absent the war declaration, and how many of the pacifists would have agreed to participate.

The agreements reached at Delaware need to be interpreted in the context of the popular, "arms linked across the sea" mood for which Wendell Willkie's best-selling book of 1943, One World,[31] is the most recognized and enduring emblem. Criticism of imperialism in general and of the British Empire in particular, which were themes of One World, diminished by the end of the war in specific relation to worries about Soviet influence. But for a few years, the notion of a species-wide solidarity—supervised by a benevolent United States and enacted in concert with the varieties of humankind—appealed enormously to Republicans like Willkie and Dulles as well as to New Dealers and to a great range of liberal Protestants. While this extravagant idealism flourished well beyond the ranks of churchmen and churchwomen, among them it took deeper root on account of the Delaware Conference's institutionalization of it. A sign of this institutionalization, and hence another indicator of the unique significance of the Delaware Conference, is the character of a second commission "study conference" held in Cleveland, January 16–19, 1945.[32]

The commission brought nearly five hundred ecumenical Protestants to Cleveland for an event that tracked the Delaware Conference of three years earlier in both its basic doctrinal content and in its organizational dynamics. The focal point at Cleveland was the Dumbarton Oaks proposal of 1944 for the structure of the United Nations, which the Cleveland Conference endorsed with a series of recommendations for revision. Prominent among these proposed revisions was the creation of a "Commission on Human Rights," the greater limiting of the powers of large nations in relation to the small, and the imperative to end colonialism and to turn responsibility for "dependent peoples" over to an international commission operated by the United Nations.[33] Press attention understandably concentrated on the relation of the Cleveland Conference's declarations to the Dumbarton Oaks proposals,[34] but what is most significant about the Cleveland Conference as viewed in historical context is its function in consolidating the political orientation established at Delaware. To be sure, a number of ecumenical Protestant leaders, most conspicuously Dulles, would in the postwar years turn away from the most left-liberal of the elements of that orientation and orient their own politics more to anticommunism. But several features of the Cleveland Conference invite attention here as they attest to the state of ecumenical Protestant leadership three years after the Delaware Conference.

The FCC facilitated a sternly controlled conference in Cleveland aided by the assuredness that its affiliates had consented to the organization's new direction and had abandoned serious quarrels about the war. The FCC office successfully mobilized delegates through most of the same denominations and organizations, even during a time when war rationing often required negotiation for travel authorizations.[35] Dulles was still the chair, but this time the new president of the FCC and a good friend of Dulles's, the forceful Methodist Bishop G. Bromley Oxnam, took a strong hand. A few years later, Oxnam would become the first president of the World Council of Churches. The drafting committees and the delegate body again consisted of a wide range of church leaders, expanded somewhat from three years before. Among the most well known of the new faces were Republican Congressman Walter H. Judd of Minnesota, who was then leading the eventually successful effort to eliminate the restrictions on Asian immigration, and E. Stanley Jones, perhaps then the most famous missionary in the world after Albert Schweitzer. In the plenary session, Jones offered a motion, seconded by Muste, pushing even further the idea of diminishing the role of the great powers in the United Nations and strengthening the role of smaller powers, but after Oxnam spoke against it the motion failed.[36] However, what most matters is what the Cleveland Conference agreed upon.

The Cleveland delegates not only explicitly endorsed the principles adopted at Delaware, but also adopted stronger language on some points. *The Christian Century* noted the diminished equivocation on economic issues, and indeed the Cleveland Conference insisted that the "right of private property" be "qualified by the public interest," presumably entailing "a larger measure of social planning and control than characterized our prewar system." And even at a time when representatives of the great ally, Britain, were known to be lobbying at Dumbarton Oaks and elsewhere against the anti-imperialism to which Winston Churchill believed Americans were naïvely attracted, the Cleveland delegates demanded that "the imperialism of the white man," which they explicitly compared to that of the Japanese, be "brought to the speediest possible end." They also proclaimed that no "sound or stable world community" can be achieved "so long as there is enforced submission of one people to the will of another whether in Korea, in India, in the Congo, in Puerto Rico, or anywhere else." The willingness to list American-controlled Puerto Rico alongside the Belgian Congo and British India, to say nothing of Japanese-held Korea, is a sign of the level of anti-imperialism that flourished at Cleveland. On domestic racism in the United States, the Cleveland declarations were no less forthright than their Delaware antecedents, asking churches to actively support legislation that would make the Federal Fair Employment Practices Commission permanent, to repeal "poll tax and other discriminatory laws," and to guarantee an end to discrimination in housing.[37]

Discrimination against black people was of sufficient concern to the FCC leaders that it was the deciding factor in the decision to hold the conference in Cleveland. Van Kirk reported to the planning group that the Cleveland hotels had directly assured him that they would welcome black delegates. Philadephia, where the FCC often held meetings of many kinds, and Cleveland were among the few major cities in the Northeast and Midwest at that time that would provide this guarantee. FCC leaders considered Philadelphia to be "too Eastern" for this particular meeting, and that appears to have been a basis, also, for the earlier decision to hold the 1942 conference on a Midwestern campus.[38] At that event, delegates stayed mostly in the homes of local church families and faculty members of Ohio Wesleyan University. Such considerations not to hold its conventions in cities where its black members would be humiliated were unusual among similarly overwhelming white national organizations of the FCC's size. Hence, the antiracist pronouncements of the Delaware and Cleveland Conferences, while well short of the measures that full-fledged civil rights organizations might have wished, were substantive.

Since the Cleveland Conference essentially validated the transformation that had been effected at Delaware, the Cleveland event is a convenient point at which to turn to my third question: In what respects did the new political orientation established at the March 1942 meeting affect the destiny of ecumenical Protestantism?

How Was Ecumenical Protestantism Affected?

In the 1940s and 1950s the influence of the ecumenical Protestant leadership was at its peak, historians often observe. Even William Inboden's recent *Religion and American Foreign Policy, 1945–1960: The Soul of Containment*, which attends carefully to the internal disagreements within that leadership, documents this climactic stage in imposing detail.[39] Among the widely recognized precursors to the historical moment are the extensive participation of the Delaware Conference's cast of characters in the founding of the United Nations in 1945 and in the proclamation of the Declaration of Human Rights in 1948. This part of the story has now been documented compellingly by John S. Nurser in *For All Peoples and All Nations: The Ecumenical Church and Human Rights*.[40] The frequency with which Niebuhr was able to consult with officials of the State Department during the presidency of Harry Truman is another well-known part of this story, as is Dulles's appointment in 1953 as President Eisenhower's Secretary of State. *Time* and other journalistic media covered the church affairs of this period extensively.

Religion was "in" as measured by a host of indicators, and despite the vaunted pluralism of American culture, religion in the 1940s and 1950s mostly meant liberal Protestantism and the other varieties of faith easily translated into its terms. This feature of the period was promoted by many conditions, including the Cold War's sharpening of a politicized secular-religious divide, the popularity of mainstream church affiliation as a basis for community in the suburbs and for upward social mobility, and the relative absence until slightly later of strong competition from Catholics and evangelical Protestants for the religious leadership of the nation. But the Delaware Conference contributed to the Protestant Establishment's high tide by bringing the extended family of ecumenical Protestants together in relation to a set of challenges understood to largely define the postwar world, especially the challenges of deciding just how the power of the United States should be exercised in the world arena, and with what other powers to cooperate.

Yet the measuring of the relative institutional influence of ecumenical Protestantism on public affairs, while a valuable inquiry, misses much of the impact of the Delaware Conference on the destiny of ecumenical Protestantism and thus on the latter's long-term role in American life. More relevant to understanding that destiny and later role are the consequences for the ecumenical Protestant community itself of the specific political orientation articulated in the conference's resolutions and reinforced at Cleveland three years later.

Even in the chastened postwar years, the positions ecumenical Protestant leaders had taken on race, empire, economic inequality, and nationalism propelled them in directions that placed them on the defensive during the McCarthy era and rendered them all the more at odds with the National Association of Evangelicals as the latter gained strength in the 1950s. By 1958, when the NCC declared itself in favor of American recognition of the People's Republic of China and of the latter's admission to the United Nations, the reaction of the evangelical right wing was, as Inboden and others have shown, apoplectic.[41] The rise of the evangelical right placed into bolder and bolder relief on the American religious map the political orientation the ecumenists had inherited from Delaware as reinforced at Cleveland.

Prominent among the directions that placed the ecumenists on a collision course with the evangelicals was the accelerated ecumenism that the Van Dusens and Oxnams of American Protestantism pursued as coterminous with the internationalism that infused their support for the United Nations and for human rights. Through their expansion of the FCC into the even larger National Council of Churches in 1950 and through their leadership in the World Council of Churches (officially established at Amsterdam in 1948, and meeting for its second convention in Evanston in 1954), the energetic ecumenists blurred denominational boundaries and diminished the standing and authority of many local communities. These men and women took seriously the Cleveland Conference's disdain for "the present structure of denominational Protestantism" as "not adequate to deal with the issues of our time" and its demand that churches seek greater unification on every level.[42]

Cold War cautions against the ability of communists to exploit decolonizing situations blunted the critique of imperialism in the world arena, but that critique was actually intensified in the one area the churchmen and churchwomen could control: missions. The fear that their own missions had participated too extensively in Western imperialism was voiced occasionally by participants in both the Delaware and Cleveland Conferences. But even as most of the ecumenical Protestant leaders of the war years expressed hopes for the future of missions, they were in the process of changing the notion of "foreign missions" to one of "world mission," with the implication that indigenous peoples were no less qualified to preach and exemplify the gospel than Methodists and Presbyterians from the United States.[43] The American Protestant foreign missionary project was subjected to increasingly severe critique from within during the quarter-century after the Delaware Conference with the result that, by the late 1960s, the mainstream denominations had drastically diminished their missionary operations and redirected most of those that remained in the direction of service rather than evangelism, and in close cooperation with indigenous authorities. In the meantime, evangelicals found fewer faults with the old missionary ideology and accused the liberals of being sellouts.[44]

But no legacy of the political reorientation of ecumenical Protestantism at the Delaware Conference was more important than an intensified opposition to antiblack racism. In March 1946 the FCC formally denounced racial segregation as a violation of the gospel and entreated its affiliated churches to work for a nonsegregated society and a nonsegregated church. David W. Wills calls this "the great landmark" in the process by which "the Protestant Establishment increasingly lent its influence to the cause of racial desegregation" because here was a position taken by the FCC itself in its full, official capacity.[45] The declarations of the two study conferences were important, but these sentiments were now strong enough to produce this official stand even on the part of an FCC that was desperately trying to keep several white southern churches in the fold. Although neither the FCC nor its larger successor, the NCC, ever pulled away from this position, the most thorough student of the NCC's engagement with civil rights, James F. Findlay Jr., finds that during the 1950s and very early 1960s the NCC was generally more reserved about civil rights than the FCC had been. The more cautious NCC was then under heavy and persistent attack for being too far to the left, and, as Findlay notes, repeatedly disappointed black church leaders who expected more from it.[46]

Still, when the early 1960s arrived, it was the NCC and *The Christian Century* that offered support to the Southern Christian Leadership Conference and other civil rights organizations, while the National Association of Evangelicals and its closely associated journal, *Christianity Today* (founded in 1956 to offer a conservative alternative to *The Christian Century*) would have nothing to do with the cause. As late as 1963 even Billy Graham, who, unlike many of his followers, refused to actually defend segregation, would not support King's March on Washington and criticized civil rights demonstrations as counterproductive. In that same year, *The Christian Century* published King's "Letter from the Birmingham Jail."[47] Martin Luther King Jr., moreover, was a product of liberal bastions of Crozier Theological Seminar and Boston University, not the more evangelical Fuller Theological Seminary. Ecumenical Protestant leadership continued, if haltingly, the path of the Delaware Conference, and in so doing was all the more conspicuously distinct from the evangelicals who came to political prominence while continuing to hold to the individualist view that racism was a problem of the human heart, not a priority for institutional engagement.

Beyond institutions, the ecumenical Protestant engagement with racism produced a number of the immediate postwar era's most sustained and probing antiracist books, including some of the most searching written by any white American prior to the 1960s. Two examples from the heart of the Protestant Establishment can illustrate this. *Racism: A World Issue* (1947) by Garrett Biblical Seminary professor Edmund Soper was a sweeping, critical account of racism worldwide, connecting Jim Crow with the practice of racial domination found in imperial, colonial systems around the globe. Soper, who grew up in Japan as the child of Methodist missionaries, wrote this book on the basis of a series of seminars on "Christianity and the Race Problem" that he convened for Chicago area academics and church leaders during the war at the invitation of the national office of the Methodist Church. Among Soper's chief consultants was George E. Haynes, the black director of the FCC's Department of Race Relations, but Soper's acknowledgments are a "who's who" of the period's leading liberal missionary theorists. It is no coincidence that Soper was also the author, four years earlier, of *The Philosophy of the World Christian Mission*, the major book that outlined the transition in missions from "foreign missions" to a vision in which indigenous peoples shared equally in the missionary project.[48]

A second example is *Color and Conscience: The Irrepressible Conflict* (1946) by Buell G. Gallagher, then a professor at the Pacific School of Religion. Not only did Gallagher call for legislation and court action against the Jim Crow system; in an era when the issue of "miscegenation" was usually avoided by advocates of racial integration, Gallagher also went on to insist that there was no sound basis for restrictions on interracial marriage and he reminded his readers of the extent of race mixing that had already taken place but was conventionally denied through the deeply racist "one-drop" rule. In a milieu in which most liberals represented the American race problem as peculiarly southern, Gallagher condemned "color caste" in every region of the country and provided examples of its ordinance. Moreover, writing as an ordained Congregationalist minister, Gallagher declared that his own vaunted Protestant tribe was being put to shame by the greater antiracist commitment of the most extremely secular of all the groups in the country, the Communist Party of the United States: "The Christian Church . . . has not produced an ethical attack on color caste which approaches the vigor and virility of the attack launched by American Communists." *Color and Conscience* was informed not only by the latest cultural anthropology of Ruth Benedict, but also by the contemporary work of black intellectuals. Gallagher thanked Alain Locke for advice, and he respectfully and repeatedly quoted W.E.B. Du Bois. Gallagher also quoted at length the declarations of both the Delaware and Cleveland Conferences on racism at home and imperialism abroad, and he cited the Malvern Conference that had inspired the FCC to convene its own study conferences. "There is enough dynamite in the Malvern declarations to blow the whole of the white man's imperialism with its racial inequities off the face of the earth—if it is acted upon," he remarked. Gallagher came within one percentage point of being elected to congress as a democrat in 1948, and he later gained fame in 1969 as the president of the City College of New York when his career was destroyed by the conflict over open admissions during which the City University trustees perceived Gallagher as too sympathetic to the demands of protesting black and Hispanic students.[49]

Gallagher and Soper were not typical ecumenical Protestants, but their writings flowed directly out of the political reorientation effected at Delaware, and they illustrate the trajectory that created enormous space between the Protestant Establishment and the growing movement of politically mobilized evangelical Protestants. In 1953, when Oxnam was brought before the House Un-American Activities Committee (HUAC) to answer charges that he was too close to communists, the annual convention of the National Association of Evangelicals (NAE) passed a resolution supporting the federal government's investigation of religious leaders for possible subversion. Indeed, HUAC's investigation of Oxnam had been prompted by a widely distributed pamphlet, *Bishop Oxnam: Prophet of Marxism*, by evangelical leader Carl McIntire, a New Jersey radio preacher with a huge national following. McIntire described the National Council of Churches as the country's "strongest ally of Russia and of the radical labor movement within the U.S."[50]

The quarrel between evangelical and ecumenical Protestantism, given enduring structure by the political reorientation the latter achieved at the Delaware Conference, would not have been so consequential for the Protestant Establishment were it not for a second development at the opposite end of the religious spectrum. Many of the reform and radical movements of the 1960s and early 1970s were overwhelmingly secular in foundation and were often led by Americans of Jewish rather than either Protestant or Catholic origin. This was especially true of feminism, but also of the antiwar movement and of the white allies of the black-led civil rights movement. If earlier left-wing movements had been discredited by associations with communism, whether real or imagined, the newer movements were less encumbered. These newer movements presented themselves as vehicles for some of the causes that ecumenical Protestants had advanced. In this context, the old claim of Dulles's generation that only Christianity could provide a sound basis for reform was persuasive to a diminished segment of their heirs: looking around them, they saw many non-Christians who were advancing many of the causes that the Protestant Establishment of old had championed. Who said one had to be Christian to do the right thing? Especially—and this is an important point too often missed—if what counted as Christian was now as credibly claimed by politically right-wing evangelicals as by the ecumenicals. The decades from the 1960s onward witnessed the expansion of post-Protestant spaces in which men and women who had grown up in ecumenical circles found engines other than the church for pursuing goals for which the church had been a primary vehicle.[51]

Prominent among those goals were the decidedly liberal aspirations set forth in the name of Christianity at the Delaware Conference of 1942, then variously defended and altered under the attacks of a Cold War–invigorated evangelical constituency that defined itself against many of these very aspirations. That the National Association of Evangelicals was founded at almost exactly the same historical moment can remind us that 1942 is a pivotal year in the history of the relation of religion to politics in the history of the United States, and can remind us, further, that the fortunes of ecumenical and evangelical Protestants have been determined to a large extent in dialectical relation to one another's religious politics as developed during the first decade and a half after 1942.

The realist–pacifist summit meeting, the concords of which were made possible by the Japanese attack on Pearl Harbor, enabled ecumenical leadership to advance liberal politics with a measure of unity and confidence that would not survive, but that sustained the "Protestant Establishment" during the years of its greatest public authority. The agreements made at Delaware were achieved within an extended family of ecumenical Protestants already quite intimate as a result of a robust network of interlocking committees, study groups, and issue-specific agencies that flourished during the 1930s despite the ferocity of the realist–pacifist debate. But the Delaware Conference brought this extended, somewhat fractious family together at a time when the conditions were right for something new to happen to it. And it did.

Notes

I want to acknowledge that my use of the FCC Papers, on which much of this article is based, was greatly facilitated by John S. Nurser, who provided me with copies he had made of many relevant documents in that collection, enabling me to find them much more quickly than had I started without his generous assistance. I also want to acknowledge the helpful comments made on the basis of a draft of this article by Martin E. Marty and R. Laurence Moore.

1. Walter M. Horton to Walter Van Kirk, November 16, 1941, Federal Council of Churches Papers, Presbyterian Historical Society, Record Group 18 (hereafter cited as FCC/PHS), Box 28, Folder 8.

2. Among the few scholars to comment on this conference even in passing are William McGuire King, "The Reform Establishment and the Ambiguities of Influence," in *Between the Times: The Travail of the Protestant Establishment in America, 1900–1960*, ed. William R. Hutchison (New York: Cambridge University Press, 1989), 127, and T. Jeremy Gunn, *Spiritual Weapons: The Cold War and the Forging of an American National Religion* (Westport, CT: Praeger, 2009), 92–93.

3. Of the many accounts of this debate, the most discerning remains Donald Meyer, The *Protestant Search for Political Realism, 1919–1941* (Berkeley: University of California Press, 1960; 2nd ed., Middletown, CT: Wesleyan University Press, 1988), although Meyer's unabashedly triumphalist narrative of Niebuhr's victory over the pacifists and isolationists leaves the impression that there is little more to be said about the political history of ecumenical Protestantism after 1941 except to chart Niebuhr's legacy. That the index to this thorough history of the political arguments of liberal Protestants right down through 1941 contains no ref-

erences to race, Negroes, or civil rights is a convenient reminder of how different the liberal Protestant conversation about politics became from the time of the Delaware Conference onward. There was of course some engagement with race during the interwar period; for an overview of this more marginal discussion, see Robert Moats Miller, *American Protestantism and Social Issues, 1919–1939* (Chapel Hill: University of North Carolina Press, 1958), 292–313. For the earlier era of engagement, see Ralph E. Luker, *The Social Gospel in Black and White: American Racial Reform, 1885–1912* (Chapel Hill: University of North Carolina Press, 1991).

4. Walter Van Kirk to Walter M. Horton, November 18, 1941, FCC/PHS, Box 28, Folder 8.

5. Undated memorandum, "National Study Conference on the Churches and the New World Order," FCC/PHS, Box 28, Folder 8.

6. See, for example, Bradford S. Abernethy to "My dear friend," January 15, 1942, FCC/PHS, Box 28, Folder 8. The Committee of Direction also included several officials of ecumenical organizations who were not heavy combatants in the realist–pacifist clash; these included Russell Clinchy of the National Conference on Christians and Jews, A. L. Warnshuis of the International Missionary Council, and Henry Smith Leiper of the then-provisional World Council of Churches. Other members of the Committee of Direction whose names would have been recognized instantly by recipients of Abernethy's letter included Harvard philosopher W. Ernest Hocking, Yale historian of missions Kenneth Scott Latourette, University of Chicago theologian Edwin E. Aubry, Methodist Bishop G. Bromley Oxnam, and Chicago Theological Seminary President Albert W. Palmer.

7. Van Dusen's account of this debate is found in *Christianity and Crisis*, April 6, 1942, 2–3. Among the other published accounts, one of the fullest is in *American Friend*, March 26, 1942, 133–34.

8. Paul Hutchinson, "Proposed Bases for a Lasting Peace," *The Christian Century*, March 18, 1942; the text of the Delaware Conference's resolutions was published as "The Churches and a Just and Durable Peace," *The Christian Century*, March 25, 1942, 390–97.

9. This handbook also carried the title, *The Churches and a Just and Durable Peace*, but the text is an extended set of commentaries on each passage of the document issued by the Dulles Commission itself in a pamphlet, *A Message from the National Study Conference on the Churches and a Just and Durable Peace*, and copied word for word in the March 25, 1942, issue of *The Christian Century*. The handbook and the *Message* are available in various archival collections, including FCC/PHS.

10. See, as examples, *Christianity and Crisis*, March 22, May 31, June 28, and July 12, 1943.

11. Reinhold Niebuhr, "American Power and World Responsibility," *Christianity and Crisis*, April 6, 1943, 4.

12. "Durable Peace," 391. Here, as throughout, when citing the resolutions of the Delaware Conference, I will reference the pages as found in *The Christian Century*, March 25, 1942, instead of as found in the *Message* (see note 9, earlier) because the *Century* is more easily available.

13. "Durable Peace," 391, 393.

14. Ibid., 391, 395.

15. Ibid., 396.

16. Ibid., 394.

17. "American Malvern," *Time*, March 16, 1942. The era's numerous "one worlders," as they were sometimes derisively called by skeptics, were quick to appreciate the Delaware Conference's having advocated "the setting up of a World Government," as it was put in an appreciative letter to Dulles by Charles Davis, the founder of the World Government Foundation, April 14, 1942, FCC/PHS, Box 28, Folder 8.

18. Minutes, Committee of Direction, Commission for a Just and Durable Peace, March 21, 1941, FCC/PHS, Box 29, Folder 6.

19. *Time*, March 16, 1942.

20. This charming and revealing fact is mentioned by William R. Hutchison, "Protestantism as Establishment," in Hutchison, *Between the Times*, 7.

21. Others included John D. Rockefeller Jr. of Standard Oil and Thomas W. Lamont, the Board Chairman at J. P. Morgan, who was a member of the commission but did not attend the Delaware Conference.

22. FCC/PHS Box 28, Folders 8 and 9; Box 29, Folder 6.

23. FCC/PHS, Box 28, Folders 8 and 9. For the operations of the Chicago group and Tittle's consultations with Dulles, see Tittle to Abernethy, February 20, 1942, Box 28, Folder 9.

24. FCC/PHS Box 28, Folder 9. Abernethy's notes show he wanted "one more Negro" on the New York committee and penciled in the names of Walter White and Adam Clayton Powell as possibilities. It is unclear if he invited either of them.

25. All of the organizations are listed in "Durable Peace," 390–91.

26. All six lectures were published as Ohio Wesleyan's "Merrick–McDowell Lectures for 1942," Francis J. McConnell, John Foster Dulles, William Paton, Leo Pasvolsky, Hu Shih, and C. J. Hambro, *A Basis for the Peace to Come* (New York: Abingdon-Cokesbury, 1942).

27. Pasvolsky's fifty-two-page, untitled document is found in PSS/FCC, Box 28, Folder 9. Roosevelt's State of the Union Address of 1944 has recently been the subject of extensive attention, for example, Cass Sunstein, *The Second Bill of Rights: FDR's Unfinished Revolution and Why We Need It More Than Ever* (New York: Basic, 2004).

28. The idea for a study group focusing on the ideal terms for world peace took form within the FCC leadership in 1940, in the context of the European war. Van Dusen and FCC Executive Secretary Samuel McCrea Cavert were considering how to go about this when Dulles keynoted an FCC conference in Philadelphia in February of that year. Dulles by this time was convinced that churches could play a decisive role in the direction of world history and that only Christianity offered a sound basis for lasting peace. At a 1937 conference on "Church, Community, and State" at Oxford, Dulles had been inspired by the intensity of resourcefulness of ecumenical leaders from both the United States and England, which he contrasted to the despair he found in other circles facing the prospect of another world war. Also present at Oxford had been Roswell Barnes, who ministered a New York City Presbyterian church of which Dulles was an elder, and by 1940 was on the staff of the FCC. Dulles's ringing manifesto for church

leadership resonated powerfully within the FCC, strongly influencing the FCC's decision in December of 1940 to establish the commission and to ask Dulles to chair it. Barnes and Van Dusen together persuaded him to accept. These early steps in the development of the Commission for a Just and Durable Peace are described in Heather Warren, *Theologians of a New World Order: Reinhold Niebuhr and the Christian Realists, 1920–1948* (New York: Oxford University Press, 1997), 98–101, and in John S. Nurser, *For All Peoples and All Nations: The Ecumenical Church and Human Rights* (Washington, DC: Georgetown University Press, 2005), 57–60. The development of Dulles's religious ideas and their direct connection to his views of American foreign policy is a topic dealt with only episodically in the considerable literature on Dulles's career, but one book is directly on point and is based on relevant archival materials in addition to interviews with Van Dusen, Cavert, and other churchmen who interacted with Dulles during the 1940s and especially at Delaware: Mark G. Toulouse, *The Transformation of John Foster Dulles: From Prophet of Realism to Priest of Nationalism* (Mercer, GA: Mercer University Press, 1985).

29. Minutes, Committee of Direction, March 21, 1941, FCC/PHS, Box 29, Folder 6. In this context, and apparently in relation to a feeling that their enterprise needed to connect more directly to local churches, the committee agreed to add "six pastors," to be approved by the FCC Executive Committee upon nomination by a subcommittee of the Committee on Direction consisting of Van Dusen (a confirmed realist), Methodist theologian Harkness (then one of the few members of the committee strongly identified with pacifism), and James H. Franklin (a Northern Baptist minister who was then president of Crozier Theological Seminary) in consultation with Van Kirk. This process resulted in the appointment of both Tittle and another prominent pacifist preacher, Congregationalist Albert Buckner Coe, but the other four added were not conspicuously identified with either faction.

30. Minutes of the Commission to Study the Basis of a Just and Durable Peace, September 18, 1941, FCC/PHS, Box 29, Folder 6. This meeting in New York City included a brief discussion of the possibility of a study conference, which remained uncertain until late October, when authorized by the FCC Executive Committee. Those in attendance at this meeting of the commission, in addition to Morrison, Niebuhr, and the members of the Committee of Direction, included Horton and Mott. Prominent figures who were members of the commission but not in attendance included Muste, Lamont, radio preacher Harry Emerson Fosdick, Moorehouse College President Benjamin Mays, and Quaker theologian Rufus Jones.

31. Wendell Willkie, *One World* (New York: Simon and Schuster, 1943).

32. It should be noted that between these two major study conferences, the commission sponsored several other smaller events, including a "roundtable" for world Christian leaders at Princeton, and circulated widely a document titled "Six Pillars of Peace," which was a condensation of the general principles adopted at Delaware.

33. *A Message to the Churches from the National Study Conference on the Churches and a Just and Durable Peace, Cleveland, Ohio, January 16–19, 1945* (New York: [Federal Council of Churches], 1945), 9–10.

34. See, for example, "Church Program for Peace Voted," *New York Times,* Jan. 20, 1945, and "Churches Adopt 'Oaks' Peace Plan, Plus Atlantic Charter," *Cleveland Plain Dealer,* January 19, 1945.

35. The Cleveland Conference was almost cancelled in November on account of the difficulties of travel at that time, but when Van Kirk wrote about this problem to Edward Stettinius, then an Undersecretary of State, Stettinius appears to have authorized an exception, probably because he realized the conference would generate strong support for the Dumbarton Oaks proposal then being pushed by the Roosevelt administration. On Stettinius's intervention, see Nurser, *All Peoples,* 109.

36. The list of delegates to the Cleveland Conference is FCC/PHS, Box 28, Folder 3. For an account of Jones's motion and its debate, see *Cleveland Plain Dealer,* January 19, 1945.

37. *Message . . . from Cleveland,* 8–9, 11, 13. *The Christian Century's* assessment is in the issue of January 31, 1945, 135–37, and 149, 157–58.

38. At its initial meeting of May 24, 1944, the Committee on Arrangements for the study conference, then being contemplated for early 1945, discussed the site at some length. The committee "voted to hold it in Grand Rapids unless RR facilities difficult, then Cleveland," because in "both Grand Rapids and Cleveland there would be no discrimination against the Negro delegates with regard to hotel accommodations. This was considered a most important point." When Grand Rapids proved difficult to get to, the committee decided at its May 31 meeting to hold the conference in Cleveland. FCC/PHS, Box 28, Folder 1.

39. William Inboden, *Religion and American Foreign Policy, 1945–1960: The Soul of Containment* (New York: Cambridge University Press, 2008).

40. Nurser, *All Peoples.* This book is especially helpful in tracing the trajectory of O. Frederick Nolde from his participation in the Delaware Conference to an increasingly important role in the FCC, including at the Cleveland Conference, but especially through the FCC's Joint (with the Foreign Missions Council) Committee on Religious Liberty. Nolde, working closely with Dulles, was the central figure in ecumenical Protestantism's pressure for more attention to human rights in the structure and operations of the United Nations.

41. Inboden, *Religion,* 94–97.

42. The Cleveland Conference's call for more aggressively ecumenical programs is found in *Message . . . from Cleveland,* 14.

43. Examples are the memorandum of A. J. Muste to the New York planning group, January 30, 1942, and Report of Commission II for the Cleveland Conference, chaired by Walter M. Horton, FCC/PHS, Box 28, Folder 1. Discussions in relation to both the Delaware and Cleveland conferences made frequent reference to the world missionary conference at Madras, India, in 1938, at which indigenous church leaders from many Asian, African, and Latin American societies protested vigorously the historically unequal relationship between the "sending" churches in the North Atlantic West and the "receiving" churches in the rest of the world.

44. This direction in the liberal Protestant missionary enterprise and the radically different outlook of evangelicals is efficiently addressed in William R.

Hutchison, *Errand to the World: American Protestant Thought and Foreign Missions* (Chicago: University of Chicago Press, 1987), esp. 177–99.

45. David W. Wills, "An Enduring Distance: Black Americans and the Establishment," in Hutchison, *Between the Times*, 172.

46. James F. Findlay Jr., *Church People in the Struggle: The National Council of Churches and the Black Freedom Movement, 1950–1970* (New York: Oxford University Press, 1993), esp. 11–47.

47. Inboden, *Religion*, 81–93, offers a well-documented account of the bitterness and severity of the antagonism toward the ecumenists on the part of the group that established, edited, and funded *Christianity Today*. The closest student of *Christianity Today* and civil rights finds that magazine consistently hostile to King and to civil rights in general from its founding in 1956 until well after 1963; see Mark Toulouse, "*Christianity Today* and American Public Life: A Case Study," *Journal of Church and State* 35 (Spring 1993), 241–84. See also Toulouse's companion article, "The *Christian Century* and American Public Life: The Crucial Years, 1956–1968," in *New Dimensions in American Religious History*, ed. Jay P. Dolan and James P. Wind (Grand Rapids, MI: Eerdmans, 1993), 44–82.

48. Edmund D. Soper, *Racism: A World Issue* (New York: Abington-Cokesbury, 1947), esp. 7–10; and Edmund D. Soper, *The Philosophy of the World Christian Mission* (New York: Abington-Cokesbury, 1943). For Soper's Chicago-area seminars during World War II, see Edwin D. Soper Papers, Garrett Seminary Library, Box 8, Folder 21.

49. Buell G. Gallagher, *Color and Conscience: The Irrepressible Conflict* (New York: Harper, 1946), esp. 170–71, 188, 215–19. For my understanding of Gallagher's remarkable career, I am indebted to research done by two University of California, Berkeley, graduate students, Gene Zubovich and Daniel Immerwahr.

50. This episode is recounted in Mark Silk, "The Rise of the 'New Evangelicalism': Shock and Adjustment," in Hutchison, *Between the Times*, 281, and in Martin E. Marty, *Modern American Religion, 1941–1960* (Chicago: University of Chicago Press, 1996), 368–69.

51. For a more extensive discussion of the destiny of ecumenical Protestantism in the midcentury decades, see chapter 2 in this volume, and my "Religious Liberalism and Ecumenical Self-Interrogation," in *American Religious Liberalism*, ed. Leigh Eric Schmidt and Sally M. Promey (Bloomington: Indiana University Press, 2012), 374–87.

CHAPTER 4

Justification by Verification: The Scientific Challenge to the Moral Authority of Christianity in Modern America

I came to appreciate the power of the concept of post-Protestantism only after I wrote this essay, but I now see the essay as in large part an account of the development of a particular type of post-Protestant mentality among American enthusiasts for a science-centered culture during the late nineteenth and early twentieth centuries. What is particular about it is the selecting out from the entire available inventory of Protestantism precisely those elements that appear to be the most continuous with science as a professional enterprise. This enterprise was then sufficiently novel to challenge the prevailing cultural order, and thus to invite, from its devotees, symbolic representations that neutralized that threat. Often, historians have observed that Victorian, Edwardian, and Progressive intellectuals embraced science with "religious" zeal, but here I detail the distinctly Protestant style and tone of that zeal. A function of religious images was to enable scientific intellectuals and their supporters to think of science as the practice of exactly the virtues for which Christianity was then most admired by educated citizens of Great Britain and the United States. Thinking of science in these terms enabled them to present scientists as the successors to the clergy as the moral models for modern living. The endlessly repeated assertion that the British agnostic scientist, T. H. Huxley, had enough "real Christianity" in him "to save the soul" of every person in the British Isles is a convenient emblem for this discourse.

That there was a genuine rivalry for cultural authority between partisans of science and the clergy is another of my themes, directed against a tendency of late-twentieth-century scholarship to mock as hopelessly anachronistic the old idea that science and religion are in conflict. I do not argue that such a conflict is inherent in some essential nature of science and of religion, but I do insist that that rival cultural programs are often organized around science and religion and that historians are better off attending to those conflicts rather than insisting that their participants simply don't know what they were talking about. Huxley and his kind envisioned a future rather different from the one preferred by the men and women who opposed the Darwinian revolution in natural history and the dissemination of the results of the historical study of the Hebrew Bible and the New Testament. Scholars of our own time who emphasize the ways in which scientific and religious practice "diverged" and became "differentiated" from one another risk obscuring this struggle, and patronizing those who waged it. I take up later variations on this struggle in several other papers, especially "Science as a Weapon in Kulturkampfe *in the United States during and after World War II," found in my* Science, Jews, and Secular Culture: Studies in Mid-Twentieth Century American Intellectual History *(Princeton, 1996), 154–174, and "The Unity of Knowledge and the Diversity of Knowers: Science as an Agent of Cultural Integration in the United States between the Two World Wars,"* Pacific Historical Review LXXX *(2011), 211–230.*

What I call an "ethic of science" was prominently affirmed in plenary addresses, manifestos, and prefaces. This ethic as I present it here is similar to Robert K. Merton's influential formulation of what he called "the scientific ethos," which Merton thought general to the scientific enterprise in all settings from the seventeenth century to the present. I believe my construct is truer than Merton's to the utterances of British and American intellectuals from about 1870 to about 1930. These savants understood the ideal scientist to be disinterested, skeptical, truthful, and objective in senses that I describe, and also committed to the sharing of inquiry's results with a global community of inquiry. To live by this set of ideals was to meet the highest of standards, to be "justified" before whatever powers mattered in an increasingly secular milieu. I call by the name of "the intellectual gospel" the notion that such a life—a life ruled by the ethic of science—was an updated version of earlier religious callings. That the old Protestant heritage divided in the late nineteenth century into a social and an intellectual gospel is the major claim of this essay. The intellectual gospel as I develop it here can be seen as a post-Protestant formation because it dispensed altogether—as the more widely studied social gospel did not—with the figure of Christ while perpetuating a set of values that its adherents learned within a Christian milieu. Science-admiring de-Christianized elites diminished the moral authority of Christianity and its institutions by appropriating for themselves many of the virtues popularly associated with the old faith.

This essay is by far the oldest reprinted here. It was first published in Michael J. Lacey, ed., Religion and Twentieth Century American Intellectual Life *(New York, 1989), 116–135. I want to acknowledge that in the intervening years several other historians have illuminated the efforts of American intellectuals to create a public culture keyed by science; the most effective and comprehensive of these studies is Andrew Jewett,* Science, Democracy, and the American University: From the Civil War to the Cold War *(New York, 2012).*

THE CHRISTIAN RELIGION AND MODERN SCIENCE, it was once thought, present real obstacles to each other's prosperity. No more, it would seem, except for fundamentalists and, at the other extreme, a few die-hard village atheists who don't realize how anachronistically Victorian is the vision of a triumphant science eventually replacing religion. Scholars and moralists of a variety of orientations now analyze the historical relationship between science and Christianity as a story not of conflict but of "differentiation" and "divergence."[1] No doubt this is an advance, but caution is in order as we invite ourselves to feel superior to John William Draper and Andrew Dickson White. Occupants of separate spheres can remain preoccupied with each other: Much of modern American Protestant thought has been reactive to the scientific enterprise, and much of that enterprise has been propelled by cognitive and moral energies drawn from the Protestant religious tradition. Moreover, divisions of labor can be invidious: "differentiation and divergence" may constitute not an alternative to "conflict" but a specification of the process by which conflict has been engaged. If our recent historiography does not openly reaffirm the once-fashionable "harmonist" perspective (science and Christianity are ultimately "harmonious"), that historiography is subtly "neo harmonist" in its dual reluctance, first, to acknowledge that beneath all the newly discovered complexities in the relations of science and Christianity there has persisted an authentic struggle over the epistemic principles that shall shape modern culture, and second, to confront in relation to that struggle the gradual and historic de-Christianization of the intellectual discourse of the United States. In overcoming this dual reluctance, this essay sets forth "neo-conflictist" caveats against the direction of recent scholarship. Hence the story this essay tries to tell is at once a story of aggression and of differentiation, of mutual engagement and of divergence.

The agents in the story are intellectuals eager to vindicate scientific inquiry as a religious calling. A major result of their endeavors in late-nineteenth- and early-twentieth-century America was to complicate the challenge presented to Christianity by science. On its simplest level, as studied by Draper and White and even as constructed by their more sophisticated successors, this challenge was strictly cognitive: What should one believe and on what epistemological basis? Where ended the authority of the Bible and of ecclesiastically supervised religious intuitions, and where began the authority of secular scholarship and science? Around these issues our studies of the Darwinian controversy, for example, properly revolve. The challenge of modern science to Christianity has been primarily cognitive, but not exclusively. This challenge also contained a more subtle, moral dimension to which our historiography has been less sensitive. The moral as well as the cognitive authority of Christianity was often at issue. This moral dimension of the scientific challenge to the authority of Christianity was encapsulated in a remark of T. H. Huxley's: the "ethical spirit" of science, quipped scientific culture's most contentious leader, entails "justification, not by faith, but by verification."[2]

"Justification" in its traditional religious meaning was a process by which the individual soul met God's standard. This was the sense of the term contained in the old Pauline maxim perpetuated by Calvinism and invoked by Huxley, "justification by faith." But the term "justification" later came to mean something quite different. When modern philosophers speak about the "justification of true belief," they do so in an entirely secular, epistemological voice. They do not necessarily imply that the state of one's soul depends on the identification and proper use of the best method for assessing truth-claims. The issue in this second sense of justification is indeed "verification." Huxley's juxtaposition of this ostentatiously scientific process with the classical Protestant affirmation of faith implied a religious function for the activity of knowing. Our obligations are not to *believe* as our inherited religious authorities have so long prescribed; our obligations, insisted Huxley, are instead to question and ultimately to *know*. "Blind faith is the one unpardonable sin." And how then are we to be "justified" before whatever powers there may be? By living according to the "ethical spirit" of modern science, by practicing "verification."

Post-Reformation defenders of the doctrine of "justification by faith" had faced the more worldly doctrine of justification by "works" and branded it a heresy—the notorious "Arminian heresy." According to this liberal doctrine, the salient sign of God's grace was not the ability to believe, but the ability to perform good works in the world. Justification by "verification" was a more radical extension of "Arminianism," singling out cognitive conduct as the salient form of "works." Had it been advanced with theological seriousness and inspired a response within the Protestant community, "justification by verification" might have been denounced as "the cognitivist heresy." But this potential drama was never played out within the church. For all the enthusiasm felt for the ethic of science by intellectuals who remained committed to Christianity, the leap was too great. To prove one's religious worth by trying to live according to the Sermon on the Mount was one thing, but to offer as such proof the conscientious application of "scientific method" to the study of nature or even to the problems of daily life was quite another, and one for which it was more difficult to find a warrant in the New Testament. Hence the notion of justification by correct cognitive conduct was not explicitly formulated as a theological alternative; the notion does not figure as a major episode in the history of modern Protestant thought.[3] It does figure largely, however, in "secularization," if this problematic term can be used to refer to the growth in size and in cultural authority of de-Christianized academic elites, and to the corresponding decline in the role played by churches in public life.

These transitions were facilitated in the English-speaking world of the mid- and late nineteenth century by the conviction that *Wissenschaft* was a religiously significant vocation. The intellectuals who shared this conviction drew on Protestantism's traditional commitment to correct belief, but placed more emphasis on this commitment exactly while responding to the epistemological transformations wrought by the successful programs of modern philological, historical, and natural sciences. What it meant to "know" narrowed considerably under the influence of these programs. Hence for men and women of Huxley's stripe, the activity of *knowing* in the modern, scientific sense came to supplement, if not to replace, the classical Christian activities of prayer, worship, good works, and obedience to ecclesiastical authority. The potential for dissonance was diminished for American celebrants of science by the predominantly respectful stance toward the modern sciences long displayed by the leading denominations.[4] The representation of the ideal scientific edifice as a "temple" became one of the most common metaphorical turns in public discussion of science. "Devotion to science," said America's favorite British philosopher, Herbert Spencer, "is a tacit worship."[5] And in one of the most famous aphorisms of Louis Agassiz, the great American zoologist declared a laboratory of natural science to be "a sanctuary where nothing profane should be tolerated."[6] Woodrow Wilson's most favorable image of science was the image of a nun at her prayers.[7] And the novelist Sinclair Lewis found it quite plausible that a budding scientist would offer a distinctive, freethinking "prayer of the scientist" upon being given access to a laboratory.[8]

A host of lesser scientists and writers relied on the same images used by Lewis, Wilson, Agassiz, and Spencer. The representation of science as a religious calling had its own conventions, routinely drawn on in public addresses and in essays on "science and culture." Champions of science made the most of these conventions when seeking to neutralize the suspicion, as the botanist Theodore Gill characterized it in 1888, that science was "an aggressive being and even . . . a demon, shoving and pushing all else away and endeavoring to throttle and kill all else." Gill's own counterimage of science is worth quoting at length because the relevant conventions are so prominent in it:

> Science is rather a goddess who is rich in attributes and ready to shower her worshipers, but coy in her gifts; she is generous only to those who worship at her shrine in sincerity and truth, and who supplement their prayers by continual labor and deeds. To such she distributes her gifts much according to their deserts. Her worshipers are generally content with their several portions, and in her temple enjoy such sweet communion and peace of mind that they envy not the lots of those outside; if at all solicitous for any outsiders they are activated by motives of philanthropy and benevolence alone to invite such to share with them. What other possible motive can there be for proselytism?

Here, then, we find not only prayer and worship within a temple, but also the spreading of the gospel for altruistic motives and the performance of virtuous labor. This hard work, moreover, is rewarded according to merit, and, in any event, assures one's existence in a heavenlike state. Gill's "goddess" of science provides a vaguely pagan variation on the otherwise Protestant theme.[9]

Only in a very loose sense, to be sure, did the celebrants of science's religious character articulate a doctrine of justification. Metaphor, not argument, was the primary mode for indicating the religious function of the scientific vocation. The explicit idea that the Judeo-Christian God actually judged individuals on the basis of their cognitive conduct, as he was said to do on the basis of "faith" or "works" in the classical doctrines of justification, was rarely expressed. Even Max Weber's widely quoted assertion that a true scientist believes "the fate of his soul depends" on his cognitive conduct should not be read too literally.[10] Weber partook of the common pattern of secularization, according to which a certain mystification of science accompanied the demystification of traditional religions. Proponents of the vocation of science often employed a set of familiar religious images to convey to themselves, and to their educated and powerful contemporaries, a continuity they sensed between the modern scientific enterprise and the inherited religious culture.

The growth and consolidation of science as a distinctive profession provided a powerful incentive to interpret secular inquiry in terms of an ethic that was congruent with Protestant moral ideals. New professions characteristically generate ideologies by which to justify themselves, but this impulse on the part of scientists was intensified by the resistance of clerical and literary elites, especially in England but also in the United States. The storied debates Huxley carried on with Bishop Wilberforce and Matthew Arnold were simply the most dramatic of many episodes in the struggle of a new scientific elite to establish a larger role for itself in education and public culture.[11] By following the "methods" and "spirit" of science, these scientific enthusiasts prophesied, we shall both advance knowledge and improve society's moral discipline.

The crucial common denominator of all formulations of "the spirit of science" was the basic presumption that science *is* a moral enterprise, that values and obligations *do* attend upon it. The new professional cadre of scientists took the lead in developing this presumption into a major theme of public discourse. In so doing, these intellectuals acted against the widespread suspicion that science was no more moral than the objects it studied. In modern times the knower and the moral agent have often been depicted as contrasting personae, defined to a large extent in opposition to each other. David Hume drew this contrast in the starkest of terms, sharpening a distinction inherited from the seventeenth cen-

tury and bequeathing to the nineteenth and twentieth a legacy of endless disputes about "is" and "ought." The ethic of science spoke directly
to this tension between the knower and the moral agent, offering "the
Scientist" as a conscientious creature of a demanding ethic. The life of
science was a life of *virtue*.

Although many specific virtues were attributed to the scientific enterprise by this or that apologist, some ideals were so consistently affirmed
that it is no mistake to refer in the singular to an "ethic of science." The
ideal scientist was "disinterested" in the sense that he (or she, techni-
cally, but the exemplary Scientist was of course presumed to be male)
held critically in check whatever sympathies he might have with one or
another potential result of his inquiries. He was "skeptical" in saving his
trust for ideas that had received a powerful empirical warrant. It was
further incumbent on the man of science to be "objective" by virtue of
subjugating private experience to conclusions verified on an intersubjective basis. This intersubjectivity, in turn, served the ideal scientist's "universalism": his commitment to developing a body of truths testable everywhere and ultimately available to all humankind. Hence the ethic of
science also entailed "discursiveness," an obligation to share the results
of one's inquiries and to take account of the results of the inquiries of
others. "Veracity," too, was imperative, as the truthfulness and sincerity
of each exchange of information were necessary to the success of the
entire, extensive, communitarian endeavor of scientific inquiry.[12] It was
primarily to these values that American and British proponents of "the
ethical spirit of science" gave homage during the late nineteenth and
early twentieth centuries.

Not every adherent of the ethic of science regarded it as a supplement to, or replacement of, a more specifically Christian ethic, but those
who did were especially prone to the temple-and-prayer vocabulary for
describing science. The most inclusive and decisively biblical of these
religious images was that of an urgent message of good news about how
to be saved: "the gospel." Richard Gregory, the editor of *Nature*, allowed
that his grandfather had "preached the gospel of Christ," his father the
"gospel of Socialism," and Gregory himself the "gospel of Science."[13]

Critics have sometimes used this and other religious terms sardoni-
cally, mocking as "a gospel of research" or "a gospel of fact" the extravagance and intensity of this or that scientific enthusiasm, and condemn-
ing as "the new priesthood" the modern scientific establishment. So
congenial is this ironic voice in our own time that it is easy to forget the
lack of artifice with which even reasonably intelligent members of an earlier generation might have advanced these terms. Without prejudice, we
can use the concept of an "intellectual gospel" to refer to the belief that
conduct in accord with the ethic of science could be religiously fulfilling,
a form of "justification."

The concept of an "intellectual gospel" invites us to recognize and keep in mind the parallels between this persuasion and another, comparable movement that flourished alongside it while drawing on different elements of a common religious heritage, the "social gospel." Our histories speak at length about the social gospel, a broad movement of American Protestants seeking, in the name of religious duty, to reform society along the lines of the ethics of Jesus.[14] Although some theologically conservative critics thought that the social gospel was a recrudescence of the old Arminian heresy, the movement was strong enough to establish itself firmly within several major American Protestant denominations and to find rigorous theological expression in Walter Rauschenbusch's classic of 1917, *A Theology for the Social Gospel.*[15] What I want to call the "intellectual gospel" bears to the hypothetical "cognitive heresy" the same logical relationship that the social gospel bore to the Arminian heresy. But the intellectual gospel was not developed as a program *for the church*; it was "heretical" only in the indirect sense that it appropriated for the legitimation of nonecclesiastical institutions a set of symbols on which churches had relied for the maintenance of their authority. The intellectual gospel was an outgrowth of Protestantism, appealing especially to liberal Protestants and to freethinkers of Protestant origin, but its merits were not debated by congregations and synods. Even Shailer Mathews, the most "modernistic" of the liberal American theologians of the 1920s, was not accused of defending "justification by verification."[16] When the intellectual gospel was implicitly condemned by Christian believers, it was condemned in the larger guise of "infidelity" or "secularism." In characterizing this extraecclesiastical movement as a "gospel," we need not lose sight of its secularity relative to the social gospel. Yet in failing to so characterize it, or in failing to emphasize in some comparable manner the roots of the scientific ethic in an inherited religious culture, we risk losing sight of the religiosity of that ethic relative to more utilitarian and materialistic affirmations of "science and technology." The intellectual gospel was a distinctive, extremely idealistic construction of the ultimate significance of science.

When admirers of the ethic of science called attention to its religious potential, they most often alluded to one or more of three specific strands of continuity with the religious culture inherited by American academic intellectuals of the late nineteenth and early twentieth century. These might be termed the psychological, metaphysical, and moral dimensions of "the intellectual gospel." The essence of each of these dimensions can be briefly set forth.

Psychologically, the "religious" character of correct inquiry was in its utter seriousness and nobility of purpose, its righteous devotion to a cause that transcends one's immediate, material interests. This psychological dimension was the most general of the three, and the most akin to claims made on behalf of any serious enterprise, including any number of arts and vocations. It was also the least specific to Protestantism and to the Judeo-Christian tradition.

Metaphysically, secular knowledge was a "religious" mode by virtue of its cosmic importance. It constituted an authentic and intense relationship between human beings and whatever powers made the universe what it was. The intellectuals who developed and popularized the ethic of science drew on a venerable tradition of respect for "the study of nature" as a means of access to God, the Creator. Protestantism and the Scientific Revolution had reinforced each other in many phases of the intellectual history of early modern Europe. The idea of "nature" and "scripture" as parallel expressions of the deity was, of course, firmly entrenched in Britain and the United States in the mid-nineteenth century. Especially in the United States both these avenues to God were distinguished from the notorious "skepticism" of the Enlightenment, which American believers routinely condemned for departing from the pious, cautious, "Baconian" study of nature and scripture in order to speculate in an ill-informed and undisciplined manner. Although the legacy of skepticism was taken up after midcentury by the intellectuals who developed the cognitive ethic, these intellectuals generally sought to assimilate skepticism into this intensely Protestant vision of empirical study as a reverent, religiously meaningful enterprise.

This task of assimilation was made easier by another tradition on which Huxley and his comrades were able to draw: the moral ideals of Protestantism itself, especially as it developed in Britain and the United States. The opportunity to perpetuate certain of these specific ideals was the third, "moral," dimension of the intellectual gospel. The classical "values of science" were far from alien to a religious heritage in which "disinterestedness" and "self-abnegation" had long been praised. Although the genealogy of the ethic of science obviously included stoic stock, as reinvigorated during the classical revival of the Enlightenment,[17] this ethic was a direct and immediate descendant of Protestantism. Hence the moral discipline of science was "religious" because it apparently carried on from the church the task of promoting certain virtues. When critics complained that science was "irreligious," it was de rigueur to respond that devoted scientists were more Christian than most clergymen. Especially was this line taken in regard to the preacherlike Huxley, of whom it was said, without irony, that in this one agnostic there was "so much real Christianity" that if its plentitude were divided up and distributed, there would be more than enough of it "to save the soul" of every person in the British Isles.[18]

The new secular gospel of which Huxley was a prominent symbol transcended the theist-agnostic divide. Huxley himself sometimes implied that Christianity was a thing of the past, to be replaced eventually by something bearing the name of "science." In the United States this view became more and more common in the early twentieth century, especially under the influence of the great secularist John Dewey, but the intellectual gospel was also absorbed by many men and women who were confident that plenty of room was left for other gospels, too, especially the one preached by Jesus Christ. This was the standard view throughout the late nineteenth and early twentieth centuries even at Johns Hopkins University, the most ideologically intense bastion of the intellectual gospel in the United States.[19] The chemist Ira Remsen, speaking in 1904 as president of Johns Hopkins, doubted that science could ever actually "take the place of religion," which would surely continue to have its own existence even while the ethical precepts of the scientific endeavor do "conform" to "the teachings of the highest types of religion."[20] Three decades later, when Dewey's influence was at its peak, the Harvard historian of science George Sarton still drew the same conventional science-religion line of demarcation, even while quoting Huxley uncritically and while extolling the intensely religious character of scientific inquiry.[21]

The line between science and religion acknowledged by Remsen and Sarton made it all the easier for institutionally responsible Christians to join in the spreading of the intellectual gospel. If even the most "religious" science fell short of becoming a new religion, surely Christianity had nothing to fear from it? Only the most theologically modernistic of the clergy and the seminarians took much interest in the intellectual gospel, but to them the notion of an intellectual gospel parallel to the social can be the least incongruously applied.[22] The support offered by this minority was, in some cases, firm and vigorous. A convenient example is Andover Theological Seminary's George Harris, one of the ablest and most learned of American Protestant theologians at the turn of the century. Harris found in the scholar's vocation "the likest thing there is" to authentic, living "virtue." Virtue itself has various embodiments, suggested Harris in 1896, and the pure, unselfish scholar's devoted, "disinterested" service to truth is the *intellectual* embodiment of virtue.[23] Harris's Congregationalist colleague Newman Smyth insisted that even the study of Jesus Christ was not "truly and profoundly reverent and religious" if carried out in a setting of "prejudice"; a genuinely "religious" approach would have to entail "the desire to find the facts as they are."[24] Of Newton's disciplining of his own preferences, the German Reformed Church's *Mercersburg Review* exclaimed in 1873, amid enthusiastic references to Bacon, Spencer, and John Tyndall, "What religious self-abnegation. . . . What a submission of the pride of intellect to the facts of the universe!"[25]

This was exactly the kind of talk William James parodied in *The Will to Believe*: "what thousands of disinterested moral lives of men lie buried" in the "mere foundations" of "the magnificent edifice of the physical sciences, . . . what patience and postponement, what choking down of mere preference, what submission to the icy laws of outer fact are wrought into its very stones and mortar." But James betrayed here an element of sympathy, even while criticizing the positivist epistemology and the agnosticism with which the intellectual gospel was sometimes connected, and while mocking the "robustious pathos of voice" in which it was so often expressed.[26] Unlike the liberal theologians quoted earlier, James was not an institutionally responsible defender of Christianity, but he was his generation's leading champion of "nonscientific" religious experience. His ironic homage to the intellectual gospel was consistent with his career-long prophecy on behalf of a science broad enough to effect what James frankly called the world's "salvation."[27]

Voices more earnest than James's, and more distant from the pulpit than those of the Andover theologians, were of course the chief agencies of the dissemination of the intellectual gospel. Preeminent among these voices were always Huxley and his contemporary British allies—including Herbert Spencer, John Tyndall, W. K. Clifford, and Charles Kingsley—whose utterances of the 1860s and 1870s remained common coin in American academic discourse long after they were joined in the 1890s by a host of native American voices. During the 1870s and 1880s the celebration of modern, secular science in a religious idiom had also gone forward in the United States, but not on the scale seen in the 1890s and in the early years of the new century when the new universities experienced their most explosive growth in size, number, and prestige.[28] Then did John Dewey explain to the Student Christian Association at the University of Michigan that the modern definition of "prayer" was the attitude of inquiry characteristic of science, and that "the building of the Kingdom of God on earth" depended as much on the spread of the ethic of science as it did on anything else.[29] Then, too, did G. Stanley Hall, as president of the new, zealously scientific Clark University, identify the spirit of "research" as the modern voice of "the Holy Ghost." Hall praised the worldwide academic community—incorporating "all groups of students inflamed with the love of truth"—as the modern equivalent of the "Church universal." The "old oracles find new voices," said Hall, "and who would and should not listen?"[30]

The writings of the American academic reformers were brought comfortably together with the foundational writings of Huxley and his British contemporaries in Richard Gregory's *Discovery: The Spirit and Service of Science*, a volume of 1916 that represents the intellectual gospel at its most romantic. Gregory quoted copiously from various and sundry paeans to "the scientific spirit," interspersing the utterances of the Victorians and their successors with inspirational passages from Bacon, Newton, Shakespeare, and Goethe. *Discovery* was brought out in American as well as British editions; it was in its twelfth printing when the kindred *Arrowsmith* appeared in 1925. Gregory himself favored the inherited religious vocabulary as much as did any of the savants whom he quoted. He spoke repeatedly of the "righteousness" and "holiness" of the calling that was the basis for his "uplifting gospel," a "gospel of light." The "temple of science" demands "sacrifices at the altar of knowledge," and "only those with sincere regard for truth will find their gifts acceptable." Entry into "the spiritual city of science" depends on a purity of heart like Sir Galahad, the knight with a "complete vision of the Holy Grail." The truly scientific mind "cannot be brought within the bounds of a narrow religious formulary," explained Gregory, "yet it is essentially devout, and it influences for good all with whom it comes into contact."[31]

Gregory dwelled on the religious piety of great men of science, including Pasteur, of whom a statue for the Cathedral of St. John the Divine had recently been proposed by Henry Fairfield Osborn, director of the American Museum of Natural History. In his pamphlet of 1913, *The New Order of Sainthood*, Osborn used Pasteur as his model for scientific sainthood. Osborn declared that the essential insights of the "faith of our fathers" were stronger than ever as a result of the "constructive, purifying, and regenerating" acts of scientific inquiry during the second half of the nineteenth century. Hence it was in a real rather than a metaphorical church—the new cathedral being built on 112th Street in New York City—that Osborn proposed the recognition of a distinctive order of saints:

> Should we not institute a new order of sainthood for men like Pasteur? Could we find one more eminent for consecration, piety, and service in life and character than this devout investigator? . . . Would not a statue of Louis Pasteur . . . proclaim the faith of the modern Church that the two great historic movements of Love and of Knowledge, of the spiritual and intellectual and the physical well-being of man, are harmonious of a single and eternal truth?[32]

Although the tone in which Osborn and Gregory spoke recalled the nineteenth century, which had produced their greatest heroes and their most treasured aphorisms, the Edwardean-Progressive works of Osborn and Gregory bear great similarity to the only slightly less romantic versions of the intellectual gospel that were enunciated during the more hard-boiled 1920s. A prominent, but insufficiently recognized, theme in the intellectual history of the 1920s is the perpetuation, in regard to *science*, of a religious idealism that was otherwise on the defensive.

The intellectual gospel was updated for this proudly skeptical decade not only by the reverent *Arrowsmith*, on the basis of which Sinclair Lewis won his greatest critical acclaim, but also by the works of historians John Herman Randall Jr., James Harvey Robinson, and Frederick Barry.[33] All proclaimed science's ability to carry on some of the salient spiritual functions of traditional religion. The same thought was expressed routinely in the popular writings of physical and social scientists throughout the decade. The biologist Winterton C. Curtis speculated in his widely discussed book *Science and Human Affairs* that "the scientific habit of mind" would "satisfy the ethical and philosophical desires which have been hitherto formulated as religion and theology."[34]

This was exactly the upshot of Walter Lippmann's *A Preface to Morals*, although this famous book of 1929 was anything but romantic. An instant classic of cultural criticism, *A Preface to Morals* caught the note of jaundiced "disillusionment" that so many American intellectuals of the 1920s associated with themselves. Hence the book's guarded advocacy of the intellectual gospel is all the more revealing an index of this gospel's appeal. Lippmann addressed what he saw as the enduring *religious* needs of his culture. These needs simply could not be met by the existing churches and their religions, he was quick to conclude, for the "acids of modernity" had eroded their foundations; the sophisticated, educated person still had religious yearnings, but intellectual integrity required that such a person turn away from the inherited, popular religions. Lippmann saw promise in what he called the "high religion" of classical philosophy. The essence of this "high religion" was a stoic "disinterested-ness" to be found in Lippmann's own day chiefly *in science*. There, more than anywhere else, could one contemplate the "mature" resignation to the limits of one's existence celebrated in *A Preface to Morals*. There, in science, the individual was to modify desire in order to meet "reality":

> And so the mature man would take the world as it comes, and within himself remain quite unperturbed. When he acted, he would know that he was only testing an hypothesis, and . . . he would be quite prepared for the discovery that he might make mistakes, for his intelligence would be disentangled from his hopes. The failure of his experiment could not, therefore, involve the failure of his life. For the aspect of life which implicated his soul would be his understanding of life, and, to the understanding, defeat is no less interesting than victory.[35]

"Hypothesis." "Experiment." "Understanding." Lippmann associated his "religion of the spirit" with ancient sages, but as he elaborated on it he spoke more and more of "the spirit of modern science." Not only did he prescribe detachment, neutrality, tolerance, universalism, and skepticism; he explicitly identified "pure science" as "high religion incarnate." The high religion has "hitherto" been "lyrical and personal and apart," but now "the scientific discipline" could bring it "down to earth and into direct and decisive contact with the concerns of mankind." Moreover, this religion was uniquely capable of surviving any and all changes in our specific knowledge about the world: "the religion of the spirit does not depend upon creeds and cosmologies; it has no vested interest in any particular truth." It alone could "endure the variety and complexity of things," because it aimed higher. "Its indifference to what the facts may be is indeed the very spirit of scientific inquiry." He smiled at those whose view of science was so naïve as to make a religion out of any given, specific set of scientific results; such people did not understand the provisional character of scientific belief, had not absorbed the insight that the religious significance of science was in its "inward principle," its spirit. To support his view of science, Lippmann quoted an essay that Charles Peirce—one of America's most forthright and consistent champions of the ethic of science—had published in *Popular Science Monthly* in 1878.[36]

Lippmann had praised "the discipline of science" long before 1929, but with a very different, more exuberant demeanor. This discipline was to promote "mastery," to enable the men and women of the twentieth century to control their fate, Lippmann had argued in 1914. Fifteen years after he had invoked the "scientific spirit" in his upbeat, bring-on-the-world *Drift and Mastery*—no less a classic of "Progressivism" than was Lippmann's book of 1929 an enduring monument of the intellectual preoccupations of that time—Lippmann called on the same device to help people adapt to "reality."[37] Scholars have noted the emotional gulf Lippmann crossed between these two books, but they have not paid sufficient attention to the fact that in both cases Lippmann turned to "the spirit of science" for his solution. The intellectual gospel admitted of formulations running across a spectrum from heady exuberance to chastened resignation, and Lippmann himself had occupied both extremes by the time he was forty.

John Dewey invites attention here because he never moved so far as Lippmann did toward the "resignation" end of that spectrum, yet he continued throughout the 1920s and 1930s to depict the life of inquiry as an essentially religious mission. Never had Dewey been more explicit and forthright about this than he was in 1934, in *A Common Faith*. This work was a reaction, in part, to a popular disillusion with science deeper than that registered by Lippmann's *A Preface to Morals*. Lippmann had given up on the idea of reconstructing society, whether by science or by any other means, but remained loyal to the ethic of science as the most defensible source of religious fulfillment. Others had reacted more sharply against the secular, humanistic currents associated with the ethic of science. Orthodox Christianity was then being affirmed against these currents by T. S. Eliot, John Crowe Ransom, and Reinhold Niebuhr.

Dewey would have none of this new orthodoxy. In *A Common Faith*, Dewey renounced once again all varieties of supernaturalism and insisted that inquiry itself could properly be described as a "religious" object. He also rejected as excessively passive the stoical outlook of Lippmann. "Faith in the continued disclosing of truth through directed cooperative human endeavor," Dewey explained, "is more religious in quality than is any faith in a completed revelation." Dewey distinguished sharply between any and all particular *religions*, which he declared to have outlived their usefulness and to have produced many destructive results, and *the religious*, a quality that might inhere in our relation to any object. The unification of the self and its harmonization with the Universe define "the religious," and this unification and harmonization can be more than "a mere Stoical resolution to endure unperturbed throughout the buffetings of fortune." This unification and harmonization can take place in relation to a systematic effort to understand and change the world. Religion is an "element" in life that must be liberated from "religions," Dewey insisted, in order that people can be free to develop this element in healthier contexts, including, above all, the practice of inquiry.[38]

The intellectual gospel did not end with Dewey any more than the social gospel ended with Rauschenbusch. The notion that conduct in accord with the scientific ethic was a form of religious fulfillment continued to be invoked, especially by people who sought to explain the nature of science to a popular audience or to defend secular cultural institutions against charges of insensitivity to the moral and religious needs of society. But the intellectual gospel was a less important feature of American intellectual life during the second third of the twentieth century than it had been during the previous fifty years. This change had a number of sources.

The very success with which cultural institutions had been secularized diminished the need to preach this particular gospel. Intellectuals who were "irreligious" in the sense of professing neither Christianity nor any other of the historic religions were generally more comfortable with their irreligion, and less moved to construct their secularity in terms that called attention to a religious heritage. Intellectuals who remained committed to a Protestant church or to Catholicism were more comfortable with varieties of neo-orthodoxy that resisted the open accommodation with "science" favored by the Protestant theological elite of the previous era. The increasing proportion of American intellectuals who had Jewish, rather than Protestant or Catholic, antecedents helped move public discourse about science away from the terms developed by Anglo-Protestant intellectuals in the nineteenth century. The intellectual fashions among educated Americans moved yet more decisively away from the extreme idealism of which the intellectual gospel was, in the 1920s, already an anomalous remnant. The worldwide political crises of the 1930s and 1940s drew proponents of the scientific ethic toward its democratic implications, rather than toward the religious virtues that had seemed so important during the Victorian "crisis of faith." The atomic bomb gave new credibility to the suspicion that demonic forces were somehow entangled in science no less than were the more wholesome forces attributed to it by the intellectual gospel. Finally, the scientific enterprise came under more critical, empirical scrutiny, rendering less plausible and less responsive to current concerns the constructions of science's religiosity popularized by Huxley and Dewey.

During the era in which the intellectual gospel flourished, however, the intellectual gospel and the social gospel divided their common religious heritage between them. Each took up and developed in relative isolation one of the two themes mentioned by Henry Fairfield Osborn, when extolling the sainthood of Pasteur: Love and Knowledge. In proposing a statue of Pasteur in the Cathedral of St. John the Divine, it was natural for even a proponent of the intellectual gospel to envisage a symbolic unification of knowledge with love, but Osborn was primarily a spokesman for an ethic not of love but of science. The social gospel accentuated and developed love as a religious ideal, trusting that other movements would pursue knowledge; the intellectual gospel accentuated and developed knowledge as a religious ideal, trusting that other movements would practice love.

The social gospel and the intellectual gospel deserve to be remembered as siblings, if not as twins. Just as the social gospel was a major tributary to the river of social reform that became a conspicuous feature of the historical landscape of the United States in the late nineteenth and early twentieth century, the intellectual gospel fed the current of academic reform that resulted in the reorganization of American culture around universities devoted largely to research. Just as the social gospel enabled a man or a woman to feel that work in a settlement house or in a Progressive's political campaign helped to bring about the Kingdom of God, the intellectual gospel enabled a man or a woman to feel that work in a university or a laboratory helped to bring to maturation spiritual seeds planted in the Bible and nurtured by Christianity. Just as the social gospel provided religious sanction for the liberal reforms carried out by the bourgeoisie in the face of tensions created by industrial capitalism, the intellectual gospel rendered a religious mission the production of the new knowledge on which the technologically sophisticated social order of modern times was increasingly dependent. Just as the social gospel inspired many church members to believe that the essence of their

Christian birthright was a set of moral teachings not dissimilar to those found in other religions, the intellectual gospel inspired many intellectuals to believe that an aura of divinity accompanied the secularization of public doctrine in response to the content, scope, and dynamic character of modern scientific knowledge. Just as the social gospel encouraged its adherents to interpret their labors in society as signs of a right relationship with God, the intellectual gospel encouraged its adherents to interpret their labors in the laboratory and the archives as signs of a right relationship with whatever gods they recognized.

But where, in the intellectual gospel, was Jesus Christ? For all its striking similarities to the social gospel, the intellectual gospel was not explicitly preached in the name of a unique Christianity. In the social gospel, men and women of Christian commitment sought to expand and reinterpret their religious tradition to make it more responsive to social and psychological conditions of modern life, but these men and women did not advance a doctrine of separate spheres, one for "religion" and one for "social reform." Meanwhile in the intellectual gospel, a spiritual intensity for which Christianity had been the uniquely powerful vehicle was transferred to an endeavor that was becoming, as our recent historiography emphasizes, increasingly differentiated and divergent from Christianity. It was to an increasingly autonomous, cognitive enterprise that ideologues of science applied the language of spiritual perfection. The intellectual gospel challenged Christianity's moral authority because this gospel intensified a connection between spiritual perfection and scientific inquiry exactly while that inquiry renounced all the more openly the Christian presuppositions that had been cheerfully acknowledged by generations of scientists.

This moral challenge did not compare in magnitude with science's cognitive challenge to the authority of Christianity, but performed a singular service in support of that more profound challenge. It equipped partisans of science with grounds for ignoring a familiar complaint of Christian moralists. Science, these complainants repeatedly insisted, was simply "about facts" and "devoid of values." If the realm of cognition is to be turned over to science, they argued, then let us remember that the realm of values is all the more clearly and exclusively the business of religion. If we are going to have separate spheres, they said, let us all remember that in the sphere of science there are *only* facts.[39] This complaint was easily neutralized by the intellectual gospel. Plainly, science embodied a demanding ethic; to do science was to affirm, to abide by, and to exemplify specific and vital values. The issues in moral philosophy begged by this confidence are beside the point of our understanding the role played by the ethic of science in making an autonomous, secular science spiritually acceptable to intellectuals brought up in the culture of nineteenth-century Protestantism. The intellectual gospel may not have been an episode in any "warfare" of science and religion, but it did function in a real struggle between rival claimants to the cultural leadership of the United States.[40]

Notes

1. This perspective has recently been displayed and consolidated in the important collection of original essays edited by David C. Lindberg and Ronald L. Numbers, *God and Nature: Historical Essays on the Encounter between Christianity and Science* (Berkeley: University of California Press, 1986); see especially the remarks of the editors, 9–10, 14. The most ambitious and polemical contribution to "neo-harmonist" historiography is James R. Moore, *The Post-Darwinian Controversies: A Study of the Protestant Struggle to Come to Terms with Darwin in Great Britain and America 1870–1900* (Cambridge: Cambridge University Press, 1979). I have sought to identify the strengths and limitations of Moore's work in my "What Is Darwinism? It Is Calvinism!" *Reviews in American History* VIII (March 1980), 80–85.

2. T. H. Huxley, "On the Advisableness of Improving Natural Knowledge," as reprinted in Alburey Castell, ed., *Selections from the Essays of T. H. Huxley* (New York: Appleton-Century-Crofts, 1948), 14.

3. Grant Wacker has reminded me that "correct cognitive conduct" of one kind or another is a standard ingredient in most religious traditions, especially the Judeo-Christian tradition. Victorian ideologists of science certainly inherited from that tradition a sense of the spiritual importance of having a proper, authoritative construction of reality. Justification even by "faith" might count as correct cognitive conduct, if one defines "cognitive" and "conduct" very broadly. But I am construing these terms more narrowly and conventionally in the interests of distinguishing the worldly practice of *wissenschaftliche* knowing from the varieties of faith preached by churches in the name of Christianity. When Huxley distinguished "verification" from "faith," he took for granted an enormous epistemological divide.

4. American Protestantism's traditionally positive perspective on modern science is discussed in George Marsden's contribution to the volume in which this essay first appeared. Of the several other works detailing this perspective, a study of "old school" Presbyterians has proved especially influential in recent historiography: Theodore Dwight Bozeman, *Protestants in an Age of Science: The Baconian Ideal and Antebellum American Religious Thought* (Chapel Hill: University of North Carolina Press, 1977).

5. Herbert Spencer, quoted, for example, in Richard Gregory, *Discovery: The Spirit and Service of Science* (London: Macmillan, 1916; New York: 1926), 41.

6. Quoted, for example, ibid., 43.

7. Woodrow Wilson, "Princeton in the Nation's Service," Address of October 21, 1896, in Arthur S. Link, ed., *The Papers of Woodrow Wilson* (Princeton: Princeton University Press, 1966) X, 31: "calm Science seated there, recluse, ascetic,

like a nun, not knowing that the world passes, not caring, if the truth but come in answer to her prayer."

8. Sinclair Lewis, *Arrowsmith* (New York: Harcourt, Brace & World, 1925; reprint, New York: Signet, 1961), 269: "God give me unclouded eyes and freedom from haste. God give me a quiet and relentless anger against all pretense. . . . God give me a restlessness. . . . God give me strength not to trust in God!"

9. The logic of this pagan variation was a logic of gender, common to defensive reactions against an "aggressive," "demonic" science that Gill represented first as "it" and then as a male (a "man of straw"). Against this aggression Gill's "goddess," like Wilson's Catholic nun, offers an ample supply of pleasing femininity. Gill's goddess of *science* is clearly a reformulation of the traditionally female *nature*; Gill's worshippers—the actual scientists—were implicitly male. Theodore Gill, "Culture and Science," *American Naturalist* XXII (1888): 489–90.

10. Max Weber, "Vocation of Science," in Hans Gerth and C. Wright Mills, eds., *From Max Weber: Essays in Sociology* (New York: Oxford University Press, 1946), 135.

11. On the relation of the professionalization of science to Victorian rivalries between "science" and "religion," see Frank M. Turner, "The Victorian Conflict between Science and Religion: A Professional Dimension," *Isis* LXIX (1978): 356–76.

12. This construction of the ethic of science differs slightly from, but is essentially in accord with, Robert K. Merton's widely cited "ethos" of science, most easily available in Merton, *The Sociology of Science: Theoretical and Empirical Investigations* (Chicago: University of Chicago Press, 1973), 267–78. I have interpreted Merton's construction in relation to the historical circumstances of the 1930s and early 1940s in my "The Defense of Democracy and Robert K. Merton's Formulation of the Scientific Ethos," *Knowledge and Society* IV (1983): 1–15.

13. Quoted by Hilary Rose and Stephen Rose, "The Incorporation of Science," in Rose and Rose, eds., *The Political Economy of Science* (London: Macmillan, 1976), 27. See also Gregory, *Discovery*, 47.

14. The social gospel has received more attention from historians than any other aspect of American religious history since the Civil War. Two of the most influential studies of the topic have been Charles Hopkins, *The Rise of the Social Gospel in American Protestantism, 1865–1915* (New Haven: Yale University Press, 1940), and Henry F. May, *Protestant Churches in Industrial America* (New York: Harper & Row, 1949). See also the contribution to the volume in which this essay first appeared by William King.

15. Walter Rauschenbusch, *A Theology for the Social Gospel* (New York: Macmillan, 1917).

16. On Mathews and the controversies surrounding his work, see William R. Hutchison, *The Modernist Impulse in American Protestantism* (Cambridge, MA: Harvard University Press, 1977), 275–82.

17. A convenient point of access to this episode, although exclusive to France, is Charles B. Paul, *Science and Immorality: The Eloges of the Paris Academy of Sciences (1699–1791)* (Berkeley: University of California Press, 1980).

18. This characterization was popularized in America by John Fiske. See, e.g., John Fiske, "Reminiscences of Huxley," *Atlantic* LXXXVII (February 1901), 283.

19. For a helpful account of the atmosphere at Johns Hopkins in the 1880s, see Hugh Hawkins, *Pioneer: A History of the Johns Hopkins University, 1874–1889* (Ithaca: Cornell University Press, 1960), 293–315.

20. Ira Remsen, "Scientific Investigation and Progress," *Popular Science Monthly* LXIV (1904): 301.

21. George Sarton, *The History of Science and the New Humanism* (Cambridge, MA: Harvard University Press, 1937), 116–18.

22. Hutchison notes in passing (*Modernist Impulse*, 165) that "about one third" of "the thirty-three most prominent leaders of theological liberalism in the period from 1875 to 1915" took "no discernible part in the social gospel." It is interesting that Hutchison's list of nonparticipants in the one liberal gospel includes several who were attracted to what I am saying amounted to a second liberal gospel: Charles A. Briggs, George Gordon, George Harris, A. C. McGiffert, Theodore Munger, and Egbert Smyth.

23. George Harris, *Moral Evolution* (London: Macmillan, 1896), 76.

24. Newman Smyth, *Old Faiths in New Light* (New York: Scribner's, 1879), 24. See also Smyth, *Through Science to Faith* (New York: Scribner's, 1902), which opened with a paean to the "pure love of truth" that ideally united enlightened theologians with scientists.

25. W. Leaman, "The Scope and Spirit of Scientific Research," *Mercersburg Review* XX (1873): 532.

26. William James, *The Will to Believe* (Cambridge, MA: Harvard University Press, 1979), 17–18.

27. I have discussed James's perspective on science and religion in *In the American Province: Studies in the History and Historiography of Ideas* (Bloomington: Indiana University Press, 1985), 3–22.

28. On the articulation of an ideology of "research" in relation to the creation and growth of these institutions, see Laurence R. Veysey, *The Emergence of the American University* (Chicago: University of Chicago Press, 1965), 121–79, especially 149–58, which focuses on the religiosity of many expressions of this ideology. See also my "Inquiry and Uplift: Late Nineteenth Century American Academics and the Moral Efficacy of Scientific Practice," in Thomas L. Haskell, ed., *The Authority of Experts: Essays in History and Theory* (Bloomington: Indiana University Press, 1984), 142–56.

29. John Dewey, *The Early Works, 1881–1898*, IV, 104–5, 368.

30. G. Stanley Hall, "Research the Vital Spirit of Teaching," *Forum* XVII (1894): 565.

31. Gregory, *Discovery*, vi, 11, 12, 27, 51, 54–55. Gregory did not cite his sources, and sometimes erred in his attributions. For example, he attributed to the University of Pennsylvania chemist Edgar Fahs Smith a rather well-known poem by James Russell Lowell that Smith had used while praising a colleague for his "self denial stern"; see ibid., 17.

32. Henry Fairfield Osborn, *The New Order of Sainthood* (New York: Scribner's, 1913), 13, 16.

33. See, as examples, John Herman Randall Jr., *Our Changing Civilization: How Science and the Machine Are Reconstructing Modern Life* (New York: Stokes, 1931); James Harvey Robinson, *The Mind in the Making* (New York: Harpers, 1921); and Frederick Barry, *The Scientific Habit of Thought* (New York: Columbia University Press, 1927).

34. Winterton C. Curtis, *Science and Human Affairs: From the Viewpoint of Biology* (New York: Harcourt, Brace and Company, 1922), 8. See also, e.g., Edwin Grant Conklin, *The Direction of Human Evolution* (New York: C. Scribner's Sons, 1922), especially 244.

35. Walter Lippmann, *A Preface to Morals* (New York: Macmillan, 1929), 209, 329.

36. Lippmann, *A Preface to Morals*, 129, 131, 239, 327–28. Lippmann quoted Peirce's "How to Make Our Ideas Clear." He cited it as reprinted in the collection of Peirce's writings edited by Morris R. Cohen, *Chance, Love, and Logic* (New York: Harcourt, Brace, 1923).

37. Walter Lippmann, *Drift and Mastery* (New York: Kinnerly, 1914); on this early work of Lippmann's, see my *In the American Province*, 44–55.

38. John Dewey, *A Common Faith* (New Haven: Yale University Press 1934) 16, 19, 26, 57.

39. For a typical rendition of this refrain, see Christian Gauss, "The Threat of Science," *Scribner's Magazine* LXXXVIII (1930):467–78.

40. Although this essay addresses the intellectual gospel in relation to American religious history and its historiography, I want to call attention to a larger frame of reference in which the cultural powers of the scientific enterprise were celebrated. Much of the discourse of twentieth-century intellectuals has been influenced by the notion that "science," rather than "religion" or "the arts," might become the decisive force in determining the contents of a superior modern culture. I have argued elsewhere that by distinguishing this "cognitivism" from the celebration of human artifice manifest in "modernist" movements in literature and the arts, we can arrive at a more accurate comprehension of the general issues that have preoccupied post-biblical intellectuals in the United States and Western Europe during much of this century. See my "The Knower and the Artificer," *American Quarterly* XXXIX (1987), 37–55. In developing my ideas about "the intellectual gospel," I have been helped by the suggestions and criticisms of Van Harvey, William Hutchison, Hugh Jackson, Julie A. Reuben, and Grant Wacker.

CHAPTER 5

James, Clifford, and the Scientific Conscience

For more than a century William James has been a favorite philosopher of persons eager to put at rest the fear that science has somehow rendered faith in God untenable. James's essay of 1897, "The Will to Believe," endures as the classic dismissal of this anxiety, still invoked reverently in our own time by Charles Taylor (in his Varieties of Religion Today: William James Revisited *[Cambridge, MA, 2002]) and by other faith-affirming thinkers throughout Christendom. Central to James's apparently successful argument was his searing refutation of the British agnostic W. K. Clifford's 1877 treatise, "The Ethics of Belief." Oddly, almost none of James's disciples show evidence of having read Clifford and of having understood the issues that James and Clifford actually debated.*

This essay is a comparative reading of "The Ethics of Belief" and "The Will to Believe" and an interpretation of each in the distinctive contexts of England in the 1870s and New England in the 1890s. I argue that Clifford displayed more sensitivity than James did to the consequences of belief. This is an ironic reversal of roles in the story of a great pragmatist who insisted, even within the text of "The Will to Believe," that "the whole defense of religious faith hinges upon" the action that faith requires or inspires. James's "The Will to Believe" should be understood not only as an artifact of its author's agony about the fate of Christianity in the age of science, but also as a product of his political complacency. Clifford had a much more modern understanding than James did of the function of belief systems in society and politics.

James was deeply ambivalent about the conflict addressed in chapter 4 in this volume. He was devoted to the ethic of science and did not object to its deployment against wildly implausible religious claims, but he was troubled by the potential of this ethic to undermine even the highly liberalized versions of Christianity espoused by the Protestants of his milieu. I show that James dealt with this ambivalence first by sharply delimiting the domain of science so that the practice of its ethic would not disturb certain classes of religious beliefs, and second, later in his career, by adopting more and more of Clifford's framework and asking that religious beliefs be vindicated through science itself rather than outside it. By the time James wrote Pragmatism *in 1907, he had quietly accepted most of Clifford's account of how one should decide what to believe.*

This essay is closely related to the one that follows in chapter 6, which addresses James's entire career and argues that The Varieties of Religious Experience *was composed in a limbo between James's abandonment of his first strategy for defending religious belief and his adoption of the second. This essay was originally published in Ruth Anna Putnam, ed.,* The Cambridge Companion to William James *(New York, 1997).*

HOWEVER DIVERSE OUR OPINIONS of William James today, we generally agree that the great pragmatist was right about one thing: the pretensions of the Victorian "positivists." James exposed the epistemological naïveté of these cultural imperialists. He celebrated openness of mind over the arrogant, dogmatic closures we associate with the nineteenth-century scientific intelligentsia. These contemporaries of Darwin ascribed to the sciences a God's-eye view, and to the world a set of hard features discoverable by men and women bold enough to replace fantasy and superstition with facts. These Huxleys and Tyndalls and Cliffords thought themselves a new priesthood, and, while telling everyone what to believe, functioned as the thought-police of their age. So deep were the roots sunk in the Western mind by this vine of conceits that we seem never to be able to get it out of our system. We attack it and attack it and attack it, and quote modern thinkers as diverse as Quine and Kuhn and Wittgenstein and Foucault against it. And we quote James. We honor him for being one of the first to take up the cause, for being among the great prophets of epistemic humility, a founder of truly "modernist" or even "postmodernist"[1] thought.

Especially in "The Will to Believe" did James vindicate the right of the average man and woman to resist the directives of the self-appointed spokespersons for science. James understood that scientific inquiry took place in a socially and historically specific matrix, and that every inquirer was both enabled and confined by cultural and psychological predilections. James's world was plural and contingent, and what features it afforded to our disciplined gaze remained, to a large extent, ontological enigmas. If the quality of James's argumentation in this legendary essay was sometimes sloppy—as has been so often lamented by sympathetic commentators[2]—the lapse has been largely forgiven in the context of the essay's prophetic role in "the revolt against positivism."[3] But we seem unwilling to forgive the chief target of James's righteous wrath in "The Will to Believe" the English mathematician W. K. Clifford. James's dispatching of Clifford was so effective that commentators on "The Will to Believe" rarely even read the arguments of the thinker James was most concerned to answer. Clifford's historical significance is, thanks to

James, akin to that of some of Socrates' more obliging stooges. He was foolish enough to voice opinions that a wiser intellect could refute with wholesome and lasting effects.

But scrutiny of what Clifford wrote reveals that he was not quite as foolish as James has led us to conclude, and that James's representation of Clifford's arguments was less than fair. Some philosophers who now claim to write in James's "spirit" might feel closer to Clifford than to James, were they to assess the two side-by-side.[4] Walking to the library to read Clifford's "The Ethics of Belief" may seem an extraordinarily simple act, but the existing scholarship on "The Will to Believe"—by far the most widely renowned of all James's essays—displays little awareness of what Clifford actually said.[5]

To call attention, as I will be doing here, to James's misrepresentations of Clifford is not simply to invite a scolding of James, nor to indulge an antiquarian's interest in Jamesiana. These misrepresentations served to conceal important intellectual ground that James actually shared with Clifford. The points genuinely at issue between James and Clifford can be distinguished from the red herrings James fed to a readership eager for any excuse to keep agnostics at bay. A more accurate understanding of James's relation to Clifford can enable us to clarify the terms on which James contested Clifford over the structure of plausibility that would obtain in the culture of educated inhabitants of the North Atlantic West. Both understood that the character of this structure of plausibility was at issue in their time. "The Will to Believe" was a distinctive moment in James's search for a scientifically respectable framework in which the essential religious sensibility of the liberal protestantism of his milieu could be affirmed. When read against Clifford, and against *Pragmatism*, which James wrote ten years after "The Will to Believe," the latter emerges as a brilliant spasm, but a spasm nevertheless. James was lashing out against a scientific conscience that held enormous power over him. In *Pragmatism*, James made a tense, but steadier and more genuine peace with this scientific conscience than he had been able to do in the jumpy, and sometimes disingenuous "The Will to Believe."

Clifford did assert that "it is wrong in all cases to believe on insufficient evidence."[6] This is the adamant, rather precious claim invariably linked with Clifford's name. The rigid, absolutist tone of the remark was made to sound silly by the practical, flexible, down-to-earth James. Our pragmatist knew that real people have to make choices between alternatives that are not always subject to clear and convincing proofs. "Clifford's exhortation" was "thoroughly fantastic" to James. It meant keeping our minds "in suspense forever." Not by such withdrawal could knowledge be expanded, and appropriate action be performed. Clifford's injunction was "like a general informing his soldiers that it is better to keep out of battle forever than to risk a single wound" (*The Will to Believe*, 24–25; henceforth cited as *WB*). Thus did James drive a cross through Clifford's infidel heart.

The victory was made more easy by the fact that Clifford lay eighteen years in the grave. James published "The Will to Believe" in 1897; Clifford died in 1879. Had "that delicious *enfant terrible*"—as James called (*WB*, 17) the brilliant mathematician killed by tuberculosis while still short of his thirty-fourth birthday[7]—been around to dispute the point, Clifford could have quoted with telling effect the very essay James ridiculed. "We have no reason to fear lest a habit of conscientious inquiry should paralyze the actions of our daily life," Clifford had explained, as though answering James directly. We encounter "many cases in which it is our duty to act on probabilities, although the evidence is not such as to justify present belief." Clifford had taken pains, then, to avoid exactly the misreading that James carried out, a misreading in which Clifford was alleged to have been oblivious to the need to live on the basis of incomplete and imperfect information. It was "precisely by" doing this, by taking chances on the basis of the best available information and observing the results, "that evidence is got whereby to justify future belief" (W. K. Clifford, "Ethics of Belief," 1877, 296; henceforth cited as Clifford 1877).

Far from advocating the passivity James ascribed to him, Clifford extolled action based on the most critically defensible belief available at any given time. What Clifford argued against vehemently was the holding of beliefs uncritically, the shielding of such beliefs from the "habit of conscientious inquiry." "Sufficiency" of evidence was a relative ideal, but James, by quoting Clifford selectively, made it sound absolute and unattainable. James thus dealt with Clifford through the classic device of appropriation and effacement: he appropriated for himself the more sensible qualifications that Clifford had built into his own argument to begin with, and then effaced these commonsense caveats from his summary of Clifford.

James was almost as cavalier on the matter of the uniformity of nature. Against the narrow construction of this principle by Clifford and his scientific compatriots James warned sagely that nature might not be so absolutely uniform, after all. Scientists refuse to look for "evidence of telepathy" because it would threaten their dogmas. To illustrate the bad faith of the scientists, James cited "a leading biologist" who told him that even if telepathy were true "scientists ought to band together to keep it suppressed and concealed." But James admitted that this unnamed scoundrel was, like Clifford, "now dead" (*WB*, 19).

What had Clifford said about the uniformity of nature? Nothing so outrageous as the sentiments of the biologist conveniently unavailable for confirming interrogation. Clifford argued that our reasoning about new experiences should begin with an assumption that these experiences can be explained by the same forces that have explained previous experiences. We assume a continuity between "what we do not know" and "what we do know." This simple assumption helps us to allocate our energies in our experiments, and to guide our actions in daily life. If what we see of the sun in our spectroscope "behaves as hydrogen under similar circumstances would behave on earth," we have good reason to think there is hydrogen in the sun. And Clifford again took pains to prevent being charged as an absolutist: he answered with a resounding "no" the question he, himself, raised: should we believe "that nature is absolutely and universally uniform?" Clifford used this preposterously extreme uniformitarianism as an example of an idea in which "we have no right to believe" (Clifford 1877, 306, 308).

For Clifford, the principle of the uniformity of nature was a guide to action, and a foundation for the asking of new questions about our world. But to believe in it as an absolute truth was an example of believing on "insufficient evidence," the very vice against which Clifford's essay was directed. James, of course, turned this around entirely, so that generations of James's readers have assumed that Clifford was one of those trusting monks of the positivist faith who believed the "evidence" was "sufficient" to believe absolutely in the uniformity of nature.

Not every impression James left about Clifford was misleading. Clifford was truly less respectful than James of the religious beliefs of the masses of humankind, beyond as well as within the Christian tradition. James was correct to identify Clifford as the voice for a sensibility different from his own. If James was inclined, as his friend Justice Holmes once complained, "to turn down the lights so as to give miracle a chance,"[8] Clifford was unattractively eager to carry the torch of the Enlightenment into the prayer room in the hope of embarrassing some pious, if misguided soul.

In several other respects, too, James left a fair impression. Clifford had more confidence than James did in the body of existing knowledge, was more inclined to stress its durability, and was less cognizant than James was of the power of a cultural inheritance to shape the course of inquiry. James was more concerned than Clifford with the psychological realities of the process of inquiry, and less piously moralistic about what the two agreed were the imperatives guiding this process. Clifford still praised a studied detachment in science that James skewered eloquently: "If you want an absolute duffer in an investigation . . . take the man who has no interest whatsoever in its results." The best investigator, James insisted in a voice appreciated by most twentieth-century thinkers, "is always he whose eager interest in one side of the question is balanced by an equally keen nervousness lest he become deceived" (*WB*, 26).

James's relation to Clifford was dominated by James's determination to protect "religious" belief from the critical spirit James himself appreciated, even as presented in Clifford's "The Ethics of Belief." James was a man of science, and deeply proud of it. Not only his earlier *Principles* (henceforth cited as *P*), but also his later *The Varieties of Religious Experience* (henceforth cited as *VRE*) were among the most formidable applications of *Wissenschaft* to any aspect of human life produced by his generation of American intellectuals. James was haunted, throughout his career-long effort to vindicate religion, by a scientific conscience.[9] This conscience he associated with Clifford more than with any other single individual. At the end of *Varieties*, for example, James invoked the long-dead Clifford once again, and in his capacity as the conscience of science. Clifford had identified "that inward monitor" that whispers "Bosh!" in one's mind when one is tempted to go beyond an "objective" assessment of experience (*VRE*, 408). In this particular instance the "conscience" served, as so often when invoked by James, to ironically prevent one from accepting as "scientific" the agnosticism preached by Clifford. The gravamen of James's disagreement with Clifford was the extent to which beliefs Anglophone intellectuals of the late Victorian era called "religious" could be held without a guilty conscience.

The core of these beliefs was an exceedingly general theism. "The essence of the religious principles for James," Edward H. Madden has cogently summarized, "was a god strong enough to ensure that moral values are not a fleeting aspect of man's short existence but have a permanent residence at the heart of things."[10] In "The Will to Believe" no less than throughout his entire career James shied away from defending more specific religious doctrines, despite the fact that his books and essays were filled with sympathetic portrayals of believers in this or that specific faith.[11]

This disposition was fully in keeping with the "essentialism" of the liberal Protestant culture of James's milieu.[12] The "essentials" of Christianity were to be affirmed, while its anachronistic overlays—the products of well-meaning if unsophisticated disciples who had projected their own cultures onto the eternal gospel—were to be cast aside. The generality of "the religious hypothesis," as James often phrased his unelaborated theism, did not go very far as theology. But as a common denominator around which the embattled Protestants of James's time and place could rally, James's formulation of the core of religion was a spectacular success. James's readers could connect to this hypothesis whatever specific beliefs they thought were implied by it. In the minds of the most highly educated segment of the population, the basic theism defended by James was the bedrock of a Christian faith that had been liberalized in response to the fear of Schleiermacher and a host of other Protestant leaders that the world's cognitive future lay with the secular, scientific intellect. Even those good Congregationalists and Episcopalians who had welcomed the emphasis on "feelings" and "conduct" following upon the scaling down of Christianity's cognitive claims remained committed, of course, to the concept of God. Hence, agnostics posed a real challenge: they undermined the remaining cognitive foundation of the Christian edifice that housed religious emotions and the social gospel.

Clifford had not attacked theism directly, nor was he forthright in his approach to Christianity. "The Ethics of Belief" was a passionate vindication of critical inquiry, and a vociferous attack on the habit of accepting, unexamined, the truth-claims that come to us from political or religious authority, social custom, or undisciplined feeling. Clifford's essay bears more comparison than it has received to a great American apotheosis of scientific method that appeared in the same year, Charles Peirce's "The Fixation of Belief" (1877). Peirce brought science to bear on the entirety of belief, explicitly including religious belief, and he did so with a spirit of moral rectitude. To "avoid looking into the support of any belief from a fear that it may turn out to be rotten," Peirce intoned with a righteous indignation worthy of Clifford, "is quite as immoral as it is disadvantageous."[13] But the beliefs of Christians figured in Clifford's text only marginally. Clifford quoted Milton and Coleridge to the effect that one should love "truth" itself above Christianity and the words of its preachers, but the religion of Clifford's readers was hidden, for the most part, behind carefully constructed stand-ins such as the "medicine-man in Central Africa," whose absurd ideas Clifford invoked coolly. Clifford's most extended example of unfounded religious belief was that of "a Mohammedan." Clifford had this imaginary apostle of a specific religion anathema to most of his readers voice the general arguments for faith common among educated Christians (the virtues of the great prophet, the miraculous events that testify to God's greatness and power, and so on). Clifford faulted these arguments as insufficiently grounded in conscientious inquiry (Clifford 1877, 297–300, 302). This was not quite Galileo inserting the Pope's arguments in the mouth of a character called "Simplicio," but Clifford's casting the Infidel Turk in the role of spokesman for "religion" had some of the same flavor.

The beliefs that get called "religious" were, for Clifford, merely cases of belief in general. Part of the power of Clifford's presentation derived from his locating of religious belief next to a variety of other kinds of belief, including scientific belief and the beliefs that inform the conduct of everyday life in the home, the workplace, and the tavern. "Every rustic who delivers in the village alehouse his slow, infrequent sentences," Clifford allowed with a patrician's sensitivity to the strivings of the respectable poor, "may help to kill or keep alive the fatal superstitions which clog his race" (Clifford 1877, 293).

Clifford's cardinal example, however, was that of a shipowner who stifled his doubts about the seaworthiness of his vessel and, putting "his trust in Providence," allowed the ship to carry its load of immigrants to their death at sea. The shipowner "did sincerely believe in the soundness of his ship," but he had "*no right to believe on such evidence as was before him*" because he had not earned it in "patient investigation" (Clifford 1877, 289–90; emphasis in original). This extended example opened the essay and provided Clifford with his major theme: that beliefs have social consequences and must, on that account, be held responsibly, which is to say, "ethically," on the basis of the best evidence to be obtained through conscientious investigation.

James's lack of attention to this theme is one of the most instructive features of "The Will to Believe," and it is a feature that becomes all the more striking if one is aware of the extraordinary emphasis Clifford had placed on the consequences of belief for social action. It is the pragmatist James, after all, who is properly remembered in the history of thought for insisting on the transcendent importance of the practical consequences of belief. And nowhere does he affirm this classically Jamesean sentiment more fiercely than in "The Will to Believe" itself:

> The whole defence of religious faith hinges upon action. If the action required or inspired by the religious hypothesis is in no way different from that dictated by the naturalistic hypothesis, then religious faith is a pure superfluity, better pruned away, and controversy about its legitimacy is a piece of idle trifling, unworthy of serious minds. (*WB*, 32)[14]

Yet nowhere in "The Will to Believe" did James indicate what actions follow from religious belief of even the most generic sort, to say nothing of any specific belief. Do men and women who believe in God comport themselves more compassionately toward their fellow humans? Do they make and sustain better families? Are religious believers more reliable citizens than are the agnostics? Are they more selfless? Are religious people more diligent in their callings than are freethinkers? James may have believed some of the assertions implied by these questions, but he neither defended nor even formulated them as claims. James managed to avoid altogether Clifford's pointed challenge about social action.

For James, the consequences of religious belief, such as they were, were worked out either within the individual psyche—James used to say that religious belief kept him sane (*VRE*, 408)—or in a celestial city: per-

haps religious believing did make more likely the believer's eternal one-
ness with God? Action in this world was not on James's agenda in "The
Will to Believe."[15] Yet James sought to leave the opposite impression, especially in his melodramatic closing calling upon his readers to envision
a decision to believe in God as comparable to worldly action in a life-or-
death situation under horrendous, physically real conditions. "We stand
on a mountain pass in the midst of whirling snow and blinding mist,"
James quoted from Fitzjames Stephen, "through which we get glimpses
now and then of paths which may be deceptive." We are obliged to make
a "leap in the dark." We cannot stand still, for if we do,

> we shall be frozen to death. If we take the wrong road, we shall be
> dashed to pieces. We do not certainly know whether there is any right
> one. What must we do? "Be strong and of good courage." Act for the
> best, hope for the best, and take what comes. . . . If death ends all, we
> cannot meet death better. (WB, 33)[16]

This philosophically obscurantist ending is another sign of the spasmic
character of "The Will to Believe." Action is mystified, and its stakes are
represented as truly momentous. A "leap in the dark" is celebrated as the
best possible mode of death. And such florid stuff is offered by someone
who, only a few pages before, had mocked Clifford for a certain "robustious pathos in the voice" (WB, 18).

Clifford called attention to the injuries done to individuals and groups
as a result of the exercise of power sanctioned by beliefs held on "insufficient evidence." For Clifford, society as a whole paid for lax standards
for belief. What of the shipowner's uncritical habits of belief? What of a
population victimized by the mystifications of priests? Did the average
citizen not need to scrutinize public questions with a more critical eye?
"The credulous man is father to the liar and the cheat," warned Clifford; social solidarity and wholesome, collective action were promoted
by "our powers . . . of judicially and fairly weighing evidence" (Clifford
1877, 294).

The ostensibly authoritarian Clifford displayed more concern about
the manipulation of the public by charlatans and frauds than did the
homespun American champion of "everyman," who betrayed an almost
aristocratic aloofness from the social matrix in which cognitive choices
are made. "The Will to Believe" defended the sensibilities of individual
souls altogether removed from the fields of social power, while "The Ethics of Belief" defended social actors from death, injustice, crime, and
exploitation that can be visited upon them by unjustified (although Clifford did not use this Foucauldian term) "regimes of truth." Foucault
would find in Clifford a soul more kindred than the James of "The Will
to Believe."

Clifford had good reason to comprehend alternative structures of plausibility as vehicles for power. British intellectuals of his generation had to contend with an established church that, in 1877 even more than when James wrote twenty years later, continued to exert enormous authority over education and public culture. It was not silly of Clifford to view the Enlightenment as an embattled cause, struggling against entrenched and resourceful enemies. But James flourished amid the enormous expansion of American universities, and in a society that treated religion as a more private matter than it was assumed to be in Britain. James thought the Enlightenment was doing so well among the educated classes that its excesses could be criticized without fear of undermining it. Clifford called attention to the "professional training" of the chemist that gave others a sound basis for listening to his testimony about chemicals (Clifford 1877, 301), while James, witnessing the most rapid and successful rise of academic professionals in history, was instead worried that professionals would intimidate the layman into undue deference.

The socially complacent American worried about the damage a strict scientific conscience could do to the peace of mind of individuals, while the politically engaged Englishman of a generation before had worried about the damage religious authority could exact on a credulous population learning only gradually the liberating potential of a critical mind. Clifford feared falsity in a social order he thought could only be improved by the truth; James defended freedom against what he saw as the cognitive tyranny of science. "Our errors are surely not such awfully solemn things," said James. Clifford spoke as though the creation and maintenance of culture was a zero-sum game and the stakes were high for all, while James spoke as though culture could expand indefinitely, making room for everyone's favorite faith without hurting anyone. "Live and let live," James urged, "tolerance" should be our ideal "in speculative as well as in practical things" (*WB*, 25, 33).

When James thus extolled laissez-faire as an adequate principle for the life of the mind he was thinking about questions on one side of a portentous divide. James distinguished between questions that could be decided "on intellectual grounds" and those that "by nature" could not (*WB*, 20). Clifford was right about the need for a scientific conscience, according to James, but mistaken about the cognitive terrain in which it was to operate. The function of James's boundary between spheres was of course to protect religious belief from critical challenge: it was all-or-nothing, either there was compelling intellectual evidence, or there was not, and in the second instance the passions were at liberty to choose our beliefs for us. James also made other distinctions discussed at length by his commentators—between options that were living or dead, forced or avoidable, and momentous or trivial—but the most salient distinction was that between intellectually resolvable and intellectually irresolvable questions. James drew the line between scientifically warranted beliefs and the rest of our opinions more sharply than the positivist Clifford did, and he pushed that line back selectively until it no longer threatened the varieties of supernaturalism favored by the most sophisticated of Protestant believers.

The absolute character of James's distinction between spheres of belief in "The Will to Believe" is worth dwelling upon because it contrasts so sharply to the more thoroughly secular approach to true belief James was just beginning to develop under the inspiration, in part, of Peirce. Although *The Will to Believe* was dedicated to Peirce, who was quick to acknowledge his appreciation for this book's title essay even while lamenting James's preoccupation with religious belief,[17] Peirce's influence on James was much more pronounced a decade later in *Pragmatism*. In that much less impetuous work, to which we will attend more extensively in a moment, James presented belief as a monolith, embracing both religious and scientific ideas, just as Peirce had done in "The Fixation of Belief." The self has an undifferentiated "mass of opinions" that is tested by the course of experience and critically revised as a result (*P*, 35). But in "The Will to Believe" James was still held in thrall by an older, highly nonpragmatic strategy for defending religious belief: the assertion of the reality of separate spheres for religious and for scientific cognition.

A host of James's interpreters have been troubled by James's refusal, in "The Will to Believe," to recognize degrees of confirmation. Even so sympathetic a reader as Gerald E. Myers, for example, has voiced "the suspicion that James has fabricated an artificial situation in which the will or right to believe applies." Intellectual evidence comes in many kinds, Myers adds, and fewer people than James supposed "assume that we hold or reject religious beliefs in a complete vacuum of evidence." It was the character and location of the line James etched between intellectual evidence and everything else that inspired Holmes's complaint that James "turned down the lights" to shield the warrants of religious faith from close scrutiny. "If we reduce knowledge, inflate ignorance, and summon feelings to center stage," as Myers puts it, "everything is set for faith's appearance" (Gerald E. Myers, *William James: His Life and Thought* [New Haven, CT, 1986], 454).

During the decade between "The Will to Believe" and *Pragmatism* James came to accept more fully an idea he had long suspected was true but had often resisted: that scientific discourse was the field on which the culture of the future would be determined. James had recognized from the start that his dispute with Clifford had to do with what structure of plausibility would prevail in the world's most advanced societies. But until around the turn of the century James episodically indulged the hope—displayed the most openly in "The Will to Believe"—that a doctrine of separate spheres would preserve a place in which traditional religious emotions could continue to flourish unintimidated.

As I have shown elsewhere,[18] *Pragmatism* was the point in James's career at which he consolidated his defense of religious belief so that it could more easily operate within, rather than outside of, scientific inquiry. He downplayed the distinction that had been central to "The Will to Believe." In *Pragmatism*, religious beliefs were to be put at risk in conscientious investigation, the better to maximize the chances of their being proven true. James feared that the agnostics would create the culture of the future if the religious believers abdicated their responsibility and left the design and execution of research programs to the likes of Clifford. There would be no one, then, to actually test "the religious hypothesis," because all of the investigators would have concluded that it was dead from the start. James was "advanced" enough to understand that the results of inquiry were deeply affected by the premises that informed it, and he was determined, in *Pragmatism*, to inspire persons with religious faith to put their beliefs at risk in the scientific arena. Religion might then have a chance to be vindicated through the *wissenschaftliche* study of the world. "What are needed to bring the evidence in," James insisted on the last page of *Pragmatism*, are the "various over-beliefs of men, their several faith ventures" (*P*, 144). James's project of defending religious belief had now come within the Cliffordian framework he had still been resisting in "The Will to Believe": "evidence" was what decided the merits of religion in the long run, and it was up to people who believed in religion to go out and get that evidence, thereby putting their cherished ideas at empirical risk. Religious faith was now integrated into the culture of inquiry. In *Pragmatism*, James was able to make the case for religion within, rather than as an exception to, the historicist and pragmatist outlook for which he is rightly celebrated as a giant of "the revolt against positivism."

A reading of "The Will to Believe" against James's chief foil, Clifford, and against James's own later work can thus remind us of the depth and intensity of the religious road James traveled to reach the formulations for which he is most honored today by persons who no longer share James's religious preoccupations. Such a reading may tempt one to resuscitate Clifford, whose critical spirit might seem attractive to today's intellectuals, troubled, perhaps, by cable television's endless string of advertisements for the services of "psychics," and by other signs that belief without sufficient evidence remains a problem in our society. But Clifford's preachy histrionics and his insufficiently historicist understanding of the scientific enterprise render him even more thoroughly Victorian than James. Both can continue to inspire our own struggles with decisions about belief, but neither can help us much without a generous portion of correction from the other.

Notes

1. For representative examples of the invoking of James as a precursor of postmodernism, see Stephen Best and Douglas Kellner, *Postmodern Theory: Critical Interrogations* (New York, 1991), 28; and James Livingston, *Pragmatism and the Political Economy of Cultural Revolution, 1850–1940* (Chapel Hill NC, 1994), 273–79.

2. Two recent examples are Gerald E, Myers, *William James: His Life and Thought* (New Haven, CT, 1986), esp. 451–52; and Samuel Levinson, *The Religious Investigations of William James* (Chapel Hill, NC, 1981), esp. 55.

3. For the classic narrative of this revolt and a typical account of James's role in it, see H. Stuart Hughes, *Consciousness and Society* (New York, 1958). For a more recent account, distinguished by an excellent treatment of James, see James T. Kloppenberg, *Uncertain Victory: Social Democracy and Progressivism in European and American Thought, 1870–1920* (New York, 1986).

4. See, for example, Richard M. Gale, "Willam James and the Ethics of Belief," *American Philosophical Quarterly* XVII (1980), 1–14. Gale characterizes (14) his own analysis of the problem of the ethics of belief as capturing "some of the spirit and thrust" of James's "The Will to Believe." But Gale could more justly be described as salvaging James by critically expanding James's argument in Clifford's direction. This is not to find fault with Gale's discussion of the ethics of belief, which is one of the most rigorous and illuminating in the literature. It is a sign of the effectiveness of James's destruction of Clifford that later philosophers arguing more in Clifford's tradition than James's can ignore Clifford and claim James as their inspiration. Another of the leading studies of "The Will to Believe" enters decidedly Cliffordian caveats against James without apparently realizing it. The thoughtful article by Peter Kauber and Peter H. Hare, "The Right and Duty to Will to Believe," *Canadian Journal of Philosophy* IV (1974), defends James by drawing out "implications" of James's argument that (1) rule out any "technique" that leads a believing subject away from seeking more evidence (339), and (2) support an actual "duty" to induce belief under certain conditions (342).

5. One of the very few philosophers to show signs of studying Clifford's essay has ended up offering a mildly sympathetic reading of it: see Van Harvey, "The Ethics of Belief Reconsidereed," *Journal of Religion* LIX (1979). Another philosopher who has actually studied Clifford's text is James C. S. Wernham, whose *James's Will-to-Believe Doctrine: A Heretical View* (Toronto, 1987) came to my attention only after this article was completed. A refreshing feature of Wernham's discussion is its sensitivity to the extent to which James misrepresented Clifford; see esp. 69–74.

6. Clifford 1877, 309.

7. For a convenient, brief account of Clifford's life and career, see Alexander Macfarlane, *Lectures on Ten British Mathematicians of the Nineteenth Century* (New York, 1916), 78–91. Clifford is a major character in the history of agnosticism, as recounted splendidly by Bernard Lightman, *The Origins of Agnosticism: Victorian Unbelief and the Limits of Knowledge* (Baltimore, 1987). Lightman points to the exceptional esteem the young Clifford enjoyed within the Victorian intellectual elite of his time. T. H. Huxley thought him "the finest scientific mind born in England in fifty years." While Clifford was dying he was attended regularly by no less a personage than Leslie Stephen himself, who then assumed the task of editing Clifford's papers and the mission of keeping Clifford's flame. See Lightman, 1987, 95.

8. Holmes to Frederick Pollock, 1 September 1910, in Mark De Wolfe Howe, ed., *Holmes-Pollock Letters* (Cambridge MA, 1941), 1, 67. I have dealt with Holmes's relation to James's pragmatism and his religious views in my *Science, Jews, and Secular Culture* (Princeton, NJ, 1996).

9. For the argument that the bulk of James's career as a philosopher should be seen in terms of James's concern with the fate of religion in an age of science, see my *In the American Province* (Bloomington, IN, 1985), 3–22. The present study of James and Clifford is an elaboration and extension of the basic interpretation of James developed in this earlier study.

10. Edward H. Madden, "Introduction," *WB*, xxvi.

11. Never was Ralph Barton Perry more accurate about James than when he proposed that James was "deeply concerned" with the right to believe, "but made no considerable use of that right." Ralph Barton Perry, *The Thought and Character of William James* (Boston, 1935), 2, 211.

12. For a helpful overview, see William Hutchison, *The Modernist Impulse in American Protestantism* (Cambridge MA, 1976).

13. Peirce's "The Fixation of Belief" was originally published in *Popular Science Monthly* 12 (November 1877), 1–15.

14. Clifford, too, held forth (1877, 298) rather "pragmatically" about belief and action: "no belief is real unless it guide our actions, and those very actions supply a test of its truth."

15. Even George Cotkin, perhaps the most assiduous of the scholars who have portrayed James as an "activist," is unable to find in "The Will to Believe" a hint of an analysis of what actions are required by theistic belief. See George Cotkin, *William James: Public Intellectual* (Baltimore, 1990), 80–81.

16. James was here quoting Fitzjames Stephen, *Liberty, Equality, and Fraternity*, 2nd ed. (London, 1874), 353.

17. "Religion *per se* seems to me a barbaric superstition," Peirce complained to James, but went on to praise the social gospel at its most social: "The clergymen who do any good don't pay much attention to religion. They teach people the conduct of life, and on the whole in a high and noble way." This letter of Peirce's to James, dated 13 March 1897, is quoted in Myers, *William James*, 605.

18. This paragraph summarizes an argument developed in Hollinger, *American Province*.

CHAPTER 6

Damned for God's Glory: William James and the Scientific Vindication of Protestant Culture

When William James died, his widow asked the Boston Congregationalist minister George A. Gordon to preach the funeral sermon because, as Mrs. James put it, Gordon was "a man of faith," which is the phrase she used to describe her late husband, too. She asked that at the service there be "no hesitation or diluted utterance" about religion. James himself had indeed said to Gordon that "you and I seem to be working toward the same end (the Kingdom of Heaven, namely)," but "you do this more openly and immediately." In the same mode, James liked to quip that he was a better Methodist than the great Boston University liberal theologian, Borden Parker Bowne. James, while dispatching a copy of his Varieties of Religious Experience *to a faith-affirming friend, allowed that the friend would probably conclude that James was "a Methodist, minus a savior." Hesitation and diluted utterances were omnipresent in James's religious talk, no matter how eager his widow was to deny it.*

The signs of James's connection with the liberal Protestant elite of his time and place are many. This essay interprets James's entire career in the light of his affinity with these people, on the one hand, and his devotion on the other to the calling of modern science. I take seriously James's many references in Pragmatism *to religious searching and indeed to "salvation," so often left out of account by secular students of James's thought. I read* Varieties *as the pivotal point in James's turn from a "separate spheres" defense of religion to an effort to mobilize a community of inquiry willing to test religious claims by experience, just as James said other claims should be tested. Against scholars who prefer to read James's corpus as a synchronic whole, I try to show that the meaning of James's various works is best grasped when his career is approached diachronically, with each text analyzed according to the stage it marks in the development over time of James's preoccupation with religion's relation to science.*

One feature of Varieties *often ignored is James's inability at the end to draw the scientific and philosophical conclusions that he has promised. He zig-zags even on the matter of whether he believes in God.* Varieties *is a classic in religious studies because of the depth and power of James's empathic identification with so many of the religious individuals whose testimony he records, not because this book has bequeathed to later generations what James so poignantly said a new "science of religions" should do. Such a science should "eliminate doctrines that are now known to be scientifically absurd or incongruous," he said, and "help bring about consensus of opinion." Varieties did not come close to doing these things. Instead, this extraordinarily influential book promoted fellow-feeling with religious seekers with a Protestant temperament, expressed guarded skepticism about fanaticism, especially on the part of self-torturing Catholic saints, and perpetuated a deeply noninstitutional, highly individualistic, and heavily mystical conception of the nature of religion.*

Perhaps the most striking fact about Varieties, *and indeed about all of James's work touching on religion, is that James never offered a serious intellectual defense of a single, specific Christian doctrine. That such a thinker could win and retain standing in Protestant America as a great champion of religion is a revealing episode in the transition from Protestantism to post-Protestantism.*

The essay was written for the centennial symposium on Varieties, *convened by Columbia University in 2002. It first appeared in the published proceedings of that event, Wayne Proudfoot, ed.,* William James and a Science of Religions: Reexperiencing "The Varieties of Religious Experience" *(New York, 2004).*

WHEN WILLIAM JAMES DIED IN 1910, his lifelong friend Supreme Court Justice Oliver Wendell Holmes Jr. remarked that when James dealt with religion, he had tried "to turn the lights down low so as to give miracle a chance."[1] Many items in the James canon feed this suspicion. Yet *The Varieties of Religious Experience,* James's most sustained treatment of religion, constitutes a proposal that even the most private, mystical experiences offered as evidence for religious belief be brought out into the open, be made, indeed, the primary subject matter for "a science of religions," an empirically oriented, publicly warranted inquiry that James envisaged as a successor discipline to "philosophy of religion."[2]

These two potentially contradictory starting points—James's self-presentation in his greatest contribution to religious studies and Holmes' skepticism toward that self-presentation—can remind us of an enduring tension at the center of James's intellectual life. The tension is between the demands of the inherited culture of Protestant Christianity, with its belief in a supernatural God potentially responsive to human striving, and the demands of modern science, with its emphasis on the intersubjective testing of claims based on the data of the senses. That James was much troubled by the apparent conflict between these demands is not a matter of dispute. That much is rightly taken for granted by virtually all James scholars, even by those who find this bit of history to be a philosophically irrelevant distraction. What is not taken for granted, even by those who find James's religious preoccupations pertinent today, is any particular understanding of the life project that this science-religion tension generated in James. Nor do James scholars agree upon just what relation *Varieties* has to James's other work. Claims about the continuity between "The Will to Believe" and *Varieties*, for example, are rarely engaged critically because many of the philosophers who address "The Will to Believe" are not much interested in *Varieties*, and many of the religious studies scholars for whom *Varieties* is a vital text have relatively little invested in the agendas that drive philosophers' interpretation of "The Will to Believe."

I want to begin by calling attention to just how the science-religion issue is displayed in *Varieties*. I will then locate *Varieties* chronologically and logically in what I believe it is fair to describe as James's career-long defense of certain central aspects of the culture of liberal Protestantism as understood and cherished by many educated Americans of his generation. This is the life project from which we today are tempted to detach James's ideas. Specifically, I will interpret *Varieties* as a product of the particular phase in James's career when he was shifting from one strategy to another in that defense. Before I proceed to the text, let me indicate telegraphically what those two strategies were, and allude to a third strategy popular in his milieu that James was concerned to discredit.

The first strategy was a highly sophisticated version of the classic "separate spheres" doctrine, an effort to protect Protestantism from science by marking off a distinctive category of beliefs that science could not be expected to touch. The second strategy was to embrace in a Peircean mode the epistemic unity of all experience and belief, and to vindicate the generic human ideals for which Protestantism was a historic vehicle within rather than outside the discursive constraints of modern science, once those constraints were properly understood. When he wrote *Varieties* in 1902, James had recently drawn away from the first of these strategies, which he had developed most fully in "The Will to Believe" in 1897, but he was not yet confident about the second, Peircean strategy, which he later employed in 1907 in the book titled *Pragmatism*. In *Varieties* James was still trying to figure out how best to carry out the second strategy, and he was also trying to decide just what it was that he wanted to vindicate scientifically under the sign of "religion." And while James was working out this transition from the one strategy to another, he remained preoccupied with the enormous appeal to his audience of a third strategy, that of absolute idealism. It is too easy today to underestimate that appeal. The absolute idealist Josiah Royce, James's Harvard colleague, was a dialectician so formidable that he was then known, after the reigning heavyweight champion, as the John L. Sullivan of philosophy. By contrast, James was a psychologist trying to do philosophy and, in the view of many philosophers, failing.

But I will return to all of that. Now to *Varieties* itself, and the specific form that the science-religion tension takes within that text.

James's ostensibly species-wide account of religious experience is deeply Protestant in structure, tone, and implicit theology. Even the categories of religious experience around which *Varieties* is organized, and the order in which James describes them, have this quality. As theologian Richard R. Niebuhr and others have pointed out, James, by moving from "healthy-mindedness" to the "sick soul" to the "divided self" to "conversion" and then to "saintliness," follows the prescribed sequence of the evangelical Protestant conversion narrative.[3] Although James presents his subject matter as generically human, and says explicitly several times that Buddhism, Islam, and Judaism as well as Christianity have been settings for religious experiences the essence of which he seeks to confront, the frequency and character of his use of Protestant examples tells us much about what was at stake for himself.

James takes the first of his many extended quotations from the writings of the seventeenth-century English Quaker George Fox. This is an interesting choice to represent the radical alterity of religious experience, as the realm James suggests is so foreign to his enlightened, modern listeners at Edinburgh and to his similarly enlightened and modern readers generally. Fox's state of mind, which James denotes as "pathological," was indeed bizarre in contrast with that expressed by the average Anglican, Presbyterian, or Unitarian of 1902. But Fox's piety was that of highly familiar dissenting English Protestantism. Fox was marginal, all right, but what he was marginal to was mainstream: the Anglo-American Protestant tradition as comprehended by James's audience. And the sensibility of which Fox was an extreme case was the widely approved sensibility of Puritan-Quaker humility. In introducing Fox's testimony, moreover, James observes that Fox brought to England a Christianity closer to that of the original gospel than England had ever seen. James describes it as "a religion of veracity," an interesting construction in a science-and-religion milieu in which the agnostic T. H. Huxley was often quoted for praising science as "fanaticism for veracity."[4] James keeps going back to Fox, and cites him another nine times at various points in the book.

One of the places in which James reverts to Fox in his pivotal discussion of saintliness, which, as John E. Smith reminds us in his introduction to the now-standard Harvard edition of *Varieties*, is the critical core of James's effort to justify religion on the basis of its results.[5] But the Protestant orientation of James's discussion of saintliness is much more pronounced than many noted. To a very large extent, these chapters on saintliness amount to a celebration of the strict observance of exactly the personal morality prescribed historically by dissenting Protestants in Britain and America. When James comes to talk about the behavioral manifestations of successful conversion, he moves quickly into a discussion of "reformed drunkards" and of males cured of "sexual temptation." This then leads to a footnote about a woman who, under the inspiration of religious experience, was able finally to quit smoking.[6] In James's two chapters on saintliness, we find ourselves right in the middle of the culture explored by James's contemporary Harold Frederic in *The Damnation of Theron Ware*, and affectionately chuckled at in our own time by Garrison Keillor.

Asceticism and charity are the two virtues on which James spends the most time in his account of saintliness, but a striking theme in his examples of charity is that of self-humbling on the part of the giver, as though the point was not so much to enhance the circumstances of the beneficiary as to diminish pride of self in the benefactor. Among James's examples are Francis of Assisi and Ignatius Loyola, both of whom James mentions for having "exchanged their garments with those of filthy beggars."[7]

Here the distinction between James's Catholic and Protestant examples becomes revealing. James refers repeatedly to the ways in which the Roman church has more or less specialized in ascetic piety. But as he alternates between Catholic and Protestant cases, a pattern emerges. After two quite benign testimonies from a Unitarian and a Methodist telling of the taking up of humble clothing and the refusing of rich food, James cites a French country priest who would never drink when thirsty and never take cover against the cold. Then James gives us Cotton Mather of Massachusetts, displaying virtuous asceticism by merely refusing to touch his beloved wife's body in her last moments of life in order that he might humbly accept her passage into God's hands. This is one of James's most gentle, attractive examples of self-abnegation, the release of a loved one. But suddenly James presents St. John of the Cross, the sixteenth-century Spanish mystic who advocates the despising of oneself, the yearning that others will despise you, and the turning of one's soul toward whatever is disgusting and contemptible. This case then slides into another Catholic example, the fourteenth-century German mystic Suso, whose account of his own physical self-mortification—sleeping on a bed of nails and the like—is one of the longest single quotations in the whole of *Varieties*. James breaks off this flagrantly masochistic and some would say mildly pornographic quotation by saying that he will "spare" us the further "recital of poor Suso's self-inflicted tortures."[8]

Several pages later James asks his readers if he might he have left an impression "of extravagance." And sure enough, he then allows that while there is much to admire in these saintly lives, he is not urging that they be "imitated." Then he launches into a vigorous critique of what he calls "excess" in "saintly virtue." The freethinkers, James admits, are on to something when they complain of certain unhealthy tendencies among the more fanatical of religious believers. Their mentality is "too one-sided to be admirable," he declares, and then provides a long quotation from a Catholic saint who James says has renounced all human uses for her asceticism. James then turns to St. Teresa, for whom he says he can feel only "pity that so much vitality of soul should have found such poor employment." This is then followed by a whole string of Catholic testimonies, including one from St. Louis of Gonzaga, whom James actually calls "repulsive." Such cases "in the annals of Catholic saintship," he says explicitly, "make us rub our Protestant eyes."[9] There is no question who the "we" or the "us" is whenever James invokes these portentous pronouns.

What casts James's treatment of Fox and other canonical Protestants into bold relief, then, is not so much his fleeting use of Muslim and Jewish cases, but the sustained treatment he gives to Catholics. One can easily get the impression that *Varieties* is a noninvidious harvest of the most intense spiritual moments of all the major religions, especially of Christianity, embracing Catholic as well as Protestant variations. But no. *Varieties* is constructed to foreground certain religious sensibilities and not others, and to present the core of religion in general as having been the most attractively manifest in exactly the cultural tradition to which James's listeners and readers were directly heir. Too often, the so-called descriptive chapters of *Varieties* are read as a rather indiscriminate reportage of random and widely dispersed "raw materials" punctuated by James's respectful commentary. But if instead we read these chapters as literary texts, with attention to his selection of quotations and their dynamic relation to one another, we gain greater access to James's center of religious gravity.

That James was being judgmental when he talked about saintliness cannot be emphasized enough, given the tendency of some readers to take the bulk of *Varieties* as merely descriptive. "We must judge," James says, and we must do so "not sentimentally," but "by our own intellectual standards." He then quotes Nietzsche's attack on saintliness as being overdrawn, but properly skeptical. Right in the middle of his discussion, James says that a goal of the science of religions is "to test saintliness by common sense, to use human standards to help us decide how far the religious life commends itself as an ideal kind of human activity." These standards, he is quick to explain, are historically specific and are grounded in a process of cultural "evolution." "What with science, idealism, and democracy, our own imagination has grown to need a God of an entirely different temperament" from that of the Catholic saints.[10]

James's frank acceptance of the idea that our gods are constructed socially on the basis of our historical experience shows just how liberal was the Protestantism with which he was comfortable. "The gods we stand by are the gods we need and can use, the gods whose demands on us are reinforcements of our demands on ourselves, and on one another." It is for us, then, said James about himself and his contemporaries, to apply to "religious beliefs" a kind of critical selection analogous to natural selection; we are engaged in "the survival of the humanly fittest" and the "elimination of the humanly unfit" religious beliefs.[11] No wonder James's funeral sermon was preached by George A. Gordon, the Congregationalist minister then known as "the Matterhorn of the Protestant Alps," who understood that religious evolution from antiquity onward had been leading up to his church in the heart of Boston.[12]

James's evolutionary language concerning the survival of the fittest religions under modern scrutiny can turn us from the aspects of *Varieties* that reveal its firm foundation in liberal Protestantism to those aspects that indicate more fully the shape and scope of the "science of religions" that James sought to establish. These elements of *Varieties* display James's sense of the scientific side of the tension that drives the work.

James defines his science of religions the most sharply against what he calls "dogmatic theology" and more generally against "philosophy of religion," the alleged character of which he conveys with quotations from such idealist metaphysicians as Josiah Royce and James Caird, and various scholastic thinkers, including Cardinal Newman. Against the propensity of this class of thinkers for "metaphysics and deduction," James calls for "criticism and induction," and for the testing of religious ideas in their capacity as hypotheses, a favorite word of James's that he italicizes in his most rigorously formulated account of what makes his science of religions different from what philosophers and theologians have done with religion in the past.[13]

Central to James's science of religion are the ideals of intersubjective testability and consensus. The severity of his presentation of these ideals is one of the least appreciated themes of *Varieties*. Although the experiences he wants scrutinized are private in origin, the idea is now to consider them in a public frame, to bring them within the scope of disciplined, empirical inquiry. The result will be a scientific distillation and evaluation of religious experience. James stresses that any philosophically sound view of life needs to take into account the totality of human experience. It was science's breadth of scope, science's ability to confront the particulars of individual experience with that of thousands and millions of other human individuals, that gave science the opportunity to build such a philosophically sound view of life. Religious claims to truth need to be integrated with our body of truths. "By confronting spontaneous religious constructions with the results of natural science," insists James, we can "eliminate doctrines that are now known to be scientifically absurd or incongruous." Our science "can offer mediation between different believers, and help bring about consensus of opinion."[14]

James is so attracted to the ideal of scholarly consensus that he uses the failure of the idealists to achieve it as a sign of the obvious inadequacy of their ideas. This is a stunning move on the part of James, who had been for so long a polemical defender of idiosyncratic minorities against the apparent tyrannies of learned majorities. And James seems to sense how remarkable a move it is, because he accompanies it with a long and defensive footnote apologizing for not even trying to meet with arguments the claims of Royce and the other metaphysical idealists.[15] He knows how odd it is of him to dismiss someone on the grounds that his or her claims have failed to win over the leaders of a professional community.

I have been quoting from the chapter titled "Philosophy," but James picks up the same themes in his final chapter, "Conclusions." There he hits hard his determination that the results of religious experience be squared with the results of the rest of experience: it is among "the duties of the science of religions," he declares, "to keep religion in connexion with the rest of Science," with the word "science" here capitalized, and not ironically as James had been inclined to do in earlier years. Even in the "Postscript," that enigmatic and disjointed indicator of the depth and texture of James's nervousness about the signals sent in the Gifford Lectures, James returns to "legitimate requirements" that must be met by any hypothesis.[16]

And it is those requirements that James believes are not met by the people he calls "medical materialists" in the first chapter of *Varieties*, titled "Religion and Neurology." There, he goes after the reductionists who dismiss Saul's transformation into Paul on the road to Damascus as an epileptic seizure, and who treat "George Fox's discontents with the shams of his age, and his pining for spiritual veracity" as symptoms of "a disordered colon." But he most adamantly condemns these cultured despisers of religion on the basis of strictly uniformitarian, scientific principles. It is the failure of the reductionists to be consistent materialists that most gives the lie to their efforts to undermine religious belief by explaining it physiologically. It never occurs to these folks, complains James, to trace to an author's "neurotic constitution" any ideas they find attractive. Why not explain through neurology the triumphs of industry and the arts and science itself? "Let us play fair in this whole matter," he remonstrates; "physiological theory" can do just as well at explaining nonreligious states of mind as religious states of mind, and in neither case would such a theory tell us all we need to know about its object.[17]

Right from the start, then, in that opening chapter, James invokes what he eventually calls his "objective conscience." This is the voice he associates with the demands of science, rightly understood: the uniformitarianism, the fair play, the public knowledge, the intersubjective testing of truth claims against the totality of human experience. In the final paragraph of his concluding chapter, James also invokes what he calls his "subjective conscience," the voice he associates with the demands of his religious heritage, with what attracts him to George Fox, with all that is implied when he speaks finally at the end of the book of himself as a "Christian."[18] Indeed, the last few sentences of "Conclusions," when James's scientific conscience and his religious conscience are brought together, constitute one of James's most compact and agonistic expressions of the tension by which so much of his life was defined.

James comes to this climactic moment, among the most moving discursive episodes in the more than forty years of Jamesean prose about this problem, when he is trying to explain what he has just declared to be his "over-belief" that God exists and that as human beings open themselves to God their "deepest destiny is fulfilled." "My objective and my subjective conscience both hold me" to that over-belief, he says. Thus fortified by this dual assertion—the two consciences finally driving him the same way, a consummation so long elusive—James then brings his Gifford Lectures to their final sentence, striking for its candid, if tentative, affirmation, in the form of a question, of liberal Protestantism's trust in the response of a benevolent God to the righteous strivings of his creatures: "Who knows whether the faithfulness of individuals here below to their own poor over-beliefs may not actually help God in turn to be more effectively faithful to his own greater tasks?"[19]

But while the Gifford Lectures end with that captivating sentence, *Varieties*, the published book does not. The religious conscience and the scientific conscience, pasted together in an act of assertion continued to pull James in different directions. So he added the tortured, six-page "Postscript," which displays his uncertainty about the issues on which he had pronounced in his concluding chapter. He expresses concern he had not been clear about his "philosophical position." Then we learn that when James had called himself a Christian at Edinburgh he did not mean "to accept either popular Christianity or scholastic theism." We learn, further, that James is a very special kind of supernaturalist, a "piecemeal" supernaturalist to be distinguished from the sort who assign the whole world to God's providence. James imagines a patchwork cosmos, with supernatural power here or there—one is not sure just where. At pains to remind his readers that he is not a theologian, yet having raised issues of an indisputably theological character, James quickly exits, saying, "I hope to return to the same questions in another book."[20] That is the way *Varieties* actually ends.

At the end of *Varieties*, then, we see James in a decidedly stuttering mode, having allowed himself to pile up example after example of religious experience while putting off the philosophical harvest. His need for a commodious science and a flexible religion was manifest, and *Varieties* had been, among other things, a search for both. But the search was not over. James managed in *Varieties* to articulate more vividly than ever before his loyalty to modern science's principles of intersubjective testability and professional consensus, and his loyalty to a worldview in which supernatural power of the sort posited by his own cultural tradition was an authentic presence and agent of undetermined scope. Neither loyalty was new to James in 1902, but now he was really out there on both.

How did he get there, and where did he go next?

At the risk of making James's life seem more of an integrated whole than it was, I want to quote a few passages from a letter he wrote to Holmes in 1868, when he was twenty-six years old. This letter was written from Germany, where James was studying the new empirical psychology in the wake of a personally distressing time in Brazil on the Agassiz expedition, and before his celebrated mental collapse of 1870 back in Massachusetts. James is telling Holmes how things are coming together for him in Dresden, how he is adopting "an empiricist view of life."

> I don't know how far it will carry me, or what rocks insoluable by it will block my future path. Already I see an ontological cloud of absolute idealism waiting for me far off on the horizon. . . . I shall continue to apply empirical principles to my experiences as I go and see how much they fit.

Here the enduring rivalry between empiricism and Hegelian metaphysics is emplotted, and the work-it-out-as-you-go style of coping with experience is essayed. Then James expresses his uncertainty about how candidly people like himself and the similarly advanced Holmes should share with the less enlightened populace their understanding that the old faiths have been discredited by Darwin and his kind.

> If . . . we must take our sensations as simply given or as preserved by natural selection for us, and interpret this rich and delicate overgrowth of ideas, moral, artistic, religious and social, as a mere mask, a tissue spun in happy hours by creative individuals and adopted by other men in the interests of their sensations. . . . How long can we indulge the "people" in their theological and other vagaries so long as such vagaries seem to us more beneficial on the whole than otherwise? How long are we to wear that uncomfortable "air of suppression" which has been complained of [by] Mill?

James continues by pondering if there might be a way to harvest something from the old religion. Perhaps we can advance "happiness among the multitudes," he suggests to Holmes, if we appropriate from "the old moralities and theologies" a piece of lumber for "our own purposes." What might that old lumber look like, once appropriated and reworked? Perhaps, James continues, we can preach "the doctrine that Man is his own Providence, and every individual a real God to his race, greater or less in proportion to his gifts and the way he uses them?" Then James, invoking the capacity of modern human beings for solidarity with one another in worldly ventures, speculates that "philanthropy" might take the place of religion "as an ultimate motive for human action."[21]

Now, James certainly did take a piece of lumber from the old religion, and he did try to build upon it a more frankly humanistic worldview that would be capable of inspiring the multitudes. The notion of human beings exercising their own "Providence," individually and collectively, was a grand leitmotif of James's creative work all the way to the time of his death. Here in 1868 we do find several of the major components of James's life project. The old religion has something we probably still need, but it has to be radically humanized, and integrated somehow into an empiricist understanding of inquiry and of the objects of inquiry. The most formidable intellectual obstacle to such a program is absolute idealism. The great empiricist John Stuart Mill is someone whose instructions are worth following. And we should respect the public and try to speak honestly to it.

These components of James's life project were visible all through the 1870s, 1880s, and early 1890s, even when he saw himself chiefly as a psychologist. They are most prominently displayed in some of the most widely quoted and reprinted of James's essays during that period, including "The Sentiment of Rationality," "Reflex Arc and Theism," and "Is Life Worth Living." These essays can be seen as warm-ups for "The Will to Believe," alongside which James reprinted them in 1897 in the book of that title. These essays sympathize with the religious believer against those hyperscientific thinkers who make what James thought was the serious mistake of assuming that science had ruled out the taking of God seriously. Yet the essays, at the same time, reflect on the value of science and condemn the perpetuation of truly anachronistic religious beliefs in a scientific age.

In these essays James invokes the strategy of separate spheres for keeping alive something of the old faith. In "Sentiment of Rationality," first published in its complete form in 1882, James draws an important distinction. He refers to "a certain class of truths" in regard to which "faith" is appropriate, and that are not supported by "scientific evidence." His favorite examples tend toward the power of positive thinking, such as believing on faith that it is really true that you have the ability to leap across an abyss in order to avoid death. But such examples are embedded in James's standard screed against W. K. Clifford and the agnostics, and his frequent empathic references to holders of religious faith. James's readers are thus invited to think of their decisions about religious belief as analogous to deciding whether "to bail out a boat because I am in doubt whether my efforts will keep her afloat." So, some truths are real for us on faith, James says, and others are real for us because of scientific evidence. He concludes "The Sentiment of Rationality" by celebrating "faith's sphere," which he describes as "another realm into which the stifled soul may escape from pedantic scruples." There are risks to this, but many people will find them worthwhile. Let people do all they can, urges James, "to mark out distinctively the questions which fall within faith's sphere."[22]

James's language does little to disguise the protective character of the separate spheres doctrine. But by the time of "The Will to Believe" he had become more cautious. The salient distinction is not as up front as it had been before, because it is now surrounded by distinctions between hypotheses that are living and dead, forced or avoidable, and momentous or trivial. "The Will to Believe" also contains a much more extensive and distracting polemic against Clifford for his absurd claim that one can never do anything except on the basis of sufficient evidence. That was a canard, as I have shown elsewhere,[23] but here I will ignore James's blatant misrepresentations of the conveniently deceased Clifford to move quickly on to the highly developed language of tolerance that most distinguishes "The Will to Believe" from the other essays in the series that employ the separate spheres strategy.

In that legendary essay, the most widely disseminated and quoted item ever to flow from James's pen, James rests the case for religious belief heavily upon a general appeal to the principle of "live and let live." James calls upon everyone to respect one another's beliefs except when those beliefs have been uncontrovertably disproved. "We ought . . . to delicately and profoundly to respect one another's mental freedom . . . then and only then we shall have that spirit" of tolerance that is "empiricism's glory." Thus James subtly relocates the question of true belief out of the jurisdiction of the laboratory and the seminar and places it instead under the jurisdiction of the polite drawing room. This sphere of tolerance applies on one side of the distinction upon which James's argument most turns: the distinction between questions that can be decided "on intellectual grounds" and those that "by nature" cannot. Clifford was right about how science worked, said James, and certainly about the need to believe "ethically." But Clifford was just plain wrong about the specific cognitive terrain in which the scientific conscience was to operate. In "The Will to Believe" James draws the line between scientifically warranted beliefs and the rest of our opinions more sharply than the positivist ever Clifford did, and James pushes that line back selectively until it no longer threatens the varieties of supernaturalism favored by the most theologically liberal of Protestant believers.[24]

But no sooner did James provide the separate spheres doctrine with one of the most successful formulations in that doctrine's long history than he began to back away from it. In the very preface to the 1897 book *The Will to Believe*, the title essay of which James had written the year before and delivered as lectures to student groups at Yale and Brown universities, James calls for the verification of "religious hypotheses" along with "scientific hypotheses" by "experimental tests." The emphasis in this preface, which asks religious believers to come out of "hiding" and actually celebrates the rough-and-tumble, "survival of the fittest" competition of religious as well as scientific ideas in the public "market-place" is strikingly different from the protective emphasis found in "The Will to Believe" itself, and in the other essays collected with it.[25] I am not sure why James began, even in 1897, to pull away from what he had just articulated so vividly. Perhaps its metaphysical character bothered him once he confronted in print what he had said. The notion that certain questions have a nature that prevents them from being decided on the basis of evidence and reasoning is, after all, in some respects very non-Jamesean. It sounds like a metaphysical principle, rather out of keeping with James's empiricist determination to take things as they come. In any event, he took a very different approach to religious belief immediately after the publication of "The Will to Believe."

The following year, 1898, James delivered at Berkeley "Philosophical Conceptions and Practical Results," the lecture that became famous for James's declaring himself a "pragmatist," for bringing the ideas of Charles Peirce out of obscurity, and for beginning the discussion of pragmatism that would animate philosophers for the next fifteen years. James quickly published this lecture in the *Journal of Philosophy* under the title "The Pragmatic Method."[26] Now, a remarkable feature of this text that is almost never discussed is the fact that it is almost entirely about God. Yet, unlike "The Will to Believe," where God talk is carefully circumscribed, the Berkeley lecture is almost never anthologized or even cited in discussions of science and religion. It is true that James says he is only using the God question as an example of the power of Peirce's principle of pragmatism. And it is true that James does not explicitly defend the claim that God exists. No doubt there are other reasons for this lecture's having found its way into the history of philosophy canon but not into the religious studies canon. But the simple point I want to make about the lecture is that in it James experiments with an epistemically monolithic context for deciding religious issues.

James does not flag this move. But he makes it. First he applies to the idea of God Peirce's principle that to get a clear idea of something, "we need only consider what effects of a conceivably practical kind the object may involve—what sensations we are to expect from it, and what reactions we must prepare." It is in pursuit of this epistemically universal method that James then analyzes how different are the effects of theism and materialism. But James reinforces the move again at the end of the lecture when he interprets Peirce as having simply sharpened the empiricist tradition of Locke, Hume, and Mill. James concludes with a ringing affirmation of the philosophical tradition of English empiricism, within which the God talk of the lecture is thus quietly embraced.[27] When James wrote *Pragmatism* in 1907 he dedicated it, after all, to the freethinking empiricist Mill, even while offering that book as a way of widening the search for God.

Before turning to that book, however, I want to note that James invokes something he calls "pragmatism" three times in *Varieties*, which, please recall, James wrote after he gave the Berkeley lecture but before he wrote *Pragmatism*. In the first use of the word "pragmatism" in *Varieties*, James invokes it against the metaphysicians who prattle on about various attributes of God; what difference could it possibly make, asks James as a self-styled pragmatist, if God has the attribute of "simplicity" or "necessariness"? Here, James is simply tracking passages from his 1898 lecture, and providing a more cogent and compelling summary of Peirce than he had managed to do previously. A few pages later, he alludes to the same pragmatic denial that metaphysical argumentation about God's attributes matters one whit. James's third and most interesting reference is on the final page of his concluding chapter, where he describes as a "thoroughly 'pragmatic' view of religion" the view that higher powers actually affect the course of the world, and are not simply in charge of it in some general, detached way. This view, he says, has generally been accepted by "common men," who have believed in "miracles" and have "built a heaven out beyond the grave."[28] Here, James associates the name of pragmatism with some very strong claims about divine agency, and it is presumably just these passages that James was most worried about when he appended his postscript, cautioning that he is not a Christian in the common man's sense after all, nor a theist in the scholastic's sense.

In that postscript James does something else that marks the transitional character of *Varieties*. He renounces for the first time, as Wayne Proudfoot has observed in a recent article in the *Harvard Theological Review*, the notion that God's guarantee of a permanent moral order is central to theism.[29] James had still asserted this in his Berkeley lecture, and he repeated it again in the conclusion to *Varieties*. Yet in the postscript James structured theism as accommodating the taking of a risk rather than the acceptance of a guarantee. "A final philosophy of religion," he speculates, will have to accept a "pluralistic" hypothesis according to which only part of the world will be saved and part will be lost, and the outcome will depend to a degree on what human beings do.[30] And here at last we are at the cusp of what James delivered a few years later in *Pragmatism.*

In that book, where he speaks repeatedly of the world's salvation, as he does in his related correspondence, James invites religious believers to risk their beliefs in inquiry, to renounce the safe harbors of the metaphysicians and to take on the materialists on their own ground, which was experience in the world.[31] Here the episteme is monolithic, the fate of religion feels less secure, but the chances of vindication ostensibly much greater than in the cloistered cognitive world of the metaphysicians and other world-eschewing believers. This is, James implies but never says explicitly, because outside is where you find the field of struggle on which the future of culture will be decided. That field is the field of intersubjective empirical inquiry. But to see how James carries this off in *Pragmatism,* we need to focus on three sequential elements of that text: its opening frame, what it declares the doctrine of "pragmatism" to be, and the final chapter, titled "Pragmatism and Religion," which unfortunately is one of the least carefully studied of all the things James wrote under the sign of pragmatism.

James's opening leaves not the slightest doubt that he wrote *Pragmatism* for people worried about the fate of religion in the face of the advance of science. The book begins by confronting the concerned soul with an obviously unacceptable choice between "tough-minded" empiricist-skeptics and "tender-minded" religious idealists. James then offers a solution: he lays out pragmatism as a middle way, suitable for those too tender to give up on God but too tough to give up on science.[32]

But when James tells us "What Pragmatism Means"—the second element in the text to which I call attention—he offers what turns out to be a natural history of belief. He describes how human beings, as a behavioral fact, form their ideas and change them in the course of experience, both individually and collectively. Especially, he points to how scientific ideas change, how ideas we take to be true in one generation are so often replaced by other ideas later. We hold to our old ideas as much as we can, but new experience puts these ideas under strain, so we graft some new idea "upon the ancient stock" while dropping some of our old opinions. The body of truth, then, "grows much as a tree grows by the activity of a new layer of cambium."[33] Although this natural history of belief echoed points James had made here and there in his previous writings, never before had he developed so sustained an account of the dependence of scientific truth upon the cognitive activities of historically situated human communities. When he used to talk about the role of preconceptions in the creation of knowledge, he would usually do so with reference to an individual mind, and while separating out from this process the religious beliefs that science—contrary to the pretensions of freethinkers like Clifford—could not touch. Now, in 1907, he nested the problem of religious belief firmly in the same matrix of inquiry with the problem of scientific belief, which is precisely where Peirce had located it way back in 1877 in "Fixation of Belief."[34]

The contrast between Roycean metaphysical idealism and pragmatism dominates the concluding chapter, "Pragmatism and Religion." There, James compares the idealists to the prodigal son, who doesn't really risk anything because he knows he can count on his father to make everything all right in the end. "We want a universe," he mocks the absolutists, "where we can just give up, fall on our father's neck, and be absorbed into the absolute life as a drop of water melts into the river or sea." This is not a realistic view of our human situation, says James. Life as actually lived, as available to an empiricist, suggests that we reside in an uncertain universe with real conflicts and real victories and real defeats. In such a world we cannot take anything for granted, including the salvation of those who are justified by faith. James is saying to members of his own religious tribe that in order to vindicate even the most rudimentary aspects of the old faith, they have got to come to grips with the radical contingency of the human process by which culture is created, reproduced, and critically revised. Once you clue into this, James implies, then you have to try to get your ideas accepted within this process of shared experience, not by ignoring it. James calls his tribe to "a social scheme of co-operative work," a project that requires its participants to "trust" each other as they work together.[35] There is no guarantee that your culture will survive without your own hard work, no guarantee that the sensibilities you hold dear will continue to find social support in the decades and centuries to come; but at least you can try to make it so. Don't let Royce tell you, James implicitly scolds, that he has proved logically that we are all embraced within the Absolute.

"Must *all* be saved?" James begins a series increasingly jagged rhetorical questions designed to undermine the ultimate cheerfulness and complacency of the idealists.

> Is *no* price to be paid for the work of salvation? Is the last word sweet? Is all "yes, yes" in the universe? Doesn't the fact of "no" stand at the very core of life? Doesn't the very "seriousness" that we attribute to life mean that ineluctable noes and losses form a part of it, that . . . at the bottom of the cup something "permanently drastic and bitter always remains"?[36]

In these final pages of *Pragmatism*, James simultaneously attacks the ide-alists and reassures his audience that he has not become an atheist. "I have written a book on men's religious experience," James says proudly of *Varieties*, "which on whole has been regarded as making for the real-ity of God." And in these final pages James reverts again and again to the problem of the world's salvation, and to the role that human beings might play in that salvation by working in harmony with God, whom James describes as "but one helper" amid "all the shapers of the great world's fate." If we do our part right, there is at least a possibility that "when the cup" of life is "finally poured off," what we drink will be "sweet enough" even if "the dregs are left behind forever."[37] How do we humans do our part to maximize our chances of gaining this sweetness?

Well, one thing we can do is to "bring the evidence in," James says, to support our "over-beliefs," including the over-belief that God exists and is responsive to our strivings. James ends *Pragmatism* with an evan-gelical call to religious believers to come out of idealist shelters and set sail on the risky seas of experience, bringing in evidence of the sort that might actually stand up in the structure of plausibility that counted in the modern, North Atlantic West. The risk, of course, was that the religious hypothesis might not stand up: perhaps experience might not confirm what one hoped it would? We need to take the "hypothesis of God," James says, inserting religion directly into the discourse of empirical inquiry, and "build it out," so that the evidence it generates can "combine satisfactorily with all the other working truths" we pos-sess.[38] James thus places the God question directly in the natural history of belief that he has presented as the core of pragmatism. This is a long way from "The Will to Believe." The distinction between questions that can be resolved by evidence and those that cannot has—quietly!—all but disappeared.

If there is any doubt about what is going on in these last few intense pages of *Pragmatism*, which rival the conclusions to *Varieties* for their com-bination of anxiety and conviction, James conflates his own call to be-lievers to throw themselves into empirical inquiry with the call of a ship-wrecked sailor who died in a storm yet through his epitaph bids others "to set sail," because "many a gallant bark, when we were lost, weathered the gale." Moreover, as soon as James quotes the epitaph, he links this bold sailing into the storm with the willingness of the old Puritans to accept an uncertain world and take chances in the hope that their risk-taking acts would be instruments for God's purposes. "Are you willing," he asks his contemporary American Protestants in the voice of the old Puritans—calling upon his friends to risk their beliefs in inquiry on the hope that they will be more commandingly vindicated—"Are you willing to be damned for God's glory?"[39]

James follows this question with an uncharacteristically perfectionist passage about the future of the globe, suggesting the possibility of saving the world by actually eliminating evil, and he does so while contrasting his mode of worldly struggle with Royce's mode of "aufgehoben":

> [My] way of escape from evil . . . is not by getting it "aufgehoben," or preserved in the whole as an element essential but "overcome." *It is by dropping* [evil] *out altogether, throwing it overboard and getting beyond it, helping to make a universe that shall forget* [evil's] *very place and name.*[40]

Now, the extremity of this last passage, nearly all of which James renders in italics, is remarkable enough. And here we have another of James's maritime figures of speech, with the hardy protagonists of James's cosmic narrative in a boat struggling to throw evil "overboard." But the passage that follows this anomalous effusion of religious perfectionism, revealing a yearning for spiritual consummation that James normally kept in the shadows, is even more interesting for anyone trying to assess what James meant by "pragmatism" and how his development of it related to the preoccupations of *Varieties*. Whoever is "willing to live on a scheme of uncertified possibilities which he trusts; willing to pay with his own person, if need be for the realization of the ideals which he frames"—and this is a secular translation of whoever is willing to be damned for God's glory—is a "genuine pragmatist."[41] This sense of pragmatism has much in common with that displayed on the last page of *Varieties*, where, as I noted earlier, "pragmatism" is associated with the doctrine that the world is the site of a struggle of uncertain outcome, in which there is at least a chance that supernatural agencies and virtuous human strivings might work together for good.

Reading the *Pragmatism* of 1907, then, helps us see what James was working toward when he wrote *Varieties* in 1902. And if we have *Varieties* in mind when we read *Pragmatism*, we are better able to grasp the depth and character of the religious concerns that produced the often enigmatic formulations James offered under the sign of "pragmatism." Shortly after 1897 James seems to have come to the conclusion that the strategy of keeping the essence of religion safely protected from the structures of plausibility being inculcated in modern societies by science was a dead end. His sponsorship of the epistemically monolithic Peirce and his adoption of what was, for James, a new label, "pragmatism," mark the start of his own risky voyage, the first substantial vessel for which was *Varieties*. He later built and sailed on other ships, most of which we continue to study, as we study *Varieties*, without attending to the course James himself had charted for them. We are not obliged to accept his priorities in order to learn from what he wrote, but we are less likely to project our own ideas onto his if we know what he was trying to do and recognize the lights and shadows that affected his vision.

Did James "turn the lights down low so as to give miracle a chance"? No doubt he did, but at the same time he replaced the fierce concept of "miracle" with the bland-sounding "the religious hypothesis." James rendered religion so general that it had a much better chance of being accepted in the modern structure of plausibility than did any particular religious doctrine. He worked from both ends simultaneously. He made science more commodious and he made religion less confined by anything that might conflict with any specific finding of science.

Two years after James was born, a close friend of James's parents wrote:

> Truth forever on the scaffold,
> Wrong forever on the throne . . .

James Russell Lowell, in "The Present Crisis," continued[42]

> Yet that scaffold sways the future, and
> Behind the dim unknown
> Standeth God within the shadow
> Keeping watch above his own.

I believe that William James always hoped, in part of his soul, that God would come out of the New England shadow invoked by Lowell, that Yahweh would speak to him from the whirlwind, show him the burning bush, let him see Ezekiel's wheel in the middle of the sky. But nothing like that ever happened. It was James's destiny rather to become his generation's most creative and conspicuous case simultaneously of the radical liberalization of Protestantism and of the radical historicization of scientific inquiry. In achieving this place in a history that we can recognize a century after the fact, I suppose James himself may have been damned, and perhaps even for God's glory, but that uncertainty in James studies is one that I leave well enough alone.

Notes

For helpful comments on a draft of this paper, I wish to thank Wayne Proudfoot, Richard Rorty, Mark Schwehn, and Ann Taves.

1. Oliver Wendell Holmes Jr. to Frederick Pollock, September 1, 1910, in *Holems-Pollock Letters, The Correspondence of Mr. Justice Holmes and Sir Frederick Pollock, 1874–1932*, ed. Mark DeWolfe Howe (Cambridge, MA: Harvard University Press, 1941), I, 67.

2. William James, *The Varieties of Religious Experience* (Cambridge, MA: Harvard University Press, 1985), 359–360.

3. Richard R. Niebuhr, "William James on Religious Experience," in *The Cambridge Companion to William James*, ed. Ruth Anna Putnam (Cambridge and New York: Cambridge University Press, 1997), 225.

4. James, *Varieties*, 15–16. For an example of the use in James's milieu of this famous phrase of Huxley's, see David Starr Jordan, "Comrades in Zeal," *Popular Science Monthly* 64 (1904), 304.

5. John E. Smith, "Introduction" to James, *Varieties*, xxxvi.

6. James, *Varieties*, 217–218.

7. Ibid., 229.

8. Ibid., 241–249.

9. Ibid., 272–283, 265.

10. Ibid., 266, 277, 295, 297.

11. Ibid., 266.

12. For Gordon, see William Hutchison, *The Modernist Impulse in American Protestantism* (Cambridge, MA: Harvard University Press, 1976), 234–244. It should be acknowledged that James's sympathies for idiosyncratic and extreme religious persuasions set him somewhat apart from the high decorum style of the liberal Protestant establishment.

13. James, *Varieties*, 342, 359.

14. Ibid., 359.

15. Ibid., 358.

16. Ibid., 402, 411.

17. Ibid., 20–22.

18. Ibid., 406, 408.

19. Ibid., 408.

20. Ibid., 409–414.

21. William James to Oliver Wendell Holmes Jr., May 18, 1868, in Ralph Barton Perry, *The Thought and Character of William James*, 2 vols. (Boston: Little, Brown, 1935), I, 516–517.

22. William James, *The Will to Believe* (Cambridge, MA: Harvard University Press, 1979), 80, 88–89.

23. See chapter 5 in this volume.

24. James, *The Will to Believe*, 20, 33.

25. Ibid., 8–9.

26. The text of "The Pragmatic Method" is reprinted in William James, *Essays in Philosophy* (Cambridge, MA: Harvard University Press, 1978), 123–139.

27. James, "Pragmatic Method," 124.

28. James, *Varieties*, 351, 361, 408.

29. Wayne Proudfoot, "William James on an Unseen Order," *Harvard Theological Review* 93, 1 (2000), 51–66.

30. James, *Varieties*, 414.

31. The analysis of *Pragmatism* developed here expands upon points made in David A. Hollinger, *In the American Province: Studies in the History and Historiography of Ideas* (Bloomington: Indiana University Press, 1985), 4–22.

32. William James, *Pragmatism* (Cambridge, MA: Harvard University Press, 1978), 13.

33. Ibid., 34–36.

34. Charles Peirce, "The Fixation of Belief," *Popular Science Monthly* 12 (1877), 1–15.

35. James, *Pragmatism*, 139–140.

36. Ibid., 141.

37. Ibid., 142–143.

38. Ibid., 143–144.

39. Ibid., 142.

40. Ibid., 142.

41. Ibid., 142.

42. James Russell Lowell, "The Present Crisis," in *The Complete Poetical Works of James Russell Lowell*, ed. Horace E. Scudder (Boston: Houghton Mifflin, 1896), 67.

CHAPTER 7

Communalist and Dispersionist Approaches to American Jewish History in an Increasingly Post-Jewish Era

Can the historic experience of Protestants in the United States cast light on the destiny of the nation's Jewish population? I think so, and in the following essay I develop an analogy between post-Protestant and post-Jewish cultural situations. I do so in the context of my effort to identify and clarify a vital issue in the study of American Jewish history: to what extent is that field properly focused on communal Jewry and to what extent might its focuses be expanded to take full account of what persons of Jewish origin have done in the world, regardless of the degree of Jewish identity they, themselves, proclaim?

This essay pulls together arguments I have offered here and there over the course of thirty-five years of writing about the Jewish experience in twentieth-century America. Thus it connects After Cloven Tongues of Fire *with an earlier collection,* Science, Jews, and Secular Culture. *A theme of several essays in each of these two volumes is the disruptive effect Jews have had on the cultural hegemony of Protestants in American life. Should that hegemony have been disrupted? Most people today could probably agree that this change in American life was a healthy one. But one's view depends to some extent on whether one is a Christian survivalist, and if so, of just what kind.*

The ways in which Christian survivalism can affect the study of modern American history is something I take up in chapter 2 in this volume. Here I simply want to observe that the basic logic of Christian survivalism might well lead some people to resent the proliferation of non-Christian populations, which undermine the standing of the United States as a "Christian nation" and thus impair that nation's capacity to serve as an instrument of the perpetuation of Christianity. Yet there are many persons committed to the survival of Christianity who take a less strict view of the matter, and have no problem with a national setting in which Jews and other non-Christians are welcomed without prejudice.

This essay began as an invited lecture for a conference of specialists in American Jewish history and was later revised and expanded as the Kutler Lectures at the University of Wisconsin. It was originally published in American Jewish History *XCV (March 2009), 1–32, where it was followed (33–72) by thoughtful commentaries from four leading specialists in the field, Hasia Diner, Paula Hyman, Alan Kraut, and Tony Michels. These discussants establish beyond doubt that what I call "dispersionist" approaches are more widely and effectively employed than my essay allows. But all kept their distance from Yuri Slezkine's* The Jewish Century *(Princeton, 2004), which I had asked them to engage. In my rejoinder (73–78) I reiterated my conviction that Slezkine, by charting and explaining the demographic overrepresentation of persons of Jewish origin in multiple domains of modernity, has provided a sound basis for the yet more ambitious expansion of the field. The last few pages of this essay overlap with a section of chapter 8 in this volume, in which I acknowledge the profound influence of the Jewish sinologist Joseph R. Levenson on all of my work, including my conception of the dynamics of American Protestant history.*

IN THE LATE 1950S, there came to a head an often animated controversy over whether the federal census of 1960 should include religious categories. The census had changed its character from decade to decade, but had always counted people by what were then called, and by the Census Bureau today are still called, "races." Never had the federal census counted people by religion. In the middle 1950s, a time when religious identity was especially popular among Americans—this was, after all, the era of Will Herberg's *Protestant-Catholic-Jew* (1955), which powerfully reinforced the idea that religious rather than racial or class identities were what really mattered in the United States—the adding of religion to the census had wide appeal. The Eisenhower administration, which participated heavily in the Cold War sloganeering that contrasted "godless communism" to the godly United States, looked favorably on the idea. Catholic groups were vocally enthusiastic about it. But Jewish organizations were at first reserved, and then increasingly hostile to it. Between 1956 and 1958, the American Jewish Congress and other Jewish organizations worked hard to stop the plan, especially by lobbying members of Congress. In 1958 the Jewish organizations were able to declare victory. The Eisenhower administration decided it was too controversial.[1]

I invoke this long-forgotten controversy, the details of which have been carefully set forth by Kevin Shultz, because the concerns voiced by Jewish opponents of the counting of Americans by religion offer a convenient window on long-term issues regarding the place of Jews in American life, the resolution of which affects the questions I address here: how do we today define the field of American Jewish history, and how does that field now relate to the larger field of American history?

The Jewish organizations of the 1950s did not want religion in the census for several reasons, one of which was a commitment to a strict separation of church and state that had always been important to Jewish organizations. This commitment had been reinforced during the 1940s and 1950s in response to Catholic and evangelical Protestant efforts to mobilize state power in support of religious education, to prohibit the sale of contraceptives, and even to prohibit the dissemination of information about birth control. So prominent were Jews in the litigation advancing church-state separation that the leaders of the American Civil Liberties Union (ACLU), as Samuel Walker has established, were desperate to find non-Jewish plaintiffs, lest the advance of church-state separation become popularly understood as a Jewish conspiracy.[2] But Shultz demonstrates that Jewish organizations were also worried that the inclusion of religious categories in the census of 1960 would draw public attention to the fact that Jews were at once a very small minority and a very visible, undoubtedly powerful presence in the society.[3]

The Jewish organizations were of course aware that many American Jews did not practice Judaism, but enough did in the mid-1950s to make a religious category almost as certain a way to distinguish the nation's Jewish population as a Jewish racial designation on the census. At issue was the marking off of Jews as a demographic entity in terms that might lend credibility to antisemitic charges that Jews were too influential and, at the extreme of popular prejudice, that they were actually engaged in a conspiracy to take over various institutions and to dominate American politics.

Catholic organizations, by contrast, had long lamented that their very high numbers were not being recognized. Catholics were a bigger deal in American life than the general public understands, Catholic lobbyists insisted. A great thing about the Eisenhower administration's plan, according to these lobbyists, was that at long last attention would be drawn to the underrepresentation of Catholics in Congress, in universities and other institutions, and in households with high income. Both Catholic and Jewish leaders had a certain stake in not making their conflict too stark and vociferous. But their disagreement was real, and Catholics were very disappointed when they lost the struggle.

Jewish institutional leaders of the 1950s were of course eager for Jews to be fully part of American life, liberated from the antisemitic obstacles that were, in that generation, being diminished in one sector after another. Yet to be recognized by a census category, and to have the number of Jews correlated with the other kinds of data collected and disseminated by the census, especially economic position, was at once a means of more complete integration—of public recognition and acceptance—and a potential marking that might complicate a tension-free incorporation into American life. So, thanks but no thanks.

And when it comes to the writing of history, just where does one show that Jews are an integral part of American history, a constituent component that needs to be fully taken into account and analyzed with the same tools that scholars bring to the study of other American groups? Where instead does one show that Jews are a special community, a thing apart from America and prior to it, a people with their own multimillennial history, the American segment of which should be told in analytic terms consistent with the story of Jews in medieval and early modern Europe and back to biblical times?

This uncertainty was explored helpfully in a recent issue of the *Newsletter* of the Organization of American Historians. Hasia Diner and Tony Michels lucidly addressed what they describe as "a large gap" that persists between "the scholarly works of American Jewish historians and the wider world of American history scholarship." They note the persistence of this gap despite the last couple of decades of rich monographic and synthetic work produced by a creative generation of specialists in American Jewish history. This gap, Diner and Michels suggest, has some of its sources in the tendencies of these specialists to avoid studying antisemitism, to ignore the relation of the federal government to Jews, and to avoid the subject of race, paying little attention to the history of racial categories and how their construction and reconstruction has affected Jews.[4]

I am persuaded by Diner and Michels, especially on this last point. More attention to how the boundaries of Jewishness have been drawn, and by whom, and in whose interests, and how the question of the boundaries of Jewishness is related to the questions not only of white boundaries, but to the questions of boundaries of other nonblack groups, might indeed bring Jewish history more fully into the race-preoccupied scholarship characteristic of U.S. specialists generally for the past half-century. But I want to add to Diner and Michels's analysis an additional suggestion. More attention might be paid to the role in history of persons of Jewish ancestry regardless of their degree of affiliation with communal Jewry.

We can distinguish between communalist and dispersionist approaches to the field. By "communalist" I mean an emphasis on the history of communal Jewry, including the organizations and institutions that proclaim Jewishness, and the activities of individuals who identify themselves as Jewish and/or are so identified by non-Jews with the implication it somehow matters. Central to communalist history is the concept of "the Jewish people." By "dispersionist," I mean a more expanded compass that takes fuller account of the lives in any and all domains of persons with an ancestry in the Jewish diaspora, regardless of their degree of involvement with communal Jewry and no matter what their extent of declared or ascribed Jewishness. To dispersionist history, the concept of "the Jewish people" means little.

The role in history played by people who were shaped by the conditions of the Jewish diaspora is a much broader site for inquiry than the history of communal Jewry. Dispersionsts confront the challenge of dealing with historical actors who were obviously shaped by the conditions of the Jewish diaspora in Europe yet affiliated only nominally or not at all with any Jewish community and/or were only rarely treated by gentiles in any special way on account of their Jewish ancestry. The secular men and women of Jewish background who did so much to advance the revolutionary movement in the Russian Empire and to staff the Soviet regime in its early decades are perhaps the most vivid examples of this social type, but relevant, too, are many scientists and financiers in the North Atlantic West, and many of the men and women who led in the development of psychoanalysis, Hollywood, modernist movements in the arts, and some other endeavors that have not been defined ethnoreligiously but that have an ethnoreligious demography. If such people are not Jewish enough for their projects and their accomplishments—nefarious or noble or morally neutral to our eyes—to be included in the mainstream of Jewish history and Jewish studies, is there nothing Jewish here to be examined?

We all know that Mordecai Kaplan, Abraham Cahan, Stephen S. Wise, and Irving Howe were figures in American Jewish history, but what about J. Robert Oppenheimer, Robert K. Merton, Thomas S. Kuhn, Walter Lippmann, Julius Rosenberg, Joyce Brothers, Benny Goodman, Ayn Rand, and Madeleine Albright?

Until very recently most of what gets classified as "Jewish history" or "Jewish studies" has been more of the communalist rather than the dispersionist variety. What has mattered is the Jewish people, as a people. But I want to suggest that a more candidly dispersionist approach to American Jewish history might promote stronger and more sustained mutual engagements with other specialists in U.S. history. This would mean the energetic exploration of Jewish demographic overrepresentation in the American worlds of finance, film, science, philanthropy, political radicalism, and other domains of modernity.

I want to linger for a moment on the word "modernity," in all its vagueness. As I contemplate the work of historians known to me who have written about Jews to one extent or another since the early 1970s, the time when I began to write about Jews, I am struck with a division in basic orientation that is not a conflict or a valid basis for a quarrel, but rather a fact about differing motivations. Some of us are interested in Jews because we want to understand the features of history that go by the name of the modern. Jews become important to us instrumentally, because as we study the cultures and societies and politics and economies of modernity, we find Jews everywhere. Some historians interested in modernity, when they keep coming across Jews, will treat Jewishness as a marginal consideration, or will simply ignore it. But others of us will try to understand whatever episode or event or movement that is before us without screening out the presence of Jews in it, but rather by confronting this presence head-on, by seeking to figure out what the Jewish presence means and does not mean.

The book of my Berkeley colleague Yuri Slezkine, *The Jewish Century*, is an example of this instrumental engagement with the history of Jews. Concerned first of all to understand the Soviet bureaucracy, he found that everywhere he looked, there were persons of Jewish background, however little they themselves made of it, or however much, indeed, Jewish identity was suppressed. Slezkine began with the historical problem he was trying to understand—the character and dispositions of the Soviet governmental elite—and he came to realize that his task would be incomplete unless he took account of the presence of Jews in the domains of modernity that he was studying.[5] I will return to Slezkine later, as I believe his work as a dispersionist has much to teach us, but for now I am simply citing him as an example of a "modernity first, Jews second" path to the study of Jewish history.

My own case is of the same kind. When I began my dissertation on the career of Morris R. Cohen, the philosopher of science, what mattered to me was that Cohen was, indeed, a philosopher of science and an agent of secular culture. I wanted to study science-related secular culture in the United States. I soon picked up on the fact that Morris Cohen was Jewish—this was pointed out to me by my Jewish then-fiancée and later wife, who somehow noticed it right away—but this had not been important to me at the start. The book I eventually published about Cohen in 1975 was quite different from the bulk of literature on Cohen written by philosophers, through which I first learned about him, and in which Cohen's Jewishness was not treated as relevant, even by philosophers of Jewish extraction who had written about his ideas and his role in the history of American philosophy. But my historian's training led me to look at Cohen rather differently than the philosophers did. I realized that Jewishness was absolutely central to understanding Cohen, and that the appeal to him of certain philosophical ideas was deeply rooted in his historical circumstances as a Jewish immigrant from Russia.[6]

Later, as I moved beyond Cohen to study other examples of scientific achievement, secular culture, and cosmopolitanism in the United States in the twentieth century, I found that I was constantly coming across Jews, many of whom affirmed Jewish identity, but some of whom, like Oppenheimer, did not make much of it, and others of whom, like Merton, took action to deflect attention away from it, if not to actually conceal it. I have written about Jews off and on for the last thirty-five years, in book after book and article after article on cosmopolitanism and scientific culture, and I have done so because Jews are there, right in the middle of my topics. I probably would not have ended up writing about so many Jews if my main interest had been the history of agriculture, or of the lumber industry, or of the military. Concerned to explain the accelerated pace of secularism among American intellectuals in the middle decades of the twentieth century, I concluded that Jews had a great influence on this specific development; hence I wrote the vigorously dispersionist essay, "Jewish Intellectuals and the De-Christianization of American Public Culture in the 20th Century."[7]

I run on about myself by way of underscoring the difference between careers like mine and Slezkine's, on the one hand, and the careers of those who study Jews because of an interest in Jews as such, on the other. The distinction I make is no way invidious. Some people are interested in Jewish history because they feel somehow attached to it personally, or they believe that the Jewish experience has lessons to offer the world that deserve to be told, or that by interpreting Jewish history in this or that way they can strengthen and enrich communal Jewry. There are a variety of motivations, and I will not pretend to list them all, or to assign any relative moral weight to these various motivations. But I believe it is fair to say that dispersionist Jewish history of the sort that Slezkine and I write is more likely to be produced by scholars who begin somewhere else—they begin with modernity, or science, or cosmopolitanism, or art, or political radicalism—and that communalist Jewish history is more likely to be written by people who begin with the idea of studying Jews as Jews. I am not saying that anyone who now does communalist Jewish history should switch to dispersionist Jewish history. There is room in the field for both approaches. But if Jewish history specialists are looking for ways to get their work more fully integrated into what we might call mainstream U.S. history, some moves in a dispersionist direction might help that cause.

An example of where a dispersionist approach might make a real difference is the study of the feminist movement of the 1960s and 1970s. In showing how different a dispersionist approach is from a communalist approach to this historical episode, I refer you to the recent, excellent book by Diner herself, *The Jews of the United States* (2004). Diner devotes six-and-one-half densely packed pages to what she calls "Jewish feminism" of the 1960s and 1970s, focusing on "the admission of women into rabbinical and cantorial school, the emergence of women as lay leaders in their synagogues, and the transformation of the liturgy in reflecting the era's regnant idea that women had an equal share in the history and destiny of the Jewish people." Diner recounts what goes on in Reform, Reconstructionist, Conservative, and Orthodox circles, attending closely to subsections of "the Jewish people" that experienced feminism somewhat differently. She is careful to observe that while Jewish feminism was "related to" the larger feminist movement in the society at large, Jewish feminism "had a history of its own," distinct from that larger movement, and was the culmination of a trend visible since the early nineteenth century, "when synagogues increasingly became the domain of women."[8]

In passing Diner devotes a few lines to the fact that "Jewish women played a powerful and formative role" in the larger feminist movement. Before rushing on to talk about her real topic, what Jewish women were doing in the various religiously defined segments of communal Jewry, Diner observes that nine of the twelve women who formed the Boston Women's Health Collective and produced *Our Bodies, Ourselves* were Jewish. In one remarkable sentence, she mentions that the Jewish women who functioned as leaders of the national feminist movement included "Bella Abzug, Vivian Gornick, Gloria Steinem, Robin Morgan, Shulamith Firestone, Meredith Tax, Letty Cottin Pogebrin," and of course, Betty Freidan and Florence Howe.[9] Diner does not mention others who might be added to this list: Ellen Willis, Alix Kates Schulman, Andrea Dworkin, and Gerda Lerner, among others. One might ask if there were any leading feminists of the 1960s and 1970s who were not of Jewish origin? Okay, Kate Millett and bell hooks, and yes, we could probably come up with a few others.

Extensive research is surely not required to vindicate empirically the proposition that the feminist movement in the United States from the mid-1960s through the mid-1970s was largely led by women of Jewish ancestry and largely of secular orientation. In what sense is Women's Liberation, as it was called at the time, a Jewish story?

One implicit answer, indeed the dominant one, is provided in Ruth Rosen's *The World Split Open: How the Modern Women's Movement Changed America*. This important and historiographically current book mentions almost every name I have just listed, but it does not address as a topic for analysis the predominance of Jewish women in the women's movement. Indeed, the word "Jew" is not in the index of this signpost work. Rosen, like so many social historians of the last generation or two, is sensitive to the demographic composition of social movements, except when it comes to identifying Jews.[10] References to the role of Jewish women in the women's movement of the progressive era are quite common in the literature of that period, to be sure, focusing on suffrage. But this is simply not the case in the substantial monographic literature we now have that touches on the development of feminism in the 1960s and 1970s.

Neither Alice Echols, *Daring to Be Bad: Radical Feminism in America, 1967–1975*, nor Cynthia Harrison, *On Account of Sex: The Politics of Women's Issues, 1945–1968*, two of the major books exactly on the topic, contains any reference to Jews or Judaism. There is no acknowledgment of the Jewish background of Jewish feminists, to say nothing of an analysis of the phenomenon, in the following works: Joanne Meyerowitz's

Not June Cleaver: Women and Gender in Postwar America, 1945–1960, Wini Breines's *Young, White, and Miserable: Growing Up Female in the Fifties,* Richard Flacks's *Making History: The American Left and the American Mind,* and Eugenia Kaledin's *Mothers and More: American Women in the 1950s.* Nancy Wolloch's important textbook, *Women and the American Experience,* explicitly notes the presence of many Jewish women in the social movements of the Progressive period, but not for any of the action after World War II. The same is true of Sara M. Evans's *Born for Liberty: A History of Women in America.* Even Elaine Tyler May, in her now classic *Homeward Bound: American Families in the Cold War Era,* has nothing to say about Jews as such beyond one reference to the importance to Jewish parents of having children to make up for those lost in the Holocaust and another reference to the approval of birth control devices by Jewish organizations.[11] In this setting, Daniel Horowitz's study of the life and career of Freidan is a highly distinctive work, directly engaging Freidan's Jewishness and is thus a signal contribution to dispersionist studies of American Jews.[12]

The historiographical circumstances of scholarship on modern feminism can be instructively contrasted to the scholarship of the last two generations on the ethnoreligious demography of the civil rights movement. We are now awash in books and articles emphasizing the Christian foundations of white as well as black participation in the struggle against Jim Crow. David L. Chappell's *A Stone of Hope* is only the most widely discussed of recent studies that explore the ethnoreligious demography of the civil rights movement and are cited constantly by political actors critical of secularism and supportive of faith-based initiatives.[13] Indeed, in symposia on the ideal role of religion in public affairs, I have been struck with how those who defend church-state separation are flummoxed when told, with some hyperbole, that it was thanks to religion that we got rid of Jim Crow. Rick Warren? Not a problem; he's a progressive on many issues, so stop worrying about religion as a bad thing in American politics.[14]

Whatever the political implications of these studies of the Protestant ethnoreligious demography of the civil rights movement, the empirical foundation is impressive. Sara Evans found that every single southern white woman whom she studied in her important book of 1976 on women in the civil rights movement, *Personal Politics,* got her start in Protestant churches.[15] That Evans is so sensitive to the ethnoreligious demography of the civil rights movement, but not, as I noted earlier, to the ethnoreligious demography of feminism, is an emblem for our historiographical situation. If Jewishness were as central to our histories of feminism as Protestantism is to our studies of the civil rights movement, the former might look more like the latter, and might be as integrated into our mainstream histories. We actually explain the sources and dynamics of the civil rights movement partly in terms of Protestantism; we almost never explain the sources and dynamics of the feminist movement in terms of Jewishness.

I want to observe, parenthetically, that the proportional overrepresentation of Jews within the ranks of white civil rights workers has been increasingly downplayed as our historical literature focuses on the Protestant matrix of the civil rights movement. Doug McAdam, the most careful scholar of *Mississippi Summer*, estimates that about one-third of the student volunteers in that endeavor were Jews, most of them, like the legendary martyrs of Neshoba County, Andrew Goodman and Michael Schwerner, not religiously observant but "freethinking Jews," in the famous phrase popularized by T. S. Eliot.[16] Some religious observers noticed this at the time. Walker Percy, the Mississippi Catholic writer sympathetic to the volunteers, noted ruefully that the movement seemed to be an expression of "the Berkeley-Cambridge axis."[17]

I will not try here to explain why Jewish women were demographically overrepresented—by how many thousand percentage points?—in the ranks of the leaders of 1960s and 1970s feminism, one of the most important movements in twentieth-century American history, although I imagine that this phenomenon can be explained in terms consistent with how we might explain Jewish overrepresentation in other radical movements. I simply underscore the point that our scholarly and popular histories take virtually no notice of this astronomically huge demographic fact about feminism. Dispersionist studies of the sort pioneered by Horowitz could change that. Nowadays, African American history is well integrated into mainstream American history. Works in that field win many prizes from the American Historical Association and the Organization of American Historians, and their authors are regularly elected to high offices. Textbooks attend extensively to African American history and also to Latino history. This is much less the case with Jewish history, which continues to be seen as a thing apart.

To be sure, recent scholarship within the field of American Jewish history has included several important steps in dispersionist directions. Andrew R. Heinze's *Jews and the American Soul: Human Nature in the 20th Century* is a salient case, demonstrating that a large swath of American popular and professional discourse about the human psyche was led by persons of Jewish ancestry, and in many cases by people who carried Jewish cultural baggage with them in their creative careers as psychologists and writers.[18] Some of the writings of Eric L. Goldstein, Tony Michels, and Joshua Zeitz might be construed as dispersionist in their attention to the impact of groups of Jews on trans-Jewish events and discourses.[19] In journalistic writings about American history, Neal Gabler's *An Empire of Their Own: How the Jews Invented Hollywood*, is a widely noted example.[20]

But the most striking pieces of scholarship known to me that vindicate the promise of dispersionist history have been written by two of my Berkeley colleagues who specialize in modern European history, neither of which has been identified with Jewish history as a field. One of these, John Connelly, studies Catholic priests who were born Jewish and converted to Catholicism, and who assign no meaning to their Jewishness. Connelly finds that in the twentieth century, the elements of the Catholic hierarchy, within the Vatican and beyond, who pushed for the renunciation of Catholic racism in general and of Catholic antisemitism in particular, were almost always Jews by birth or by one generation removed. Among Connelly's examples is Johannes Osterreicher, who got his start in virulently antisemitic Vienna in the early 1930s, and eventually had a distinguished career teaching theology at Seton Hall University in New Jersey. But Connelly has many examples. He has discovered specific meetings in the Vatican during the early build-up to Vatican II in which every priestly participant in the room was a convert who had been born a Jew or was the son of a convert. As Connelly states his central argument about the dynamics of Catholic antiracism in Europe from the 1920s through the 1960s, "the Catholics who opposed anti-Semitism with the greatest conviction were of Jewish origin."[21]

What makes Connelly's analysis interesting for my purposes is that he is talking about a collection of people who actually renounced Judaism, and rejected Jewish identity altogether. They are worth thinking about because they hint at a legacy of Jewish experience extending even beyond the abandonment of Jewishness, and even within an organization—the Roman Catholic church—with a history of suspicion of converts for harboring secret Jewishness.

My second Berkeley colleague is Slezkine, already famous for his finding that in the Soviet government, people born as Jews were extravagantly overrepresented. Aware of the antisemitic discourse linking Bolshevism to Jews, as advanced particularly by the Nazis by also by antisemites in the United States and elsewhere, Slezkine's research nevertheless brought him face to face with the fact that the secret police was the most demographically Jewish organization within the Soviet state. Here, again, we have a group of people who were born Jewish and rejected both Judaism and Jewish identity, and indeed denied that their Jewishness had any meaning at all. In that sense, they are like the Jews who converted to Catholicism and then took leadership positions within the Catholic hierarchy. Some critics of Slezkine insist that his subjects were not really Jews, and thus should not be studied in a Jewish context, and that to classify them as Jews is to reinvigorate a discredited discourse.[22]

But in fact, Slezkine's explanation for Jewish Bolshevism does not track the old antisemitic discourse, with its essentialist assumptions and its charges of concerted efforts to achieve world domination. On the contrary, Slezkine focuses on the material conditions of Jewish life within the Pale of Settlement, on the world-historical role of service nomads in relation to landed and warrior-status populations, on the history of antisemitism in Russia, and on the special opportunity that communism presented, at least in its early years, for the utter and complete renunciation of blood-and-soil nationalism in the interests of a truly egalitarian, universalist social order. *The Jewish Century* is a radically demystifying book, following closely upon the social theoretical ideas of Ernst Gellner. Selzkine is forthright about the monstrousness of the miscalculation made by the Jews who put their faith in the Bolshevik project. He speaks movingly of his own Russian Jewish grandmother who gave her life to the Soviet cause and died firmly convinced that it had all been a mistake and that her life had been wasted. But Slezkine provides us with a compelling instance of a distinct pattern of behavior in a non-Jewish context of people whose lives were significantly formed by historical conditions that were unquestionably Jewish.[23]

The cases of Connelly and Slezkine can remind us of an important methodological issue. There is always a danger of overdetermination: one can try to explain too much with reference to a Jewish background. But that is where statistics are helpful: when descendants of the diaspora are found to be overrepresented, the greater the overrepresentation the more incentive should there be to consider explanations grounded in the conditions of the diaspora. In approaching this methodological issue, we can be assisted by the well-established practices of our colleagues in other fields. The overrepresentation of Asian Americans in certain sectors is now being analyzed with reference to the distinctive preimmigration history and immigration patterns of Americans of Japanese descent, Chinese descent, Bengali descent, and so on. The extraordinary overrepresentation of Americans of Korean descent in colleges and in the professions, we are told, results not from some innately Korean drive to dominate, but from the fact that an overwhelming majority of adult immigrants from Korea are college graduates and are fluent in English. The overrepresentation of African American males in prisons is explained by our social science colleagues with reference to slavery, Jim Crow, and the larger history of the institutionalized debasement of black people. Similarly, the overrepresentation of Jews in other social locations can be explained by the same methods. Genes are not the issue, nor are mystified notions of ethnoracial essence. History is the issue.[24]

This more thoroughly historical way of thinking opens the way to a candid public discussion of "Jewish influence," a term from which one might be enabled to remove the scare quotation marks on account of the recognition that the "influence" at issue is not derived from some tribal mystique, or from some centralized authority driving Jews to take over this or that institution in the interest of some quasi-secret agenda. The demystification of Jewish populations, including the acknowledgment that many historical actors who get classified as Jews are not part of communal Jewry, facilitates this more relaxed discussion. The Jewish population is far from monolithic; even, indeed, the population that identifies with communal Jewry is far from monolithic. Recognition of the diverse and dispersed character of the population descended from the European diaspora helps to diminish the hold of old prejudices, and equips us to better particularize our arguments when we speak of the demographic overrepresentation of Jews in this or that social space. If the Protocols of the elders of Zion are still being circulated in Cairo and Riyadh, we in the United States should not be intimidated into limiting our own inquiries and public debates to the terms set by the evil men and women who promote such long-discredited lies. The notion that it is "bad for the Jews" to proclaim the truth about their central role in modern history plays subtly into the implication that there is indeed a conspiracy afoot. Why hide the truth, if it is indeed innocent?

Yet it should be acknowledged there might be costs to moving the field of Jewish history in more dispersionist directions, even if among those costs is surely not the inviting of new pogroms. What costs? The field can become more amorphous, and its boundaries harder to define and to maintain. Scholars without Hebrew and Yiddish can be taken more seriously than has often been the case within the guild of Jewish history. The need for a solid grounding in medieval history would probably become less important. The United States would become a major site for the study of Jews, rather than a marginal one. The people who are accustomed to exercising leadership in the field might find themselves with more and different company than in the past. There might be pressure to revise syllabi. The philanthropists who so generously support Jewish history—and have made it the most highly capitalized subfield within the entire discipline of history as manifest in departments of history in public as well as private higher education—might be less enthusiastic about dispersionist studies than about communalist studies. The benefits of the change might outweigh the costs, but some things valued by many people in and beyond the field might be diminished in the process.

I don't know how much resistance there is to dispersionist approaches, but in reading reviews of Slezkine's book I have been aware of the rapidity with which his implications for an enriched, expanded study of Jews have been recognized by scholars not closely associated with Jewish history, and how ambivalent has been the reaction of many scholars closely identified with the study of Jewish history.[25] Some specialists in Jewish history seem not to realize that Slezkine is opening up the entirety of modernity to them as a field where their skills and learning as Jewish history specialists can be put to effective use in a vastly enlarged domain, and to greater recognition by historians and the public. Communalist approaches, whatever their virtues, simply do not engage the challenge that Slezkine, more compellingly than anyone else, has issued. I hope for an honest and collegial division of labor, not a circling of the communalist wagons.

I hasten to acknowledge that until now I have been speaking as if the gap addressed by Diner and Michels was entirely a product of decisions made by specialists in Jewish history, too concerned, perhaps, with maintaining the security and authority that comes with well-established boundaries and a small amount of turf. But this is not the case. There is another side to this unsatisfactory collegial relationship, and I now want to turn to that other side, to dispositions within the mainstream of the profession that appear to have inhibited the more complete integration of the scholarship of American Jewish history into American history generally. Diner and Michels are cautious and nonaccusatory about this dimension of the situation, but I want to push their envelope a bit further.

One aspect of American Jewish history that makes it potentially significant in the larger context of American history as a whole is the story of how Jews negotiated a place for themselves in an overwhelming Christian society, and how they developed and maintained a set of communal institutions, many of them secular in orientation, that perpetuated a significant amount of cultural particularity even while individual Jews became increasingly prominent in American politics, science, the arts, and so on. One might think that this story, on which a number of communalist-oriented historians have written with distinction and at length, would attract the attention of mainstream historians interested in the history of identity formation and cultural diversity as general phenomena, which have been huge preoccupations of American historians for the last forty years. One might even suppose that the Jewish case of group identity, filled with material for the scrutiny of how economic position and education and language and religion and morphological traits affect one's destiny in America, might offer lessons for understanding the destinies and strategies of other minority groups, and might even offer practical ideas for historically disadvantaged groups today. Feeding this speculation is the appropriation of the concept of the diaspora by and on behalf of non-Jewish groups, and the modeling of Kwanzaa on Jewish rituals.

But I hope it is fair to observe that mainstream scholarship has been slow to recognize and appreciate Jewish history in relation to the larger prehistory and history of cultural diversity in America beyond the general point, made frequently, that Jews were among the white groups who defined themselves as nonblack. In addressing this reluctance to embrace and energetically explore the Jewish case of group identity and cultural diversification, I want to look above and beyond the history profession for a moment to focus on the dynamics of the multiculturalist movement of the last three decades. The dynamics there are simpler and cruder than what we see displayed in the historical profession as such, but in the popular multiculturalism of the schools and the colleges and universities, we can see an ideological atmosphere that also affects the historical profession.

The key point about multiculturalism is that there has been almost no place in it for Jews. Multiculturalism has been organized largely on the basis of the ethnoracial pentagon, our mythical, five-part structure with cultures ascribed to color-coded communities of descent, often in recent years labeled African American, Asian American, European American, Hispanic or Latino, and Indian or Native American. On this map of culture in America, Jews are invisible, except in very detailed versions of it that show the cultures ascribed to subgroups, in which case we find Jews, along with Poles and Irish and Italians, and so on, within the part of the map labeled European American.

The ethnoracial pentagon draws on a long history of demographic categories, but only in the late 1970s did this particular way of mapping culture in America become dominant. Cultural diversity was certainly mapped before the 1970s, and in those earlier projections, Jews were not only visible, but prominent. Horace Kallen, the philosopher who popularized the term "cultural pluralism," had Jews very much in mind in his writings of the 1910s and 1920s. Virtually all of the influential commentators on cultural diversity between then and the 1960s— including Alain Locke, Louis Adamic, Will Herberg, Milton Gordon, and Nathan Glazer—were highly conscious of Jews.[26] Herberg's 1955 classic, *Protestant-Catholic-Jew*, successfully promoted the idea that Jewishness was one of the three most important categories by which Americans could be categorized.[27] Yet even the heavy demographic overrepresentation of Jews in the cultural industries, including academia, the fine arts, film, and journalism, has failed to get Jews on the standardized multicultural map of the United States as drawn since the 1970s. Considered as a map of cultural diversity in America, the ethnoracial pentagon is rather like the Mercator projection of the globe, in which Greenland and Patagonia and Spitzbergen are huge, while Nigeria and Indonesia and Peru are tiny.

But the appeal of the pentagonal vision of cultural diversity during the 1980s and 1990s was very deep, and to understand this appeal may be also to understand why mainstream historians of the period paid close attention to monographs about African American, Asian American, Latino, and American Indian history, but relatively little to American Jewish History. The pentagonal cultural map of America made excellent sense in the context of the *Bakke* decision of 1978 concerning affirmative action. Remember that Justice Lewis Powell's epochal opinion in *Bakke* treated skin color as a predictor of culture. Powell said that colleges and universities could give special treatment to ethnoracial groups, as one of other considerations in the admissions process, so long as it was understood as means of advancing the goal of cultural diversity. In Powell's famous words, our nation needs leaders exposed to "the ideas and mores of students as diverse as this nation of many peoples."[28] Powell saved affirmative action, for a while, at least, by translating it into the terms of culture. The result was to encourage the trend we saw in the 1980s by which educational programs designed to increase appreciation of cultural diversity, and to diminish ethnocentric prejudices, were increasingly allied with affirmative action programs.

If affirmative action was essentially an enterprise in cultural diversity, and if cultural diversity was measured in terms of standardized ethnoracial categories, it made perfect sense for multiculturalist initiatives to be organized on the basis of the affirmative action map, which was pentagonal from the time of the Equal Employment Opportunity Commission's first employment forms, issued in 1966. Just as a Mercator projection of the globe served the specific and valuable purpose of enabling a flat wall-hanging, so, too, did the pentagonal map of culture serve the specific and valuable purpose of affirmative action. One of countless examples that might be cited is one from my own campus.

In the late 1980s, the Berkeley faculty senate enacted a new requirement for the bachelor's degree. In order to graduate, you needed to complete a course on what was called "American Cultures," and this was defined in terms of the standard pentagon, with the proviso that any course licensed to fulfill the requirement had to deal with the cultures of at least three of the pentagonal groups.[29] This enactment followed the standard line of the 1980s, according to which ethnoracial groups were assumed to be relatively autonomous, enduring, analogically structured entities, each with its own culture and its own color.

Even by the mid-1990s this way of looking at ethnoracial groups was subject to considerable criticism, especially on the grounds that culture and color did not go together quite as easily as Powell and the various multiculturalist initiatives implied. But the complaints were also heard that there was no place in this map for Arabs, and that religion was inappropriately downplayed in a scheme for culture, given the fact that culture, however defined, had long been assumed to include religion. This was not the federal census, after all; this was a series of programs for the study of culture. Where was Islam, it was asked, well before Nine-Eleven? Now and then someone complained—at Berkeley, and in other settings where the same orthodoxy was in place—that Jews were ignored, but the rejoinder was quick and cogent: the main point of multiculturalism was color, and Jews were white, and a second point of multiculturalism was inequality, and Jews were doing very well in the United States. So, cool it, the collegial message was: let these programs deal with the needs of Americans color-coded as black, brown, yellow, and red in contrast to the empowered white demographic block. Fussing about the particularity of Irish, Jewish, Italian, and Polish Americans, and so on, could even be seen as vaguely racist, pushing the interests of a privileged group when other, more disadvantaged groups needed the support multicultural programs could provide.

Hence students of Jewish history from the late 1970s onward were surrounded by a transdisciplinary academic discourse of group identity that systematically deemphasized religion, yet the religious component in Jewish history was vitally important. This pervasive discourse of identity privileged color, yet color did not distinguish most Jews from white people in general. This discourse of identity downplayed the linguistic and historical particularity of the different descent communities within each of the color-coded segments of the pentagon, yet for Jews, linguistic and historical particularity was basic to group identity. This discourse nested issues of identity and culture in a matrix of unequally distributed power, and often aspired to allocate social benefits on the basis of demographically proportional representation, yet Jews were the richest and most empowered of any of the society's prominently recognized ethnoracial groups. This discourse placed great emphasis on the barriers that minorities faced in the United States, yet the Jewish case constituted the most dramatic instance in all American history of a stigmatized descent group that had been discriminated against under the protection of law suddenly becoming overrepresented many times over in social spaces where its members' progress had previously been seriously inhibited. All this is to suggest that the story of how Jews found their way in America could come across, in the 1980s and 1990s, as a distraction, if not a threat. The Jewish case was just plain inconvenient.[30]

The generation of monographic scholarship in the field of American Jewish history surveyed by Diner and Michels and too often ignored by the historical profession as a whole coincides almost precisely with the period of the hegemony of the ethnoracial pentagon. But things are changing. Misgivings about this prevailing discourse of identity have been voiced more and more often in these early years of our new century. Not only has the recognition of the reality of marriage and reproduction across the pentagonal lines increased sharply, but the differences between the various Asian groups have become widely asserted and analyzed, giving new credibility to distinctions within the "European American" segment of the pentagon. Are Americans from Turkish Anatolia "Asian Americans"? From Lebanon? Iran? The category of Asian American has run up against difficulty even in the case of people whose background is in Sri Lanka, India, Pakistan, and Bangladesh. But often, affirmative action was interpreted to include South Asia but to end at the Khyber Pass. Why? Are Afghani Americans and Pakistani Americans so different? These questions are piled on top of uncertainties about the significance of distinctions between the classically Asian American groups, the Chinese, Japanese, and Koreans. Most important of all, the character and boundaries of blackness have been called into question in terms that were unthinkable when the pentagon's ordinance was established in the 1970s.

Among the fascinating features of the Obama era into which we have now been launched is the honest uncertainty displayed by many commentators on just what Obama's blackness means. And if the meaning of blackness has been destabilized, what, then, of other identities? Blackness is the pivotal concept in the intellectual and administrative apparatus used in the United States for dealing with ethnoracial distinctions. Doubts about its basic meaning, boundaries, and social role affect ideas about whiteness, and all other color-coded identities. These uncertainties make it easier to contemplate a possible future in which the ethnoracial categories central to identity politics would be more matters of choice than ascription; in which mobilization by ethnoracial groups would be more a strategic option than a presumed destiny attendant upon mere membership in a group; and in which economic inequalities would be confronted head-on, instead of through the medium of ethnorace. The more that politics during the Obama era move in this direction, reflecting the destabilization of color-coded identities and the greater recognition of economic inequalities and their historical matrix, the more opportunity there is for culture to be released from the pentagonal map and the more opportunity there is for the study of group identities to be engaged with conceptual sophistication and a strong empirical foundation.

The decline of the ethnoracial pentagon thus opens up promising opportunities for American Jewish history. Not only are groups and cultures within the pentagonal blocks now more readily engaged, but also the boundaries between the pentagonal blocks and between the subgroups within them are increasingly recognized as blurred and historically contingent. Moreover, as scholars engage the particular histories of Asia-derived populations of Americans, many of which have high educational and income levels, historians of some Asian American groups become welcome allies to historians of American Jews: all are studying natal communities apart from the dynamics of affirmative action, for which most Asian American groups are no longer counted as eligible.

A real benefit of the decline of "identity politics" in the United States is a greater capacity to appreciate and to critically engage ideas and practices that owe much to "identity groups" but are no longer confined by them. The insight that the creative influence of religious and ethnic communities often lasts well beyond the time when individuals and families have been deeply embedded in such communities is behind today's buzz about "post-Jewish," "post-black," "post-Catholic," "post-Polish," and so on, and the more comprehensive notion of "postethnic."

To denote the domain of experience and possibility beyond the ethnoracial pentagon, some of us use the word "postethnic." A postethnic social order would encourage individuals to devote as much—or as little—of their energies as they wished to their community of descent, and would discourage public and private agencies from implicitly telling every citizen that the most important thing about them was their descent community. Hence to be postethnic is not to be anti-ethnic, or even color-blind, but to reject the idea that descent is destiny. It is also to release economic inequalities from the discourse of ethnicity and race, and to promote direct and honest confrontation with those economic inequalities. And it is to recognize the effects of descent-community-related experiences that survive the diminution of affiliation with the community of descent.[31]

Post-Jewishness, as defined by the organizers of a highly successful exhibition of post-Jewish art at the Spertus Jewish Museum in Chicago in 2008, emphasizes voluntary rather than ascribed Jewishness. "The post-Jewish generation," in the words of the Spertus catalogue, "focuses on self-definition and on balancing lived experience and heritage in intellectual and daily practice," fostering "an internal, highly personal consciousness as to how one connects with Jewishness today."[32] Hasia Diner does not employ the concept of post-Jewishness, but in her conclusion to her history of 346 years of Jewish experience in America, she speaks in an idiom almost identical to that of the Spertus catalogue. Speaking of the elasticity of definitions of Jewishness and of norms for Jewish practice, Diner allows that by the year 2000, "on some level all American Jews, not just the growing number of converts, had become Jews by choice." In a sentence that could apply exactly to the artists of the Spertus exhibition, Diner speaks of a population of Jewish ancestry that, "whether they affiliate or not, continue to invest their Jewishness with meaning," however elastic and unpredictable that meaning might be.[33]

But post-Jewishness in this sense, like postethnicity in its various other instantiations, is not for everyone. Some people are deeply attracted to styles of communal life in which the individual submits to the authority of tradition as he or she understands it. To these people, the old rules do matter. Some communitarian theorists even celebrate this acceptance of unchosen authorities, and declare the appreciation of, and submission to, an unchosen fate as the mark of a profound mind. Post-Jewishness, like all varieties of postethnicity, is a classically liberal disposition.

To be sure, there are so many "post"s these days—postmodern, post-colonial, postfeminist, poststructural; recently somebody called me "post-WASP"—that one has to bring a certain skepticism to the whole enterprise of "post"ing things. Perhaps this practice does reflect a weakness in our vocabulary, a lack of invention? When I first advanced the concept of postethnicity in essays of 1992 and 1993, I was looking for an alternative to "cosmopolitanism," which seemed too encumbered with ambiguous historical baggage. The term "postethnic" implies a strong legacy from the past, but a refinement of that legacy in relation to new opportunities and constraints. A postethnic perspective recognizes and encourages voluntary affiliations and is suspicious of involuntary ones while not denying their historical ubiquity, and tries to balance an appreciation for the indispensable function of natal communities with a capacity for making new communities and for developing multiple identities. It is a term somewhat like "postwar," in that it implies the relevance of a past to defining a particular present, yet it recognizes that something has changed, something is over. From the postethnic point of view, the part of ethnicity that is "over," like the war in "postwar," is the old idea that descent is destiny, that regardless of an individual's wishes he or she is essentially defined by the group into which he or she was born. That old idea is classically "ethnic," rather than postethnic. The part of ethnicity that is not over, from a postethnic point of view, is whatever in that ethnic heritage individuals choose to affirm and develop.

The key postethnic principle is affiliation by revocable consent, meaning that individuals ought to be free to devote as much—or as little—of their time and energy as they wish to their community of descent. Classical ethnic conservatives like Kallen used to say, "you can't change your grandparents," as if this was a knock-down argument against ethnoracial liberals. But the postethnic response is that the meaning of one's grandparents is not given, but is contested and negotiable. You may not be able to change your grandparents, but you need not become cultural clones of them. Politically, a postethnic perspective actively encourages strategic enclaving; what it opposes is the assumption that people are deeply obligated in the nature of things to make common cause with others of the same skin color, morphological traits, and kinships system. Postethnicity considered as an ideal is a choice-maximizing ideal, an ideal that encourages cultural and political dynamics responsive to individual perceptions and ambitions. Postethnicity considered as a condition is the experience of being able to really choose.

Hence the value of terms like "postethnic" and "post-Jewish" and "postcolonial" and "postwar" is that they convey an honest recognition of the limited character of the change that is being addressed, that is, the war still does a lot to define the postwar period of American history, colonialism defines a great deal of what we mean by postcolonial, and ethnicity defines a lot of what we mean by postethnic. It is a way of speaking that appeals to people who are looking for ways to recognize a particular past without being captured by it.

The growing appeal today of the concept of "post-Jewish" invites reflection on how markedly the conversation about Jewishness has changed in the last half-century. In an extensively documented article in a recent issue of *Jewish Social Studies*, Susan Glenn reminds us that the concept of "Jewish self-hatred" was omnipresent in late 1940s and throughout the 1950s and much of the 1960s with reference to Jewish engagements with non-Jewish society and culture. In that milieu, authenticity and psychological health consisted in living Jewishness to the fullest as defined by the self-appointed guardians of tradition, while inauthenticity and pathology began with the subsuming of Jewish issues under human rights concerns and other more universalist frames of reference.[34]

The magazine *Commentary*, which in the 1950s was such an important outlet for the writings of "The New York Intellectuals," was routinely attacked as a hotbed of self-hating Jews. In Glenn's summary, these New York writers, such as Harold Rosenberg and Clement Greenberg, "openly expressed uncertainty about the meaning of their own Jewish identities, demanded individual rather than collective definitions of Jewishness, and advocated individual rather than group solutions to the various states of ambivalence and identity confusion." For this, and for suggesting, as Lionel Trilling sometimes did, that Jewish life was by definition parochial and provincial, the *Commentary* crowd was said to be "self-hating." And of course nothing marked Jewish self-hatred more strikingly than marrying outside the Jewish community, which was on the increase from the mid-1950s onward.[35]

Glenn finds that the most vociferous and eloquent contemporary critic of these uses of the concept of "Jewish self-hatred" was the great sociologist David Riesman. In a series of essays of the early 1950s, Riesman attacked what he called Jewish chauvinism, and denounced the label "self-hating Jew" as an unattractive form of policing, of keeping Jews from exploring the larger world. It was sort of like calling a

New Dealer a communist, a form of red-baiting. Glenn also reviews the controversies of the early and mid-1960s surrounding the work of Hannah Arendt and Philip Roth, and concludes that by the middle of the 1970s the discourse of Jewish self-hatred had played itself out.[36] No doubt she is correct, but I remember vividly than as late as 1975, when I published an article titled "Ethnic Diversity, Cosmopolitanism, and the Emergence of the American Liberal Intelligentsia," which tried to establish the historic function of what Isaac Deutcher called "non-Jewish Jews" in twentieth-century American history, a number of people told me that the people I was writing about—Trilling, Alfred Kazin, Greenberg, Riesman, Franz Boas, Morris Cohen, and so on—were self-hating Jews, and they did not understand why my article did not make this obvious point.[37]

In looking again recently some of Riesman's essays from *Individualism Reconsidered*, his great book of 1954, perhaps a more profound mediation on the United States than his more famous book, *The Lonely Crowd*, I was wondering what Riesman would make of the concept of post-Jewishness, and whether the term, as we use it today, might even be applied to him? Could Riesman himself be credibly called "post-Jewish?" Could Harold Rosenberg? Clement Greenberg? Indeed, how many of the so-called self-hating Jews of the 1940s and 1950s might today be welcomed in a more relaxed discourse as post-Jewish?

Closer to home, I wish I would have had an opportunity to ask my late colleague, Amos Funkenstein, what he would make of the post-Jewish concept. I speculate about this because Funkenstein, who considered himself a secular humanist religiously even while strongly identifying himself as a Jew, wrote with great penetration about Jewish history and about the dynamics of Jewish identity. In one of the last essays he published before his death, Funkenstein argued forcefully in favor of styles of Jewishness that openly and proudly defined themselves, generation after generation, in dialectical relation with non-Jewish experiences. He criticized as a romantic conceit the quest for "what is original and therefore autochthonous in Jewish culture, as against what is borrowed, assimilated, and alien." Historically, my colleague insisted, "even the self-assertion of Jewish culture as distinct and different is [inevitably] articulated in the language of the surrounding culture." There is no primordial Jewish identity to be threatened by the acids of modernity, Funkenstein declared; the very conception of Jewishness as primordial rather than historically contingent is an example of borrowing, in this case from Herder and other German romantics.[38] I cannot speak for Funkenstein, but his final writings, and some conversations I had with him shortly before his death, enable me to hope that he would welcome the concept of post-Jewishness as now being developed.

Since both the post-Jewish concept and the notion of dispersionist scholarship seem to unnerve some people, I want to invoke, as heuristics, post-Protestantism and what might be called communalist and dispersionist approaches to the study of Protestantism in the history of the United States. Central here are people whose lives were significantly formed by Protestant conditions but who have drifted away from, or even renounced, Protestantism. The secular and quasi-secular legacies of Protestant cultural conditioning provide us with yet another window on the ways in which a natal community influences individuals long after they have drifted away from, or even renounced, that natal community.

The vast sanctuaries built by the Methodists and Presbyterians and Congregationalists in the center of almost all American cities and towns are rarely full, and many have been sold to other organizations, often Pentecostals. But the millions and millions of people and their children who left those huge downtown churches did not just disappear. The much-debated decline of numbers in the old, mainline Protestant denominations does not mean that the cultural influence mainstream Protestantism has evaporated. The domains in which that influence is visible can be called post-Protestant.

A widely understood artifact of post-Protestantism is the career of John Dewey, whose gradual movement from Congregationalism to atheism is a prominent theme in studies of Dewey. Books by Bruce Kuklick and Neil Coughlin addressing Dewey's career might well be described as dispersionist studies of Congregationalism.[39] William James is often seen as more religious than Dewey, but when James wrote his greatest book about religion, *The Varieties of Religious Experience*, he was able to affirm his belief in not a single Protestant doctrine even as he was celebrated for having saved religion from science. James is a good candidate for the archetypal post-Protestant.[40] Yet another relevant case is Elizabeth Cady Stanton, a resolute freethinker who so scandalized Gilded Age and Progressive Era women's rights activists by attacking parts of the Bible for their sexism that she was essentially dumped for the more conventional Susan B. Anthony. Yet Stanton spoke casually of "our Protestant idea of individualism," and otherwise comfortably embraced a Protestant heritage while renouncing most of its preachers and theologians.[41] We have countless studies of the legacy of Puritanism for secular America, for which the title of Sacvan Bercovitch's *Puritan Origins of the American Self* can stand as an emblem.[42] Very recently, discoveries in the early writings of John Rawls enable us see the deeply Protestant foundations of *A Theory of Justice* and other major works of the late twentieth century's most accomplished and influential ethical theorist.[43] Many historically informed readers of the work of the atheist philosopher Richard Rorty have found echoes of his grandfather, the great social gospel theologian Walter Rauschenbusch; Rorty, too, might be counted as post-Protestant.[44]

Among historians who have worked on the history of Protestantism in the United States, one can distinguish between communalists and dispersionists. Prominent communalists would include Mark Noll, George Marsden, D. G. Hart, Richard Bushman, Grant Wacker, and Harry Stout, all of whom study the institutions and ideologies of professing Protestants with special attention to the adhesives that make for the preservation of Protestant communities.[45] By contrast, we might call by the name of dispersionists Richard Fox, Lisa McGirr, Laurence Moore, Bruce Kuklick, Henry F. May, Sacvan Bercovitch, and me. We are dispersionists for focusing on aspects of American life created and sustained by people with a Protestant background whose measure of commitment to Protestantism is dubious, and sometimes mostly a matter of ancestry.[46] Perhaps it is significant, further, that Noll, Marsden, Hart, Bushman, Wacker, and Stout are all devoted members of the Protestant community, and are avowedly Christian believers, while the dispersionists are less conspicuously so, and several of them—especially Kuklick, Moore, and myself—are quite outspokenly far over on the freethinking end of the spectrum of spiritual orientations.

By way of exploring what a post-Protestant sensibility can look like today, I want to focus on a single, widely acclaimed recent piece of fiction: Marilynne Robinson's 2004 best-selling novel, *Gilead*.[47] This book has developed a huge and enthusiastic constituency among Americans of Protestant background who no longer identify as religious Protestants. I am told that Robinson herself continues to attend church near her home in Iowa City, but what I want to say about *Gilead* follows less from its intentions than from its reception.

This story of a small-town Congregationalist minister and his family in the Midwest of the 1950s has almost nothing in common with the Protestantism that dominates the media today, as personified in televangelists like Senator's McCain's erstwhile ally John Hagee and the political lobby of the religious right. Insofar as the style of liberal Protestantism Robinson's novel appears to espouse is alive today, it is in rapid retreat within American Protestantism and in the American nation. The book is all the more credible because it is so clearly rooted in the 1950s past. Many readers whose understanding of Protestant culture in America has been formed by what they see on television tell me that they simply do not recognize as Protestant the sensibility displayed and analyzed by this novel.

What *Gilead* does for post-Protestants is to display a set of Protestant themes that play very well beyond Protestantism, while criticizing another set of Protestant themes that most post-Protestants are quite happy to leave in the super-Protestant custody of James Dobson and Pat Robertson and Mike Huckabee and the leaders of the National Association of Evangelicals. The protagonist of *Gilead* is an aging minister with a young wife and a son to whom he writes Robinson's novel in the form of a meditation on his own life as a minister and that of his father and grandfather, also ministers. This protagonist is a man of great humility, who while practicing his faith conscientiously is subject to frequent self-doubt. Has he understood his duty correctly? Has he acted upon it wisely? Moreover, his ministry has been carried out in constant dialogue with the Enlightenment. He was a proud, lifelong subscriber to *The Nation*. He kept up with liberal causes. His freethinking brother left the church early on and gave to our hero a copy of Ludwig Feuerbach's *Essence of Christianity*, a slashing critique of Christian orthodoxy. Our hero says near the end of the novel that he never preached a sermon expressing ideas that he did not think could pass muster with his long-estranged, freethinking, Feuerbach-reading brother. And at the very end, when our hero has his final conversation with a young man whom he worries might take up with his young wife when our hero dies, he gives that young man—the son of his closest friend and his own namesake—his personal, dog-eared copy of Feuerbach. Repeatedly in *Gilead*, Robinson warns against varieties of political zealotry that have been justified in the name of religious faith. She provides her hero with a father who spent several years hanging out with the Quakers partly in revolt against our hero's abolitionist grandfather for having participated in John Brown's massacre of slaveholders in Kansas. Throughout *Gilead*, the virtues of decency and humility are advanced, and self-interrogation is the chief mode of operation.

Now, there are many things in the Protestant cultural inventory other than decency, humility, and self-interrogation, and there are many places to find these virtues other than Protestantism, and that's part of the point. *Gilead* functions not as an emblem for an entire Protestant past, but for the part of the Protestant past most appreciated by educated post-Protestants who dislike the kinds of Protestantism they see the most prominently displayed in the early twenty-first century. *Gilead* is very different from another famous book about Protestant preachers, Sinclair Lewis's *Elmer Gantry* of 1927, which could be called anti-Protestant rather than post-Protestant.[48] By the same token, Kevin McDonald today—I am thinking of his book, *The Culture of Critique*—would be an anti-Jewish writer rather than a post-Jewish writer.[49] *Gilead* is for many post-Protestant reviewers and readers a link to a kind of Protestantism they still find appealing if they do not define their own lives by it.

No doubt the parallels between post-Protestantism and post-Jewishness, and between communalist and dispersionist studies of Protestants and Jews, can be pushed too far. Protestantism is a religious rather than an ethnoracial category, yet in this country historically Protestantism has been demographically based largely in people whose ethnic ancestry is British, German, Dutch, and Scandinavian. The very notion of White-Anglo-Saxon-Protestant derives from this association. Unlike Jews, American Protestants do not have in their recent historical memory persecution of the sort that might drive individuals to conceal, renounce, or aggressively retain a Protestant identity—although this is matter of time and degree, as I am reminded when I reflect on the fact that Protestant ancestors of my own were murdered by Catholic terrorists a few centuries ago. Protestantism has been a majority persuasion in the United States, unlike most other communities to whom the prefix "post" is now applied. Rarely is an American of Protestant background portentously instructed that his or her identity is Protestant; the whole dynamic of ascribed identity applies less to white Protestants than to any other population group in the United States. Affiliation by revocable consent applies to Protestants, too, and in vast numbers, and this has always been true, given the voluntary nature of Protestant affiliation in general and of denominational affiliation in particular. You might say that Protestants have always been postethnic in the specific sense that they have long had affiliation by revocable consent and have not had to struggle to get this principle accepted for them. That is why the post-Protestant phenomenon can be a heuristic for thinking about other situations in which the principle of affiliation by revocable consent is gaining more credibility. The more choice that Jews have about just how Jewish they want to be, the more does the historic situation of Jews become like the historic situation of Protestants, and the more relevant to post-Jewish studies do post-Protestant studies become.

I want to conclude these collegial reflections by acknowledging what might be construed as a Jewish source, many steps removed, for my own interest in Jewish history. No, it's not a Jewish ancestor, although there are many Jewish Hollingers in the United States, all of whose ancestors seem to have come to this country from Romania. I am often wrongly assumed to be one of them. My Jewish connection is very different. It has to do with scholarly writings about China.

Earlier, I spoke of myself as interested in Jews because I was interested in the cosmopolitanism so prominent in modern societies, especially the United States. I have studied Jews instrumentally, because I found so many of them in those domains. But I came to my interest in cosmopolitanism to begin with by way of inspiration from Joseph Levenson, an orthodox Jew whose Jewish-preoccupied studies of Chinese history turned out to be the setting in which I decided I wanted to study cosmopolitanism. When I was a graduate student at Berkeley in the 1960s, I read, at the suggestion of graduate students in Chinese history whom I had come to know through the free speech movement and the antiwar movement, all three volumes of *Confucian China and Its Modern Fate* (1965).[50] These friends told me to read it because they knew I was training to be an intellectual historian, and they said I'd find Levenson interesting, methodologically. I certainly did, but beyond Levenson's correctly anticipated methodological value I discovered something entirely different and much more important.

Levenson was interested in the world-historical dynamic of provincialism and cosmopolitanism, and more specifically in the ways historical actors dealt with the threats and opportunities presented by a traditional community's contact with modern formations of larger scale, if not global in scope. This was true of *Confucian China and Its Modern Fate*, but more explicitly in the work he did immediately thereafter, including the posthumously published *Revolution & Cosmopolitanism: The Western Stage and the Chinese Stages* (1971).[51] It was Levenson who first engaged me with the tension between cosmopolitanism and provincialism, and with the questions of identity, peoplehood, and nationality that have dominated my work. Nothing of Levenson's did more to shape me intellectually than an article of 1967 titled "The Province, the Nation, and the World: The Problem of Chinese Identity."[52] This essay helped me formulate for U.S. history the chief questions on which I have worked for forty years. Levenson came at the right time for me. I was ready to go in directions I did not recognize until I saw them in Levenson's work. But Jewishness, I later learned, was essential to Levenson's work.[53]

I learned this from many sinologists, but above all from Levenson's own most distinguished student, Frederic Wakeman, author of many works on Chinese history and a president of the American Historical Association. Wakeman, a gentile like me, was Levenson's successor at Berkeley and later my own colleague there. He taught me that Levenson's deep brooding about the destiny of communal Jewry in the North Atlantic West was at the core of all of his writings about China. A dispersionist studying the modern historiography of China would be obliged to count Levenson's work as an example of Jewish influence. Thus we have a case of my hauling coal a long way to Newcastle: I figured out what I wanted to study in the North Atlantic West by reading an interpretation of Chinese history that was in large part a projection onto China of the story of Jews in the United States and Europe. So it was that I, a son of Idaho raised in a small Anabaptist sect, found my career-defining preoccupations, including a cosmopolitanism commandingly exemplified by Jews, when connections made through a political movement brought me into contact with the work of an orthodox Jew addressing the cultural dynamics of the modernization process through a meditation on Confucian China's encounter with communism.[54] Now, that's dispersion for you.

Notes

This essay began as the keynote address at the Scholars' Conference on American Jewish History, sponsored by the Academic Council of the American Jewish Historical Society and held on the campuses of the University of Southern California and the Hebrew Union College-Jewish Institute of Religion, Los Angeles, June 1, 2008, and was developed further as the Stanley and Sandra Kutler Lectures at the University of Wisconsin during early 2009. For discussions during the past several years of the issues addressed here I wish to thank a number of colleagues, friends, and family, especially Carol J. Clover, Mark Galanter, Susan Glenn, Joan Heifetz Hollinger, Daniel Horowitz, Thomas W. Laqueur, Herbert Lewis, Deborah Dash Moore, Ruth Rosen, Yuri Slezkine, and David Sorkin.

1. Kevin M. Shultz, "Religion as Identity in Postwar America: The Last Serious Attempt to Put a Question on Religion in the United States Census," *Journal of American History* 93 (Sep. 2006): 359–84.

2. Samuel Walker, *In Defense of American Liberties: A History of the ACLU* (New York: Oxford University Press, 1990), 220.

3. Schultz, "Religion as Identity."

4. Hasia Diner and Tony Michels, "Considering American Jewish History," *OAH Newsletter* 35 (Nov. 2007): 9, 18.

5. Yuri Slezkine, *The Jewish Century* (Princeton: Princeton University Press, 2004); Slezkine, "The USSR as Communal Apartment, or How a Socialist State Promoted Ethnic Particularism," *Slavic Review* 53 (Summer 1994): 415–52.

6. *Morris R. Cohen and the Scientific Ideal* (Cambridge, MA: MIT Press, 1975).

7. This essay appears as chapter 2 of my *Science, Jews, and Secular Culture: Studies in Mid-Twentieth Century American Intellectual History* (Princeton: Princeton University Press, 1996).

8. Hasia R. Diner, *The Jews of the United States, 1654–2000* (Berkeley: University of California Press, 2004), 351.

9. Ibid., 350.

10. Ruth Rosen, *World Split Open: How the Modern Women's Movement Changed America* (New York: Viking, 2000). Rosen does emphasize (for example, on page 265) the secular character of modern feminism, a crucial point often ignored in today's rush to give credit to religion as an inspiration for progressive movements in American history. Rosen now generously acknowledges that her book is weakened by not addressing and trying to interpret the overwhelmingly Jewish leadership of modern feminism. She has observed (in an e-mail to me, May 22, 2009) that these Jewish women "embraced the secular universalism of social justice causes and felt uncomfortable with the parochialism of Jewish communal life." Unlike the Protestant women who had joined the civil rights movement in the context of their church experiences, "most of the feminist leadership came to the movement with a sense of social justice that may have come from their Jewish culture, but not from their religious experiences." These feminists of Jewish ancestry "were proud to be Jews, but they were outraged to see anyone— blacks or themselves—treated as less than equals in American society," and they are best seen as continuing a tradition of Jewish radicalism in labor unions and

elsewhere: "Look back at the struggles by young textile workers in the early years of the 20th century and once again, you see Jewish women leading the fight for collective organizing," and "even further back and you see Jewish women in the Pale of Settlement engaged in marketing and commercial life." Rosen summarizes that "Jewish women had a history of being actors in public life, as opposed to women of Italian or Slavic descent," and "they brought their experience and knowledge of political and public participation with them as immigrants."

11. Alice Echols, *Daring to Be Bad: Radical Feminism in America, 1967–1975* (Minneapolis: University of Minnesota Press, 1989); Cynthia Harrison, *On Account of Sex: The Politics of Women's Issues, 1945–1968* (Berkeley: University of California Press, 1988); Joanne Meyerowitz, ed., *Not June Cleaver: Women and Gender in Postwar America, 1945–1960* (Philadelphia: Temple University Press, 1994); Wini Breines, *Young, White, and Miserable: Growing Up Female in the Fifties* (Boston: Beacon Press, 1992); Richard Flacks, *Making History: The American Left and the American Mind* (New York: Columbia University Press, 1988); Eugenia Kaledin, *Mothers and More: American Women in the 1950s* (Boston: Twayne Publishers, 1984); Nancy Woloch, *Women and the American Experience* (New York: Mcgraw-Hill, 1996); Sara M. Evans, *Born for Liberty: A History of Women in America* (New York: Free Press, 1989); Elaine Tyler May, *Homeward Bound: American Families in the Cold War Era* (New York: Basic Books, 1988).

12. Daniel Horowitz, *Betty Friedan and the Making of "The Feminine Mystique": The American Left, the Cold War, and Modern Feminism* (Amherst, MA: University of Massachusetts Press, 2000). See also Joyce Antler, *The Journey Home: How Jewish Women Shaped America* (New York: Free Press, 1997).

13. David L. Chappell, *A Stone of Hope: Prophetic Religion and the Death of Jim Crow* (Chapel Hill: University of North Carolina Press, 2004).

14. A prominent representative of this discussion is E. J. Dionne Jr., *Souled Out: Reclaiming Faith and Politics after the Religious Right* (Princeton: Princeton University Press, 2008).

15. Sara M. Evans, *Personal Politics: The Roots of Women's Liberation in the Civil Rights Movement and the New Left* (New York: Knopf, 1979).

16. Doug McAdam, personal conversation, July 12, 2008. McAdam's influential study on the 1964 volunteers is *Freedom Summer* (New York: Oxford University Press, 1988).

17. Walker Percy, *Signposts in a Strange Land* (New York: Farrar, Straus, Giroux, 1991), 330.

18. Andrew R. Heinze, *Jews and the American Soul: Human Nature in the 20th Century* (Princeton: Princeton University Press, 2004).

19. Eric L. Goldstein, *The Price of Whiteness: Jews, Race, and American Identity* (Princeton: Princeton University Press, 2006); Tony Michels, *A Fire in Their Hearts: Yiddish Socialists in New York* (Cambridge, MA: Harvard University Press, 2005); Joshua Zeitz, *White Ethnic New York: Jews, Catholics, and the Shaping of Postwar Politics* (Chapel Hill: University of North Carolina Press, 2007).

20. Neal Gabler, *An Empire of Their Own: How the Jews Invented Hollywood* (New York: Crown Publishers, 1988).

21. John Connelly, "Catholic Racism and Its Opponents," *Journal of Modern History* 79 (Dec. 2007): 813–47.

22. Slezkine, *Jewish Century.*

23. Ibid., vii.

24. In this paragraph and in several others, I draw upon my earlier essay, "Rich, Powerful, and Smart: Jewish Overrepresentation Should Be Explained Instead of Avoided or Mystified," originally published in *Jewish Quarterly Review* 94 (Fall 2004): 595–602, and reprinted in my *Cosmopolitanism and Solidarity: Studies in Ethnoracial, Religious, and Professional Affiliation in the United States* (Madison: University of Wisconsin Press, 2006), 154–65. For a recent and convincing discussion of the genes versus environment issue in the study of Jewish intelligence, fully consistent with the arguments that Slezkine and I have been making, see Richard E. Nisbett, *Intelligence and How to Get It* (New York: W. W. Norton, 2009).

25. Sheila Fitzpatrick's review in the *London Review of Books,* for example, can be contrasted in its worldview and scholarly orientation with Steven Zipperstein's negative review in the *American Historical Review.* See Fitzpatrick, *London Review of Books,* Mar. 17, 2005, 3–5; and Zipperstein, *American Historical Review* 112 (Apr. 2007): 463–65.

26. The cultural pluralist discourse of the 1940s is well represented by Alain Locke and Bernard J. Stern, eds., *When Peoples Meet: A Study in Race and Cultural Contacts* (New York: Harper, 1942; rev. ed., 1946), in which Jews are frequently mentioned. For a cogent summary of Locke's own views, see Margaret Just Butcher, ed., *The Negro in American Culture: Based on Materials Left by Alain Locke* (New York: Mentor, 1956), 221. The redoubtable pluralist Louis Adamic addressed the Jewish case frequently, including in what is perhaps his most famous book, *From Many Lands* (New York: Harper, 1940). Milton Gordon's classic, *Assimilation in American Life: The Role of Race, Religion, and National Origins* (New York: Oxford University Press, 1954), drew repeatedly and with widespread academic and popular influence on the relation of Jews to his topic. Nathan Glazer's extensive contributions to sociology from the early 1950s onward attended carefully to the place of Jews in American society, but his most famous work in this domain was the major book co-authored with Daniel Moynihan: Glazer and Daniel Moynihan, *Beyond the Melting Pot: The Negroes, Puerto Ricans, Jews, Italians, and Irish of New York City* (Cambridge, MA: Harvard University Press, 1963).

27. Will Herberg, *Protestant-Catholic-Jew: An Essay in Religious Sociology* (Garden City: Doubleday, 1955).

28. *Regents of University of California v. Bakke,* 483 U.S. 265, 311–13 (1978).

29. Regulation 300, *Regulations of the Berkeley Division of the Academic Senate of the University of California,* adopted April 1989.

30. In this paragraph and at several other points in this essay, I draw upon my earlier piece, "Jewish Identity, Assimilation, and Multiculturalism," in *Creating American Jews,* ed. Karen Mittleman (Philadelphia: National Museum of American Jewish History, 1998), 52–59.

31. These ideas I have developed in a number of places, especially in *Postethnic America: Beyond Multiculturalism,* 3rd expanded ed. (New York: Basic Books, 2006); and in "Obama, the Instability of Color Lines, and the Promise of a Post-ethnic Future," *Callaloo* 31 (Fall 2008): 1033–37.

32. Staci Boris, ed., *The New Authentics: Artists of the Post-Jewish Generation* (Chicago: Spertus Press, 2008).

33. Diner, *Jews in the United States*, 358.

34. Susan Glenn, "The Vogue of Jewish Self-Hatred in Post–World War II America," *Jewish Social Studies* n.s. 12 (Spring/Summer 2006): 95–136.

35. Ibid., 109.

36. Ibid., 119.

37. "Ethnic Diversity, Cosmopolitanism, and the Emergence of American Liberal Intelligentsia," *American Quarterly* 27 (May 1975): 131–51.

38. Amos Funkenstein, "The Dialectics of Assimilation," *Jewish Social Studies* n.s. 1 (Winter 1995): 10–11.

39. Bruce Kuklick, *Churchmen and Philosophers: From Edwards to Dewey* (New Haven: Yale University Press 1985); Neil Coughlin, *Young John Dewey* (Chicago: University of Chicago Press, 1973).

40. I have addressed this in chapter 6 in this volume.

41. Elizabeth Cady Stanton, "The Solitude of Self," *The Woman's Column*, Jan. 1882, 2–3, reprinted in *Elizabeth Cady Stanton and Susan B. Anthony: Correspondence, Writings, and Speeches*, ed. Ellen Carol DuBois (New York: Schocken Books, 1981), 246–53; and *The Woman's Bible*, 2 vols. (New York: European Publishing Company, 1895–1898).

42. Sacvan Bercovitch, *The Puritan Origins of the American Self* (New Haven: Yale University Press, 1975).

43. See, for example, Joshua Cohen and Thomas Nagel, "Faith in the Community: A Forgotten 'Senior Thesis' that Signals John Rawls's Future Spiritual Force," *Times Literary Supplement*, Mar. 20, 2009, 12–14.

44. See, for example, Casey Nelson Blake, "Public Life and Public Commitment: From Walter Rauschenbusch to Richard Rorty," in *A Pragmatist's Progress? Richard Rorty and American Intellectual History*, ed. John Pettigrew (New York: Rowman and Littlefield, 2000), 85–101.

45. For an especially successful example of scholarship in this mode, see George Marsden, *Reforming Fundamentalism: Fuller Seminary and the New Evangelicalism* (Grand Rapids, MI: Eerdman's, 1987; 2nd ed., 1995). In some cases, these scholars also study the decline of Protestant hegemony. Marsden, for example, explains how the university as an American institution gradually ceased to be a mechanism for the support of Protestantism. See Marsden, *The Soul of the American University: From Protestant Establishment to Established Nonbelief* (New York: Oxford University Press, 1994).

46. See, for example, Kuklick, *Churchmen and Philosophers*.

47. Marilynne Robinson, *Gilead* (New York: Farrar, Straus and Giroux, 2004).

48. Sinclair Lewis, *Elmer Gantry* (New York: Harcourt, Brace, 1927).

49. Kevin Macdonald, *The Culture of Critique: An Evolutionary Analysis of Jewish Involvement in Twentieth-Century Intellectual and Political Movements* (Westport, CT: Praeger, 1998).

50. Joseph R. Levenson, *Confucian China and Its Modern Fate: A Trilogy* (Berkeley: University of California Press, 1965).

51. Levenson, *Revolution and Cosmopolitanism: The Western Stage and the Chinese Stages* (Berkeley: University of California Press, 1971).

52. Levenson, "The Province, the Nation, the World: The Problem of Chinese Identity," in *Approaches to Modern Chinese History*, ed. Albert Feueurwerker, Rhoades Murphey, and Mary C. Wright (Berkeley, University of California Press, 1967), 268–88.

53. For accounts of Levenson's extraordinary career and for several meditations on its significance, see *The Mozartian Historian*, ed. Maurice Meisner and Rhoades Murphey (Berkeley: University of California Press, 1976).

54. I have told this story about Levenson at greater length in chapter 8 in this volume.

Church People and Others

When I agreed to write for a book made up of answers to the question "Why and how did you become a historian?" my main purpose was to tell the story of how I, as a specialist in modern U.S. history, had been importantly formed by a provocative interpretation of the history of China that I read as a graduate student. This autobiographical fact seemed to me unusual enough to make it worth telling. But as I filled out the piece, trying to provide a more comprehensive answer to the question, I realized I could not do so honestly without discussing the intensely Protestant atmosphere in which I had grown up. Hence this essay can now serve as an account of Where I Was From, *to adopt the past tense employed purposively by Joan Didion in the title of her memoir about her California origins. Didion writes from New York, and thus is no longer a Californian. I write from a secular perspective, and am no longer a Protestant. But Didion's California past defines her in many important ways, and so, too, does my Protestant childhood have much to do with my secular adulthood.*

Since so much of After Cloven Tongues of Fire *is about ecumenical Protestants, and since I grew up as an ecumenical Protestant, I want especially to call attention to the part of this essay that reflects on a methodological and ethical concern that I picked up from my youthful encounter with the work of the sinologist Joseph R. Levenson. If all historians are inevitably the creatures of their own time and place, yet obliged to see and analyze aspects of the past that are more than mirrors of one's self, how does one guard against projecting too much of oneself onto the screen of the past? My colleagues who worked in the China field explained to me that Levenson, whose study of Chinese history was formative for me, had projected so much of his own preoccupations onto China that his interpretation of Chinese history, for all its architectural and prose grandeur, was highly idiosyncratic and often simply wrong. This cautionary tale, as I recount here, has stayed with me and is especially on my mind when I write about American Protestantism and about the post-Protestantism of which I am surely now an example. When does a personal frame enable a historian to see historical realities that others might not see, and when does it become, instead, a bias? It is not my place to offer an evaluation of my own case, but I take this opportunity to testify that I have worried about getting this right while writing the essays collected in this volume.*

This essay was originally published in James M. Banner Jr. and John R. Gillis, eds., Becoming Historians *(Chicago, 2009), 101–121.*

WHEN I WAS A CHILD IN IDAHO, I learned that human beings were divided into groups. There were church people, who were good, and not-church people, who were bad. Within the ranks of the church people, there were more refined distinctions. Mormons, Catholics, and Pentecostals went to the wrong churches. Methodists, Presbyterians, Brethren, Mennonites, Lutherans, Quakers, and Congregationalists were prominent among those who went to the right churches. I did not know that it was possible to divide people up into groups on any basis other than what churches they went to, or whether they went to church at all, unless they were Japanese or German. I knew about the Japanese as a separate group because my parents told me how dreadful it was that Americans of Japanese ancestry had been taken from their homes and put into camps during World War II. I assumed this had been done by not-church people, but later found out that it was more complicated. I knew about the Germans because when my mother sent relief packages to her cousins in Germany right after the war I discovered that having German ancestors was an important part of me, and that because of my father's German heritage from a migration much earlier than my mother's, our family was Pennsylvania Dutch even though we did not live anywhere near Pennsylvania and had no ancestors from Holland. Most Germans in Germany were not-church people, my mother explained, and that is why there had been a war, but her cousins most definitely went to a Lutheran church. I did not meet a black person until I moved away from Idaho, and I did not realize that Jews were a contemporary presence, rather than merely a group that flourished in biblical times, until I was in the seventh grade in California and met a boy named Stan Swerdloff who went to church on Saturdays but who was not a Seventh Day Adventist.

I also knew about Indians, and that's how I got started as a historian. Or, more precisely, it was in reading about the Nez Perce Indians after moving away from Idaho that I became interested in becoming a historian. But once I really got going as a historian, some years later, what most engaged me was a tension between cosmopolitan and provincial impulses that assign significance—or deny it—to distinctions between human beings based on race, ethnicity, religion, location, and nationality.

Our family had moved to California by the time I started reading about the Nez Perce, but we often went back to Idaho to visit an aunt and I retained a strong Idaho identity as a teenager. I was fourteen when I first decided I wanted to be a historian, and the decision was marked by the buying of *War Chief Joseph*, by Helen Addison Howard and Dan McGrath. This was the first book I bought with my own money, earned by mowing lawns. I had read a library copy, but loved it so much I was determined to have a copy of my own. When this biography of the great Nez Perce chief arrived in that summer of 1955 by mail-order from the

Caxton Printers in Caldwell, Idaho, I felt a personal connection to the writing of history that I had not felt in reading library books, or even the few history books owned by my parents. The following spring, I had mowed enough lawns to enable me to buy Bruce Catton's three-volume history of the Army of the Potomac.

Why the Nez Perce and the Civil War? I was approaching history through specific local settings that were meaningful to me. The Idaho with which I identified was the land of the Nez Perce Indians, and thus the story of the Nez Perce was "ancient history": the part of the past that came before "we" did—the European-derived settlers who, I was often told, had simply stolen Idaho from the Indians. The American Civil War was also "local" for me because my father had grown up on a farm just north of the Gettysburg battlefield, and the stories he and his siblings told of life in Gettysburg evoked for me a past larger than Idaho's yet equally accessible to me personally.

My father and my aunts and uncles were present in 1913 at the 50th anniversary of the battle. Their recollections of the Confederate and Union veterans I had heard long before I first saw the photograph of the aged Blues and Grays shaking hands in Ken Burns's PBS documentary. At fourteen I thrilled to Catton's account of Gettysburg in *Glory Road,* and even more to "Toward the Dunker Church" in *Mr. Lincoln's Army* —still affecting as I read it again more than fifty years later because there Catton's description of the battle of Antietam centered on a tiny church in which my own great-grandfather may have preached before the war. No ancestor of mine had fought in the Civil War (as German Baptist Brethren, or "Dunkers," and Mennonites, they refused military service on scriptural grounds). But the notion that the two greatest battles of the nation-defining struggle over slavery had taken place partly on ground that the Hollingers had owned or on which they had worshiped gave me a connection to Catton's books akin to that felt by descendants of the soldiers.

My attraction at the age of fourteen to a career as a historian was not quite a desire to celebrate my own ancestors, or even to find fault with them. Chief Joseph and Gettysburg were most important as local points of access to a more general engagement with the ways in which contemporary life had been shaped by previous events. Why this engagement at fourteen, rather than some other?

I fell into history largely because it seemed the most accessible to me of all learned endeavors at a time when I was in the process of deciding that I'd like to be a professor of one kind or another. In a moment, I'll talk about why I was attracted to academia in general. But history was appealing in part because I could pick up widely praised works of history and absorb them with pleasure and understanding. Catton's *Stillness at*

Appomattox was just then being hailed as a masterpiece, although not so much by professionals, I later learned, as by lay audiences and journalists. I was less comfortable with what samplings I managed of other fields, of whose character I understood even less than I understood history. Theology and philosophy, to both of which I felt attracted, were less welcoming, at least as I encountered them. The analytic vocabulary in both cases was too technical for me. And neither of these subjects was taught in junior high school. Science and math were taught, but neither grabbed my attention so firmly as did the fields I later learned to call the humanities and social sciences. English literature I knew only as novels and poems and plays, not as criticism. I was engaged by what was called "social studies," but even the best teachers of that amorphous subject did not put me in contact with sociology, economics, and political science the way an eighth-grade history course seemed to put me in touch with what historians did.

Only geography seemed remotely as accessible as history, but I never heard about individual geographers by name the way I heard about Arnold Toynbee and Will Durant, and, of course, Bruce Catton. I loved *National Geographic,* and in later years defended it against critics unable to forgive its bourgeois ethos and its too-often patronizing view of societies beyond the North Atlantic West. This magazine opened up countless worlds for me, symbolized by the wonderful maps, dozens of which I still own. The journey from the local to the global has to start somewhere, and for many of us growing up in the 1950s *National Geographic* was not a bad starting point. But *National Geographic* did not translate geography into the terms of a vocation, unless it might be that of explorers like Admiral Richard Byrd. I did try to imagine what it would be like to be a writer or editor for that magazine, but the prevailing popular culture and the junior high schools of the day did not encourage me to see geography as a career. They did enable me to see history in that way.

Am I suggesting that I went for history because it appeared to be easy? Yes. History was one learned pursuit that I thought I understood well enough to see myself in it. That was the key. By why was I, at fourteen, so inclined to say "I'd like to become a college professor" whenever I was asked what I wanted to do when I grew up? That was more complicated, psychologically and culturally. I am not certain that I understand it even now. But I do know one thing for sure: a powerful factor was the deep respect both of my parents had for learning itself.

My father had earned his high school diploma at the age of thirty-three, having gone to night school for three years while working forty-hour weeks as a shoe salesman at a Sears store in Chicago. He came there to begin the education he needed to become a minister. He later worked his way through college, too, painting houses, and even through a theological seminary, although by the time I reached adolescence he had left the ministry and was earning a living again as a self-employed house painter. My father, who never put any pressure on me to pursue any particular calling, said little, then or later, about this huge change in his life. Yet as an early teen I was puzzled and privately disturbed by the obvious gap between how he spent every working day and the education he had struggled to attain and of which he remained proud. He remained active in the church, and did some guest preaching. One of my uncles, who also painted houses for a living, had no schooling beyond the eighth grade. Another uncle, who had completed high school, was a school custodian. My mother, who had been a high school home economics teacher before she stopped working outside the home when I was born, was much more direct in encouraging me to read and to stretch myself intellectually. I sensed that she wanted me to make a life in which education would be put to good use. Both of my parents spoke with reverence about great scholars and great universities.

"He's got a PhD," my father used to remark of this or that visiting speaker at church, or, more often, of someone who appeared on the TV shows of Alistair Cooke (*Omnibus*) and Dave Garroway (*Wide Wide World*) that we watched every Sunday afternoon. I absorbed my parents' awe for people with doctorates. I later came to see my parents' respect for learning as part of a secularization process. They inherited a feel for the value of biblical learning, but they had come to believe that all truth was sacred. My parents never gave up the religious faith, away from which I gradually drifted, but I understood even as a teenager that biblical scholarship and other kinds of learning were somehow part of a single intellectual piece. By pursuing learning, I would be carrying on a family tradition of sorts, even though the many preachers in my father's "Pennsylvania Dutch" ancestry had all been farmers with very little schooling. They were "called" to the ministry by their congregational peers in classic Anabaptist fashion, but continued to live as farmers. My father had been part of a generation that sought to modernize the Brethren ministry.

Yet academia was remote. One aunt whom I rarely saw approached it late in life, earning her master's at age fifty-eight. She taught education at Gettysburg College and was the only one of my father's siblings to remain in Pennsylvania and to leave the Brethren (she married a Presbyterian). She contributed to the mystique of elite higher education by repeatedly telling us, during occasional visits to the West Coast, the story of once having seen the great scholar Owen Lattimore standing outside the library at Johns Hopkins. "He was smoking a cigarette during a break from his research," she invariably said, as if the mere sighting of such an important academic in an informal moment was a moving experience.

The closest I came to viewing the academic life during my high school years was meeting some faculty members at our local denominational institution, La Verne College. Those people, whom my parents and I met in church, usually got their PhDs at mid-career. "He's working on his PhD at USC," it was said of one La Verne professor after another. I got the impression that the PhD was an enormous undertaking, achieved fairly late in life, and that to teach at USC, like Frank C. Baxter, the English professor whose local program, *Shakespeare on TV*, I watched every week, was the pinnacle of academic achievement.

Given the apparent difficulties of getting into academia, I needed a path to it that I could reasonably hope to actually travel. History, being uniquely accessible, was that path, and choosing it happened simultaneously with my starting to tell people that I expected to become a "college professor." It is ironic that my idol, Bruce Catton, was not a college professor, did not have a PhD, and dropped out of Oberlin College without even completing his bachelor's. I did not know this at the time, of course, and I associated Catton with all that talk about having a PhD. Moreover, what I thought historians did had little relation to the more realistic conception to which I was later introduced. Indeed, it may be misleading for me to claim that I had decided at the age of fourteen to be a historian. What I eventually became was rather different from the practice exemplified so wonderfully by Bruce Catton.

The latter meant telling stories about the past and making sure that the documentary record supported the stories. This conception stayed with me through my high school years, when I wrote term papers on the Nez Perce. I had no grasp whatsoever of the hermeneutic problem. Like most high school students and most readers of Bruce Catton's books, I assumed a single and permanent historical truth that was there to be discovered. Indeed, had I any inkling of the challenges of historical interpretation as I later faced them, I cannot imagine having started down the historian's path. I suppose I might have eventually gotten there from some other domain, but I was able to hold fast throughout high school to my ambition of becoming a historian because I had very little idea what it really involved. One might say that I became a historian because I did not know what I was doing.

During my senior year in high school teachers encouraged me to consider a career in law or business, but I shied away from both. Our family knew intimately not a single lawyer or businessman. I had the impression that colleges and universities were more rationally stable and ethically sound settings than courtrooms and corporations, less subject to the abuses of charismatic authority. I would not have used this phrase then, but my suspicions of charismatic authority had developed in high school in response to television and film portrayals of lawyers and businessmen, who seemed to get ahead—in terms of money and status—by manipulating people with sheer force of personality. My parents' greatest living hero was the self-effacing missionary doctor Albert Schweitzer, and they were never comfortable with profit-making, rather than merely life-sustaining endeavors.

My concern about charismatic authority was accentuated by discussions of religion with other high school students. Many of the latter were evangelical Protestants, deferring to an emotional preaching style violently at odds with the plainer style of the Brethren and Mennonite tradition. The families of these young people generally took Billy Graham as their hero, and I remember being shocked that youths who went to church every Sunday, and were good at quoting scripture, had never heard of Schweitzer. My mother had been raised in the Church of the Nazarene, and had fled that denomination's florid altar calls to join the more reserved Brethren. She warned me against the revivalist sensibilities of some of my high school friends. Although I was not considering the ministry as a vocation, my contacts with Southern Baptists moved me further from anything associated with charisma and the playing on the emotions of one's fellows. Hence I finished high school with a renewed resolve to become a professor of history, a job I associated with reason, fair-mindedness, and lack of avarice. It was a secular vocation of which church people of my kind could approve.

College changed my understanding of what it meant to be a historian, but not much. As a history major at La Verne College, which I entered in 1959, I found the study of facts comforting. I was good at memorizing details, and did much better on multiple-choice tests than on the essay examinations which required a facility for abstraction and a capacity to mobilize facts in support of an argument. Nevertheless, while at La Verne I did encounter two understandings of what historians did that were, for me, "post-Catton." Both sustained my vocational choice while expanding my horizons, yet continued to protect me, so to speak, from what I would encounter in graduate school. One of these understandings was embodied in the work of Arnold Toynbee. The other was the Amherst Pamphlets.

I actually read only snippets of Toynbee's prodigious *A Study of History*, but at La Verne I often heard it said that Toynbee addressed the *meaning* of history. *All* history. Toynbee generalized; he had a "theory" of history. He had apparently discovered the dynamics by which entire civilizations rose and fell on the basis of the same kind of detailed evidence that Catton used to explain General Grant's military success in Virginia. I had been accustomed to thinking of the historian's calling as a modest and manageable one, but Toynbee, or I should say the image of Toynbee, made me wonder if history might be a successor-subject to theology and philosophy. I had yet to hear of Vico, nor did I have a sense of the claims that the ostensibly particularizing study of history might make on the domains of the generalizing social sciences. The buzz about Toynbee gave me a hint of a grander dimension of historical study. I was intimidated by this, and also attracted to it. Perhaps the path I had chosen at fourteen had more possibilities than I supposed? Above all, what I heard said about Toynbee got me brooding about "meaning." Catton had implied something of what the Civil War "meant," but he never said it explicitly; rather Catton left me with the impression that the meaning of events was transparent in their accurate description.

This impression was challenged more directly by the Amherst Pamphlets. Popular with the history professors at La Verne, these practical, 100-page, double-columned paperback anthologies of prominent scholarly writings on major questions introduced me to the idea that responsible scholars could offer conflicting interpretations of historical events. The basic character of episodes like the American Revolution and Jacksonian Democracy could be contested. Properly called "Problems in American Civilization," these pamphlets were known popularly by the name of Amherst College because its American Studies faculty designed them for the D. C. Heath publishing company.

The Amherst Pamphlets encouraged students to evaluate conflicting interpretations, usually presented in the form of two easily summarized alternatives. *The New Deal: Revolution or Evolution?* is the title of one of those I still own. The mood was put in the introduction to another I have kept on my shelves all these years, *Reconstruction in the South*. "The reader will have to determine," declared Edwin C. Rozwenc, "whether the Reconstruction of the South must be judged to have been primarily 'a blackout of honest government' resulting from political rule by ignorant Negroes and villainous white carpetbaggers and scalawags, or whether the story of Reconstruction should be written in terms of 'quietly constructive' political and social achievements." Reexamining this pamphlet now, what I find most striking is not the antiquated construction of the issues and the heavy tilt toward what we now recognize as a deeply racist interpretation of Reconstruction. (Rozwenc described the excerpt from W.E.B. Du Bois as written with "racial feeling" but said nothing of the sort about the several white supremacist writers he anthologized, including Woodrow Wilson.) Rather, what hits me now is that there were two sides—and only two—to every story, or at least to most of the stories historians tell. This made it easier to deal with conflicting interpretations: historians debated questions in straightforward terms, and, like a courtroom jury, decided them either one way, or the other. That simplified the matter of "meaning": an event meant one thing, or it meant another.

One nonacademic experience at La Verne affected my later choices as a historian. During the fall of 1960 while driving through Oklahoma with seven other La Verne students, one of whom was black, I saw with my own eyes racial segregation in public accommodations. Our group was returning from a national meeting of Brethren youth leaders in Ohio. Our Volkswagen microbus broke down on Highway 66 near the town of Vinita, Oklahoma, where, while the vehicle was being repaired, we found we could not eat or sleep in the same facility. We were not "freedom riders." We had neither the political sophistication nor the personal courage to undertake such a project. We were simply Californians caught by surprise. During the two or three days it took to repair the vehicle we could sleep and eat together only in the homes of members of the nearest Church of the Brethren, in Bartlesville. One of our hosts, a beautiful young mother of two children in whose home I stayed, explained to me with great patience that we young Californians would approve of segregation if we lived in the South and saw "how the Negroes actually live, you know, the dirt and all." Eventually, having been immersed in a racially segregated society for several days, we resumed our journey on Highway 66 back to La Verne. On the way, we tried a pancake house in Amarillo, Texas, but were again turned away.

The experience of segregation marked all of us in ways that did not always register immediately. One of the travelers, my closest friend at La Verne, transferred the very next year to historically black Howard University, partly because he wanted to engage the parts of the world we encountered in the South. I did not see him again for another forty years, but at our reunion he and I immediately began talking about that incident and the ways in which it had changed each of us. We both remembered seeing our fellow student weeping disconsolately, and were glad we cannot remember what we said to her, because neither of us could imagine that it was up to the occasion. That so tame an incident could mark us white students so vividly is no doubt a sign of how insulated we were from major features of the society in which we lived. But my own engagement with the history of the black-white color line dates from that experience.

I felt increasingly isolated at La Verne during my four years there. My three closest friends—two others, in addition to the one Howard-bound—left after the sophomore year for other colleges. Almost none of the remaining students shared my academic ambitions. I spent more and more time in the library exploring what my friends regarded as obscure periodicals. I was befriended there by the campus's handful of foreign students, some of whom saw me reading *The Manchester Guardian Weekly* and were pleased to learn that I cared about what was going on in Africa and India. I regularly read essays and reviews in *Partisan Review* and

Hudson Review. As editor of the campus newspaper, I imitated the *Hudson*'s enthusiastic reviews of foreign films. These movies I saw in the neighboring town of Claremont, site of a number of colleges, including Pomona College, that were much closer to the academic mainstream than La Verne. To Claremont's Village Theater I took several uncomprehending dates. "What was that about," the girl would ask about *Virgin Spring,* or *L'Avventura,* or *La Dolce Vita.* Not that I was so wise about Bergman, Antonioni, and Fellini. I just wished that others I knew were as engaged by their movies as I was.

My difficulty in finding college friends, male or female, who were interested in the same issues I was renewed my determination to go forward in academia. I appreciated the personal qualities of many people I got to know at La Verne, but I was looking for a different kind of intellectual community. I felt I belonged somewhere else, but I was not sure where. History was the strongest undergraduate major at La Verne, reinforcing my vocational choice. I joined the American Historical Association and what was then the Mississippi Valley Historical Association (later the Organization of American Historians). Professional journals, along with the *Hudson Review,* which I liked so much I actually became a paid subscriber to it, now came directly to my dormitory room. My friends were amused, but they put up with my peculiarities. They knew I was headed for someplace really different from La Verne, and they wished me well.

That someplace turned out to be Berkeley. Shortly after arriving in the fall of 1963, I was immersed in a practice built around the making of arguments. That historians were mostly in the business of making arguments was implicit in some of my previous experience, especially through the Amherst Pamphlets, but I had not fully absorbed it. The other graduate students, in and out of class, talked about assessing so-and-so's argument about this or that, or about how they were making this or that argument in a paper they were writing. Most people who become historians probably get that from the start, and thus know what they are doing when they decide to go into history. It was more like being a lawyer than I had realized. For me the insight, however elementary, came late, and I could quickly see that nearly all of the other graduate students I came to know that first year were a lot better at making arguments than I was.

I decided to specialize in colonial American diplomatic and constitutional history because in those fields, it seemed to me, arguments were easier to make without having to know much about social theory and other modern discourses of which I was so much more ignorant than were the other students. Wrong again. Even in those ostensibly less theoretically entangled subfields, I was out of my depth. My first research paper, based on a reading of the *Archives of Maryland* from 1634 to 1670, was close to a disaster. I studied all the documents and reported what seemed to be their most important content, but could not figure out what they meant, except in the most literal of terms. What was my argument? What assumptions about human behavior enabled one to explain the actions of magistrates? The instructor, Winthrop D. Jordan, then teaching his first graduate seminar at Berkeley, was terribly generous, but also made abundantly clear in both written and oral comments that I did not know what I was doing.

Finding my way as a historian that first year at Berkeley was made more difficult by the distractions of culture shock. The transition from La Verne to Berkeley was not easy for me. In making friends with other graduate students, I soon learned to shut up about my own background because the graduates of Columbia and Harvard were stunned when I told the truth, and implied that I was from a distant and exotic country. One emblem for the culture gap was the practice of moderate social drinking, which was altogether new to me. La Verne banned the consumption of alcohol out of deference to the Brethren tradition (I Corinthians 6:19, to the effect that the body is the temple of the holy spirit, which was understood to ban smoking, too). Before arriving at Berkeley I had never been at a social event, even a dinner in a private home, at which wine was served. I had never met an atheist or a communist, and had met so few Jews that I had trouble distinguishing them from persons of Italian extraction.

Toward the end of that year a graduate student from New York rather awkwardly asked me (this was while drinking coffee in the Mediterranean Café on Telegraph Avenue, then a favorite hangout for humanities graduate students), "If you don't mind a personal question, I'd like to know what it feels like for someone like you to be a member of a minority group." I had no idea what he was talking about. Then he, incredulous, explained that he knew me to be an Anglo-Saxon Protestant, and that most of the graduate students in our circle were Jewish. I had not yet learned how to read the signs, nor to assign to them the socially prescribed significance.

Yet amid these striking novelties, that first year at Berkeley was as thrilling for me as it was unsettling. I met people who really did share my intellectual interests. I felt I was in the right place, however challenging and numerous were the changes I had to make in myself in order to function in that new environment. Many of my new acquaintances from New York and New England and San Francisco were humane and responsive as well as intellectually acute. Some others, however, made me feel like a hick. I can see why meeting someone like me tested whatever generosity of spirit they possessed: I *was* a hick by their standards! At the time I was too willing to accept their standards and to take their superciliousness as something I deserved. It took me too many years to realize that most of the people who treated me as a hick had their own problems to deal with—hidden from me by their superior social skills—the working out of which entailed being condescending toward me.

The following year was easier for me personally, and was enlivened by the career-transforming experience of reading the works of Perry Miller. Here was a really different kind of history: intellectual history, and directed at the history of theological and philosophical ideas, yet it was more rigorously argumentative than what I had been reading in diplomatic and constitutional history, to say nothing of Bruce Catton, or even most of what appeared in the Amherst Pamphlets. It was also literary in the finest sense: Miller was a compelling and even commanding writer, and by then I had realized that very few works by professional historians of the United States reached the prose standard attained by the better works in European and Asian history. Had I read Miller earlier, I probably would not have been prepared to appreciate his work. But I encountered Miller at just the right time. More than a year of professional immersion had prepared me to understand and appreciate something so very different from what I had previously understood history to be. Intellectual interests of my own that I had not yet found a way to explore suddenly came into play. It was a bracing, integrating experience. The immediate setting was the graduate seminar on colonial America taught by another then-junior professor, Robert L. Middlekauff. He assigned not only both volumes of *The New England Mind*, but also *Jonathan Edwards* and several of the essays in *Errand into the Wilderness*. Week after week of that fall of 1964, I alternated between Puritan theology and the free speech movement. Both proved to be exciting.

I invoke the free speech movement in relation to becoming a historian because at that time, generated by issues in free expression closely connected to the civil rights movement and by quarrels over the role of universities in society, it invigorated interaction among Berkeley graduate students. I was quickly absorbed into a larger, more interactive community. Conversations about contemporary political affairs and about whatever we were reading in our classes or were teaching to undergraduates as teaching assistants somehow got connected in one long, informal seminar that lasted all day and well into many nights. My social integration into a community of intellectually ambitious and politically engaged graduate students meant that I was no longer "bowling alone," to pick up on Robert Putnam's popular figure of speech. I found every aspect of life lived to a higher degree of intensity just as Putnam argues that interactive behavior in one domain can promote it in other domains as well. Discussions about the professional merged with conversations about the political. Yet lines could be drawn. Middlekauff's sympathy for the free speech movement was undisguised, but my friends and I admired his professionalism and when we went to his classroom in Haviland Hall, we knew we were there to talk about Puritanism, and we did. The moral intensity of the free speech movement and of the seventeenth-century Puritans and of Miller himself all spun into one another, without getting in each other's way.

Miller's *The New England Mind* did more than any other work to reveal to me the promise of intellectual history as a specific kind of scholarship. The essays collected in his *Errand into the Wilderness* did more than any other writings to provide me with a sense of what it meant to write an analytic essay on a historical question. Richard Hofstadter performed the latter service for most historians of my generation who were attracted to the analytical essay as a genre, but despite my respect for Hofstadter's work, especially his *American Political Tradition*, I found Miller to be a more ambitious writer and more capable of achieving empathic identification with historical actors different from oneself. Miller, an atheist, showed great appreciation for the hold of religious ideas on previous generations, while Hofstadter seemed less able to get out of his own generational and ethnoreligious skin. Once I focused on writing analytic essays, I found the form more challenging and satisfying than the sort of narrative history Catton had led me to emulate. I never lost my appreciation for good narrative history, but part of Miller's impact on me was to convert me to the analytic essay as my favored genre. To this day, most of what I write takes that form. Finally, I knew what I was doing methodologically, at least as judged from the perspective of the historian I eventually became.

Figuring out what I was doing substantively, rather that methodologically, came about through reading scholarly books and essays about China. This may seem odd, since I as a specialist in U.S. history have never worked in the field of Chinese history, never even took a course in it, and cannot read a word of Chinese. Graduate students in Asian history, whom I probably would not have gotten to know without the cross-field connections created by the free speech movement (and its successor, the antiwar movement), often talked about one of their professors, the esteemed sinologist Joseph R. Levenson. "If you are going to be an intellectual historian, you've got to read Levenson," they would say.

Immediately after passing my U.S. history orals in the spring of 1966 I read all three volumes of *Confucian China and Its Modern Fate*. I was captivated by the vast scope of the enterprise, and, subversive as this may be of an authentically sinological focus, I was captivated even more by Levenson's use of Western European categories to interpret Chinese history. He was constantly citing European and American philosophers and writers, and representing aspects of the Chinese past in their terms. I was enthralled by his conclusion to volume three that the Confucian bureaucracy's aestheticism and antispecialized amateur ideal had rendered China incapable of defending its culture against the scientific-rationalist-specialized energies of the West: Confucianists never "had to fight Jonathan Swift's battle of the books, for the ancient against the modern," because "when the issue arose in China it was post-Confucian, forced in China because it had come to the test in Europe first, and Swift had lost."

I was also attracted to Levenson's combination of abstraction (he meditated on the difference between "*historical* significance" and "historical *significance*") and playfulness. He was not afraid to have fun, even if some readers suspected that levity took precedent over *Wissenschaft*. He loved language, as Miller did, but Levenson let himself go in ways that the more austere Miller did not. At the end of his imposing trilogy, having written a conclusion to his third volume, he added, characteristically, this note to the reader: "Having concluded roundly, let us conclude squarely with a concluding conclusion." He then brought all three volumes to a close. Levenson wrote "musically," it was often said. No wonder a book of essays dedicated to his memory was titled *The Mozartian Historian*. Levenson's books, chapters, pages, and paragraphs were all subject to a certain architectural design. I could understand readily why some China specialists found Levenson's approach insufficiently empirical, but I was reading these volumes less for their truth-value than for their conceptualization and style. Beyond all that, however, I discovered something else in Levenson that was altogether unexpected and that proved to be much more important.

Levenson was interested in the world-historical dynamic of provincialism and cosmopolitanism, and more specifically in the ways historical actors dealt with the threats and opportunities presented by a traditional community's contact with modern formations of larger scale, if not global in scope. This was true of *Confucian China and Its Modern Fate*, but more explicitly in the work he did immediately thereafter, including the posthumously published *Revolution and Cosmopolitanism: The Western Stage and the Chinese Stages*. It was Levenson who first engaged me with the tension between cosmopolitanism and provincialism, and with the questions of identity, peoplehood, and nationality that have dominated my work. It was also Levenson's obvious projection onto China of some of the dilemmas of Jewish identity in the West that propelled some of my investigations of the history of Jewish intellectuals in the United States. Nothing of Levenson's did more to shape me intellectually than an article of 1967 titled "The Province, the Nation, and the World: The Problem of Chinese Identity." This essay helped me formulate for U.S. history the chief questions on which I have worked for more than forty years.

Ostensibly about China, this remarkable essay is, like so much of what Levenson wrote, a meditation on the effect of the modernization process on localities in Europe and the United States as well as China. Laced with references to Trotsky, Freud, Emerson, Blake, Levi-Strauss, Alan Tate, Henry James, Marx, Hume, Dickens, Lawrence, Proust, Ortega y Gasset, Yeats, Michelet, and a variety of Chinese thinkers of whom I had never heard, this essay amounted to a magnet drawn through the canon of world literature and philosophy charged with picking up bits of discursive metal defined by provincialism or cosmopolitanism. For me, it was a de facto anthology of shorthand references to aspects of history about which I wanted to learn more. "Yeats, like Tagore with his cosmopolitan culture," runs a typical sentence, "was as far from a lost Bengal or Connemara as any faceless victim of standardized mass society." Someone with a better education than I had might have been less dazzled by Levenson's learning. But as with Miller, Levenson came at the right time for me. I was ready to go in directions I did not recognize until I saw them in Levenson's work.

Why was I so engaged with the tension between provincialism and cosmopolitanism? No doubt being from Idaho and the Brethren, surrounded with Ivy League graduates and others from backgrounds very different from my own, usually more broadly educated, had something to do with it. I understood what it meant to be provincial. Nobody else I knew in graduate school had grown up with the view of human groups I summarized at the start of this essay. I also understood—without, I hope, judging provincials, in Idaho and elsewhere, too ungenerously for being what history had made of them—what it meant to try for a more capacious life, one that embraced more of human possibility. "Variousness and possibility" was the theme of another work I was reading in 1967, Lionel Trilling's *Liberal Imagination*. I was especially affected by the essay on *The Princess Casamassima*, in which Trilling connects James's hero in that novel, Hyacinth Robinson, to the "Young Man from the Provinces," equipped with "poverty, pride, and intelligence" as a standard character in modern literature. Such a young man "stands outside life and seeks to enter," wrote Trilling, and seeks entry usually by going to the metropole. Of course I thought of my father, penniless and alone, hitchhiking to Chicago during the depression summer of 1933 from Saskatchewan, where, after departing Gettysburg, he had tried to make a living as a wheat farmer. And I thought of myself, more fortunate than my father, yet also recognizable as a variation on the type.

In 1967 I switched from the intellectual history of the eighteenth century to that of the twentieth; largely because it was about the twentieth century that I thought I had the most to learn, and potentially the most to contribute to the study of provincialism and cosmopolitanism. Henry F.

May, the director of my dissertation, was wonderfully kind in putting up with a period of indecision, during which I dropped a dissertation topic on John Locke in America, in which May had been vitally interested, and took up instead, the career of the Jewish cosmopolitan philosopher of science Morris R. Cohen. By then, I knew what I was doing. Perhaps for the first time? At least I felt that I was making an informed decision between viable alternatives, rather than being pushed and pulled by circumstance, and ending up with position achieved largely by default.

The China connection thus amounts to a hauling of coal to Newcastle. Levenson's sensitivity to the dynamics of provincialism and cosmopolitanism in the North Atlantic West, especially as those dynamics affected Jews in relation to the Enlightenment, framed his study of Chinese history. Yet it was in reading Levenson on China that I came to recognize the questions about the United States that most engaged me. And so it happened: a son of Idaho and of a small Anabaptist sect, having been inspired by a Harvard atheist's studies of New England Puritanism, found his career-defining preoccupations when connections made through a political movement brought him into contact with the work of an orthodox Jew addressing the cultural dynamics of the modernization process through a meditation on Confucian China's encounter with communism.

Was there a more efficient way for me to get from Idaho and La Verne to Morris Cohen, Jewish intellectuals, and the tension between cosmopolitanism and provincialism in American culture? No doubt there was. Perhaps this turn in my life, which I make so much of here, is simply another instance of my not knowing what I was doing? I don't think so. Rather, I take it as an example of how an individual makes his or her decisions on the basis of an inventory of possibilities that happen to be at hand. You play, as they say, the cards you are dealt. Levenson was one of the best cards I was ever dealt. I never met Levenson, who died in 1969 in an accidental drowning in the Russian River at the age of forty-nine. I was still in Berkeley that spring, finishing up my dissertation. I went to his funeral.

During the years after Levenson's death, when China specialists warned me more and more often of the peculiar nature of Levenson's "take" on China, Levenson's example ended up presenting me with yet another gift: a profound cautionary tale. Levenson seems to have weakened his interpretation of Chinese history by projecting too much of himself into his subject. I wanted my own pursuit of the cosmopolitanism-provincialism dynamic to be heuristically informed by my own experience, but not captured by it. Would my ambivalence toward the provinces known to me, and my attractions to many varieties of cosmopolitanism, prevent me from seeing and proclaiming the most warrantable of the truths embedded in my objects of study? Whatever the answer to this question, the frequency with which I have interrogated myself in its terms is another way in which Levenson's writings affect me to this day.

My Levenson-inspired self-interrogation has been keyed by Idaho and the Brethren. My trajectory away from what a great antiprovincial called "the idiocy of rural life" has made it too easy for me, I have reminded myself repeatedly through the decades, to treat in too frosty a fashion worlds of the sort from which I myself had come. Having found the cultures of my upbringing too confining, there was a danger that my appreciation for the cultures of my adulthood would blind me to the needs many people have for tightly bounded communities and to the dignity that can attend on a provincial life. I have also been aware of the possibility that I would blind myself to the particular virtues of the kind of Protestantism with which my life began. This self-interrogation has affected most of what I have written, especially *In the American Province* (1985), *Postethnic America* (1995), and *Cosmopolitanism and Solidarity* (2006).

But the very attraction to cosmopolitanism and the self-interrogation about it that defines so much of the historian I became is deeply embedded in my Brethren past. I want to elaborate a bit more on that past. Most important was a formidable universalist strain in Christianity that came to me through the Brethren.

The German Baptist Brethren were anything but universalist. This sect was ethnically defined for two hundred years before its name became Church of the Brethren in 1908. The Brethren remained a largely descent-defined denomination in fact long after it ceased to be so in name. During the years of my upbringing, however, Brethren leaders were in a decidedly ecumenical phase. I was exposed to a certain selection of Brethren themes, focusing on service and inclusion. This was the agenda of the educated elite of the church, especially the editors of denominational periodicals and the professors at the denominational colleges and seminary. These leaders wanted to make the Brethren more like the Methodists, that is, to walk humbly in the Lord but to do so in a more modern manner, less suspicious of the world. The old Brethren tradition had been highly sectarian. The celebration of Christmas was too worldly (the view of my grandfather). Women were to be excommunicated ("churched" was the Brethren term) for not wearing the proper bonnet (the fate of my aunt who married a Presbyterian and became a professor at Gettysburg College).

In this new ecumenical context, universalist sentiments flourished. Galatians 3:28 taught that in Christ there is no Greek or Jew, no male nor female, no slave nor free. The second chapter of Acts advanced this universalist vision at its most radical and dramatic, presenting the reader with a mythic moment when the curse of Babel was revoked and all the tribes of the earth could understand each other as they spoke the gospel with cloven tongues of fire. In church in Idaho and later in California, we used to sing "In Christ there is no East or West, In Him no South or North; But one great fellowship of love, throughout the whole wide earth" (Hymn 362 in *The Brethren Hymnal*, edition of 1943). I soon learned to take this extravagant idealism for what it was, the enunciation of an ideal rather than the summary of a practice, but the ideal was presented to me with sufficient vigor that I know it had something to do with my engagements as a historian.

The work of another Berkeley professor of Levenson's generation, with whom I did not study, led me to conclude that I should engage the cosmopolitanism-provincialism problematic through the cultural functions of science and the ways in which science was defined by public moralists. It was also in 1967 that I first read Thomas S. Kuhn's *The Structure of Scientific Revolutions*. Kuhn had left Berkeley by then, but the memory of him was still vivid in Dwinelle Hall and every "with-it" graduate student had read his great book. The issues to which Kuhn introduced me led me to choose, as the topic of my dissertation, the career of a philosopher known for his defense of science as a foundation for culture.

Kuhn led me not only to Morris Cohen, but also to a sharpening of the methodological principles I had derived from Perry Miller. Kuhn's account of the dynamics of scientific communities spoke to the dynamics of other kinds of discursive communities in much the same way that Levenson's account of Chinese history spoke to other cases of the tension between provincialism and cosmopolitanism. During the next several decades I would repeatedly call the attention of colleagues to the methodological good sense embedded within Kuhn's understanding of how science works. But Kuhn's legacy in the Berkeley of my graduate years consisted also in the contribution he made to the department's remarkable focus on intellectual history.

Berkeley in the 1960s was truly an extraordinary place to do intellectual history. At the time I did not recognize this distinction. Of the Berkeley historians I have already mentioned, Kuhn, Levenson, and May were primarily intellectual historians, but Jordan and Middlekauff, too, were then doing important work in intellectual history. I served as a research assistant for Jordan's *White over Black: White Attitudes toward Negroes in America, 1550–1812*. May's lecture course on the intellectual history of the United States since 1865 has always been a model for my own, and has affected the character of the source book, dedicated to him, that I have co-edited in many editions with Charles Capper, another Berkeley PhD from that era. But there were many more intellectual historians, including William J. Bouwsma, the Renaissance and Reformation specialist, in whose historiography seminar I wrote what would become my first published article (on Perry Miller). I did not study with Carl Schorske, Samuel Haber, Hunter Dupree, Nicholas Riasanovsky, Adrienne Koch, George Stocking, or Martin Malia, but I invoke their names here to mark the department's exceptionally strong representation of intellectual history during the time that I was deciding just what kind of historian I wanted to be.

I was lucky to have been at Berkeley when I was. Indeed, so much of what I have narrated here seems to me a story of luck, mostly good. I am breaking off this account in the late 1960s because by then the basic foundation of the historian I became had been established, mostly by the remarkable people with whom I came into direct or indirect contact as a graduate student at Berkeley. Nearly all of these Berkeley people, as it happened, were not-church people, including Joan Heifetz Hollinger, whom I married in 1967. But the good luck goes back even prior to Berkeley, back to the church people. From my parents and their religious culture I derived a set of basic resources that served me remarkably well as I proceeded to a life very different from the ones they had led. Long after I left the ranks of church people, my favorite scripture remained Amos 9:7, in which those who think their group superior to others are urged to cool it: "Are you not like the Ethiopians to me, O people of Israel?" I was lucky enough, also, to go through the state of California's junior high and high schools at a time when these schools actually delivered—magnificently!—on the promise of public education.

Perhaps the luckiest thing of all was simply to have been part of a small enough generational cohort to enable me to gain admission to a place like Berkeley on the basis of my unimpressive qualifications. Having served now on the admissions committee of the same department that admitted me, I know full well that I would not be accepted at Berkeley now. An irony of my career is that nearly all of the graduate students I now teach at Berkeley are better than I was at their stage, yet here I am, one of their professors. I hope they have a streak of luck as good as I have had, but I fear that many of them will not. There are not enough jobs now. And this brings me to another instance of generational good luck.

When I went on the job market in the fall of 1968, I told my doctoral mentor, Henry May, that I did not want him to nominate me for any job south of the Mason-Dixon line or in the cities of New York and Chicago. The brass of it now seems incredible. Was this yet another case of my not knowing what I was doing? In terms of taste and tact, probably yes. But cognitively, I acted on the valid understanding that there were plenty of jobs. I wrote in a matter-of-fact way, simply registering a set of preferences as to where I did and did not want to live. The job market was so flush that it did not occur to me that I would not get a job, and a good one. Some of us were able to develop full careers as historians because the institutional support was there to enable us not only to get started, but to stay with it, and to act upon whatever intellectual ambitions we had developed as graduate students. Talent and enterprise? Of course they play a role. But those of us who became historians under the fortunate circumstances of the 1960s should never forget how much luck had to do with it.

CHAPTER 9

Enough Already: Universities Do Not Need More Christianity

Have American colleges and universities moved too far from the Protestant cultural frame that long defined so many of them? I do not think so, but the question is contested. This essay arose from my participation in a three-year consultation convened by the Lilly Endowment (hence I refer frequently to "the Lilly Seminar") in which I found myself surrounded by colleagues worried that higher education in the United States had become too secular. The controversy goes well beyond the Lilly group, and is a variant on issues about the nation as a whole I address in several of the other essays collected in this volume: what has been the place of religion in the public affairs of the United States, and what should it be?

Persons worried about the decline of Christianity's role in American higher education are often reluctant to confront honestly the honorable reasons men and women have had over the course of the last two centuries for rejecting Christian commitment, or drifting away from it, or restricting it to a private realm. If Christianity is basically right and its hold on the North Atlantic West is justified by its truth value, the logic of mystification proceeds, then its decline among the intelligentsia must be the result of misunderstanding or fraud. Those making this argument are often blind, moreover, to how intimately and persistently the affirmation of Christian values by faculties and administrators in our society has been historically bound up with discrimination against Jews, and in blatant forms as recently as the 1940s. When a prominent professor of Christian ethics accused me during a session of the Lilly Seminar of being a "secular triumphalist," I responded by asking if she could offer a nontriumphalist narrative of the integration of Jews into American universities after World War II. She gazed at me with bland incomprehension. Another tendency I have found frustrating in the colleagues with whom I argue in this essay is their effort to conceal a campaign to reestablish Christian culture hegemony under the guise of a "pluralism" that reduces the entirety of modern scientific thought to simply one of a number of "paradigms." Hence I practice in this essay the hermeneutics of suspicion.

This essay was first published in Andrea Sterk, ed., Religion, Scholarship, and Higher Education: Perspectives, Models, and Future Prospects *(Notre Dame, 2002), 40–49. A decade later I made a more exasperated complaint against the ongoing movement to restore Christianity to epistemic privilege under the guise of pluralism, "The Wrong Question! Please Change the Subject!"* Fides et Historia *(Fall 2011), 34-37.*

UNIVERSITIES HAVE REASON TO BE PROUD OF HAVING CREATED, within the most Christian of all industrialized societies of the North Atlantic West, a rare space in which ideas identified as Christian are not implicitly privileged. Our leading colleges and universities once shared in a pervasive Protestant culture, to which they owe a great deal. Now, however, mainstream academia maintains a certain critical distance from the Christian project. This critical distance is consistent with the drift of science and scholarship in the North Atlantic West. Not everyone is happy about this critical distance. The very topic "Religion and Higher Education" generally carries an implication that something is amiss. Higher education has gone too far in a secular direction, it is sometimes complained, and now pays too little respect to religious commitment in general and to Christian commitment in particular. I find this complaint hard to credit.

In defending mainstream academia's critical distance from Christian commitment here, I will not be suggesting that the men and women who are caught up in secular academia's workings are able always to live by the rules of fairness they espouse. Nor is my point that modern learning has so fully exhausted the intellectual resources of the classical religious traditions that it can responsibly pay no attention to them. I stress these disclaimers because I find that anyone who resists the movement to bring more Christian commitment back into academia is accused of being an uncritical defender of the status quo. At issue, rather, is *whether these imperfect academic communities can be improved by diminishing the critical distance from Christian cultural hegemony that they have achieved only after a long struggle.*

I put the question in this way because without this question there turns out to be little to discuss. I assert this with some conviction after three years of conversation within the admirably collegial Lilly Seminar. The overwhelming majority of the members of this seminar displayed a commitment to Christianity (I believe I was one of only four out of thirty who did not). Within this majority, a great many displayed a persistent if elusively articulated sense that American higher education was too aloof from religious commitment. Just where and how is this aloofness problematic? To this question the seminar was not able to come up with a coherent, agreed-upon answer. Of specific complaints from one concerned Christian or another there was no shortage, but most of these complaints proved too weak to generate sustained support even from coreligionists. Everyone in the seminar agreed, to be sure, that crude religion bashing could not be defended, that the serious academic study of religion should be higher than it now is on the agenda of several scholarly disciplines, and that this society needs a variety of kinds of institutions of higher education, including some that are religiously affiliated. And almost everyone agreed, after some friendly interrogation, that Christians were so well treated in the United States, even in elite academia, that it was a mistake to represent Christians as "victims." Many of the seminar's most animated discussions were well off the topic. It was common to grouse about this or that aspect of contemporary American academic life—its failure to live up to its own stated ideals was a favorite theme of some—but eventually someone would point out that what we were discussing was not much related to religion.

So, one might ask, what's all this about? The Lilly group was a seminar in search of a problem. But every now and then the search succeeded. In almost every such moment, a close reading of the transcripts will confirm, the problem proved to be some version of the question I italicized earlier.

Here, in these post-seminar reflections, I want to sketch several of the arguments I made during the seminar. In so doing, I will voice a skeptical perspective on the higher-education-and-religion conversation as it is now being pursued in the United States.

Many of those who want to reform academia in a more religious direction turn out, upon scrutiny, to be hoping to change the structure of plausibility taken for granted by the prevailing epistemic communities, but are slow to articulate and defend this program of reform. This initiative should be brought out into the open and debated. To do so, we need to begin with a familiar distinction.

Motivation and warrant; origins and verification; discovery and justification. These are three versions of an old distinction about science and scholarship that was drawn too sharply by the logical positivists, and by some of the theorists who preached against "the genetic fallacy." We now are quick to acknowledge that our decisions about what shall count as a standard for true belief may owe something to what motivates us to make a claim, or to hope that the claim may be proven true. And we are quick to acknowledge, too, that the prevailing modes of warrant in the epistemic community within which we work may also become part of our motivation for advancing a claim: we may be motivated to advance certain ideas because they are likely to be found true within a community whose approval we desire. But once these and other such caveats are entered against the old distinction, it can serve us well when we talk about religion and contemporary learned communities.

The personal circumstances of any individual inquirer exercise an important influence over what topics he or she will pursue and what approaches to those topics he or she will find attractive. There is no reason to doubt or lament this fact about inquiry. An individual's religious orientation may help to motivate an inquiry, a working hypothesis, and/or a specific claim one hopes to vindicate. But when it comes to warranting the claims made, what matters most are the rules, formal and tacit, of the relevant epistemic community. Those rules are of course contingent, and often contested. But that such rules exist, and are important, will be understood by anyone who has sat on a journal's editorial board, served on a prize committee, attended a tenure meeting, dispensed grant money, or helped an academy decide who should be elected to membership. If those rules fail to reflect a given religious orientation, then that religious orientation loses its salience in the warranting process. Even if an individual or a particular group finds that biblical evidence, or the evidence of immediate religious experience, helps to convince them of a particular truth, other kinds of evidence will be required to persuade the larger epistemic community of sociologists or physicists or historians.

I stress the cogency of this simple distinction between motivation and warrant because so many people have proven eager to avoid it. Often, the initiative to change warranting rules is obscured when a Christian believer says he or she simply wants to be able to declare a worldview openly. That sounds like an affirmation of a motive, and a request to be heard sympathetically when one affirms the motive publicly. When asked if this is all that's meant—when invited, that is, to accept the distinction between motivation and warrant, and to keep religion on the one side of it—some will see the point and say, "yes, the warranting process, if it is to work in a community that includes nonbelievers as well as believers, must operate by that community's structure of plausibility." Fair enough. Yet others will equivocate. It's "more complicated," they will say. They will complain that the rules of the mainstream academic communities are too narrow. There almost always follows a call for "tolerance," for a more "pluralistic" setting in which a variety of outlooks are entertained.

Pluralism in this context usually means accepting forms of evidence and reasoning that were once plausible within disciplinary communities in the social sciences and humanities but are no longer. There was once a time when scholars in the North Atlantic West took for granted a shared Christianity. In that bygone era, the boundaries of the epistemic community and the boundaries of the community of faith were largely coterminous. But now the boundaries of the epistemic communities that define discussion in the learned world are no longer coterminous with the Christian community of faith, and this fact appears to create discomfort on the part of some Christians. There are good reasons, too obvious in the intellectual history of the last three hundred years to bear repeating here, why the prevailing epistemic communities now have the boundaries that they do, and why these communities, as a consequence of their relative de-Christianization, no longer count biblical evidence and other religious experience particular to Christianity as relevant to the assessment of a truth-claim or an interpretation. At issue, then, is not whether learned communities should be tolerant or intolerant, pluralistic or nonpluralistic, flexible or inflexible, open or repressive; at issue rather is the specific direction the always ongoing revision of the epistemic rules of these communities should take.

An incident that took place during a meeting of the Lilly Seminar can illustrate the importance of the motivation-warrant distinction, and can also illustrate the ease with which this distinction can be obscured or evaded by well-meaning discussants who are eager to get Christianity more involved in the academic process. A speaker criticized the political science discipline, and presented his critique as growing directly out of his Catholic commitment. I asked him to specify the relevance of Catholicism to the critique. Was it simply a personal context in which he had developed the critique, and indeed a motive for thinking in this direction? Was the critique one that only Catholics would be able to develop? Could non-Catholics accept the critique? (It was manifest by this time that many non-Catholics in the room accepted the critique, so the significance of this question was all the more apparent.) Could the critique be justified on grounds that had nothing whatsoever to do with Catholicism? If the latter, was the relevance of Catholicism not confined to the context of motivation, and largely irrelevant to the context of warrant?

The speaker and several others struggled for some time with these questions. Several were determined to keep Catholics in possession of the critique, while eager to see it shared with the rest of the world. Eventually, one position won strong support in the group. It was as follows. Sure, non-Catholics can appreciate and make use of this critique, but if they detach it from the matrix out of which it came they will be failing to credit Catholicism for producing the critique. Catholicism is the inspiration for something valued by the larger community; hence the nurturing of Catholicism is in the interests of the larger community. We do not want to cut off this source of inspiration, which might happen if we neglected the tree from which the fruit was picked. This tree is likely to bear other good fruit. The questions I had raised, while provocative, were beside the point. What really mattered was the connection between good ideas and their matrix.

This position is remarkable in several respects. First, it invites the retort that when ideas we like come from matrices we dislike we do not make the nourish-the-tree argument. An example is the Nazi campaign against cancer and tobacco, many features of which prefigured programs that are now counted as wholesome in medical and public-health communities of the United States. We do not say, "Hey, this cancer breakthrough shows that the Nazi tree could bear good fruit, so let's see if trees of the fascist species bear other good fruit in regard to, say, race or retardation or government organization." Second, the position does not take into account the possibility that a lot of non-Catholics might have come up with the same ideas on their own, which would diminish the argument for watering the Catholic tree. The harvest of many orchards needs to be assessed before we can be sure just where our agricultural energies are best spent. Third, the position takes no account of the distressing possibility that when the entirety of the cherished tree or orchard's harvest is assessed, it will be found to produce as much noxious fruit as sweet. Most matrices for cultural production have negative as well as positive potential. Fourth, the position finesses the motivation-warrant issue by (1) agreeing that the critique might be justified within a community of warrant that recognizes no Catholic principle, while (2) demanding that the larger community give points to the Catholics for coming up with the critique that proved of value to the larger community. This proposed trade-off concedes that whatever gives an idea any claim to a distinctly Catholic character is no reason for a larger community to accept that idea, but expects in return that the larger community will continue to recognize the idea's Catholic character. This move neutralizes the potential of the motivation-warrant distinction to sever from the faith community an idea that promises to enhance the standing of that faith community in the larger world.

This last point invites elaboration. The greater proportion of the inventory of valuable ideas that can be traced to Christianity, the less sense it makes for the prevailing epistemic communities to maintain the critical distance from it that distinguishes them from their counterpart communities of past centuries. Hence there is a tendency to credit religion in general and Christianity in particular with producing and sustaining a host of valuable aspects of contemporary culture, title to which might well be claimed, or at least respectfully shared, by other parties. At work here is a familiar dynamic in the struggle for possession of cultural capital. It works as follows.

Ideas the value of which is recognized in a large social arena will be claimed by particular groups as their own contribution. One of the means by which groups achieve, maintain, or lose relative power in a multigroup arena is to be identified or not identified with highly valued items in the common cultural inventory. What endows an item with the capacity to function as cultural capital is the prestige it enjoys among many groups. This dynamic has been especially visible in recent years among ethnoracial groups, rather than among religious groups. Consider the following well-known examples. Some Afrocentrists claim the culture of ancient Egypt as the contribution of a descent community that embraces African Americans of the present day. Some educators have asked that the Iroquois Federation be given credit for having inspired vital aspects of the constitution of the United States. An earlier example is the assertion that democracy is owed to the sturdy Saxons of the primeval German forests who then carried it to England and finally to America. Another is Madison Grant's notorious insistence that Jesus Christ belonged not to the Jewish community of descent but to that of the Nordics, by way of the Savior's long-obscured Greek ancestry.

I choose extreme examples to identify the dynamic, not to deny that some claims of this order are true. Indeed, Christianity itself is so massive a presence in the last two millennia that it is not difficult to proliferate credible and convincing claims about how many of the things almost everyone today appreciates came to us through a Christian chain of cultural transferal. The point of understanding the dynamic is not to turn us away from honest inquiries into the historic path by which valuable practices, artifacts, ideals, and doctrines have been created, transferred, preserved, and critically revised. Rather, the point is to be better able to approach critically claims of this kind in a context in which the party making the claims is concerned about its standing in relation to other groups, in this case non-Christian groups. Do we owe Catholicism credit for our colleague's critique of political science? The question needs to be considered in relation to this dynamic.

The need to keep this dynamic in mind is all the more compelling when we see someone assigning to their favorite group credit for cultural commodities that are highly generic. The rule of thumb is this: the more generic the commodity claimed, the more suspect the claim should be. It is common to hear Christianity associated with a set of general virtues, including humility, generosity, decency, charity, and spirituality. Now, Christianity's ordinance has been so large that it is indeed within a Christian context that millions of people have seen the generic virtues articulated and exemplified. When you practice the classic virtues especially well, someone will say, honestly and without artifice, "Oh, you *are* a good Christian!" When you hear that, you are likely to be quite far removed from the faculty club. But I invoke this charming mode of praise to call attention to a presumption that has proved durable even in some academic circles. The presumption is that behaving well and being religious and being Christian are somehow part of the same thing. Another episode from the Lilly Seminar can illustrate this presumption.

One member of the seminar expressed the concern that without the sustaining influence of religious communities, academia was having a hard time transferring "spiritual values" from one generation to the next. This person backed off when he was reminded that lots of non-Christians, even atheists, had proven capable of practicing these virtues as well as Christians could, and even of transferring them to their young. But what I found remarkable was that so able and sensitive a scholar could write and speak as he did in the initial iteration. He was not engaged in a power ploy, I'm sure, but he inherits and sometimes works within a frame of reference that, when it operates in an arena of diverse religious orientations, functions to advance Christianity by reserving to it a unique leadership role in the wholesome project of enabling people to be good.

A closely related incident, this about cosmology rather than ethics, betrayed the same presumption that Christianity owns the title to some very generic cultural material. In this instance, a member of the seminar observed that the knowability of the world and the capacity of humans to grasp parts of its nature were distinctly Christian presuppositions, and that historians, in particular, simply could not do their job effectively without this Christian cosmology. When I asked this colleague if Thucydides and Gibbon and Perry Miller operated on Christian presuppositions despite their lack of Christian commitment, he said yes. Christianity has title, it would seem, to metaphysical and epistemological realism. This view was met with some skepticism in the seminar.

But even many of those who were skeptical about this particular example remained attracted to the basic outlook I have been analyzing here, which can be seen as a "fallback" position on behalf of the cultural project of Christianity. It is a fallback position in the sense that this project, after losing influence over the rules by which truth is established, lays a more adamant claim to being the inspiration, indeed the cultural matrix, out of which arises those truths that do not actually conflict with the project as understood by its current supervisors. Hence there is now so much more talk of Christianity as a set of insufficiently tapped resources, not as a standard for belief. This is another step in the historic process of secularization.

I have been proceeding here in the mode of the "hermeneutics of suspicion," but only for the purposes of bringing out aspects of the conversation on religion and higher education that are often hidden. In concluding, I want to pull back from this mode and call upon my religiously committed colleagues to recognize the virtues of the critical distance mainstream academia now maintains toward Christian commitment. Now that academia is emancipated from a Protestant hegemony, the evils of which surely require no belaboring here, it has proved to be a setting in which Catholics, Protestants, religious Jews, agnostics, atheists, and more recently Muslims are able to work together in creating good science and scholarship, and in sustaining good teaching programs for graduate and undergraduate students. I believe we should rejoice in this.

Unless we suppose that the religious believers who function well in this environment are somehow less authentic in their faith commitments than those who do not so function, we must surely consider the possibility that the line dividing religious from irreligious scholars is not terribly important, after all, for the purposes of higher education. If it is more important for such purposes—I am not talking about life as a whole, but about higher education—than I grant here, surely our reformers need to provide an analysis of those of their coreligionists who live so successfully within the present system. Is their religion less authentic than that of the reformers?

I sometimes think that our reformers are in the thrall of a parochially Pauline model of religious authenticity. Diaspora Judaism represents an interesting contrasting model, eschewing evangelical modes. And there are other styles of religious commitment and practice. The choice between models of religious authenticity is relevant to teaching as well as to science and scholarship. I am often dismayed at the loose talk about "formation" that I hear from religiously committed colleagues. I wish these colleagues would attend more to the intellectual content of the subject matter they teach, and less to their own conceptions of the moral needs of their students.

Perhaps our reformers need to be reminded that Christianity marched into the modern era as the strongest, most institutionally endowed cultural program in the Western world. Its agents tried through a variety of methods, some more coercive than others, to implant Christian doctrines and practices in as much of the species as possible. Yet as the centuries went forward, this extraordinary presence in world history lost some of the ground it once held. Christianity after the recent end of the century prophesied in 1900 as "the Christian Century" is less triumphant in the North Atlantic West than it was in 1500 or 1700 or 1900. The fate of Protestant culture in the United States is but a fragment of this larger drama of the transformation of the North Atlantic West from a society heavily invested in the cultural program of Christianity to a society in which Christianity found it harder and harder to retain the spiritual capital of its most thoughtful and learned members.

If Christianity's continuing adherents include some of the world's most thoughtful and learned men and women—as I believe they do—let them continue to bear witness as they will. But let's not forget that outside secular academia, Christianity continues to be the cultural norm, not the exception, in the United States. Our society is one in which voters in 2000 could choose between two more-Christian-than-thou presidential candidates: one, George W. Bush, who declared his favorite philosopher to be "Christ," and another, Al Gore, who claimed to solve ethical dilemmas by applying the old formula of Charles Sheldon, "WWJD" (What Would Jesus Do?). Enough already.

Universities should not surrender back to Christianity the ground they have won for a more independent, cosmopolitan life of the mind. There are plenty of things wrong with higher education in the United States today, but a deficiency in Christianity is not one of them. Of all the parties to our cultural conversation, none has had a greater abundance of opportunities to be heard in the United States than Christianity.

CHAPTER 10

Religious Ideas: Should They Be Critically Engaged or Given a Pass?

Either/or, I say. Either *religious ideas are not an appropriate justification for public policy in the United States* or *they are subject to the same rules for discussion that apply to ideas about the economy, race, gender, the environment, historical events, and the multitude of other topics Americans discuss openly and sometimes even contentiously with one another. This essay voices frustration with the trap that many faith-affirming politicians have increasingly sprung on doubters: "If elected to office I will act in keeping with my religious faith, but any journalist or rival politician who asks a skeptical question about my faith is biased against religion." Religious ideas are thus sheltered from the public, critical scrutiny to which other ideas are commonly subject. This protection of religion would not be such a problem if religion were a private matter, as in the past it has so often been understood to be. But increasingly we live in an atmosphere of both/and, not either/or: religion is both a legitimate foundation for public policy and protected from critical examination.*

*Above and beyond the question of religions role in electoral politics, this essay also pushes religious liberals to argue more forthrightly than is common nowadays with rival voices within their own communities of faith. Perhaps religious liberals could diminish the standing of ignorant and obscurantist ideas, and encourage faiths consistent with modern standards of cognitive plausibility. After all, Protestant liberalizers have long engaged in vigorous contestation of the claims made by religious conservatives; liberal religion itself has generally been created out of more conservative religion. Such is the story of William Ellery Channing, Harry Emerson Fosdick, John A. T. Robinson, and countless others. Reinhold Niebuhr was willing to publically attack the evangelical preacher Billy Graham in 1957 for promoting a child-like faith. There is some of that today, but just how little is revealed in a symposium organized by the Center for American Progress (*Debating the Divine *[Washington, 2008]) largely for the purpose of assessing the arguments I had made in this essay. In that symposium, several leading ecumenical thinkers display reluctance to engage evangelicals as sharply as I urge them to do, and they continue to worry that secularism, not the obscurantist versions of faith, is the big problem.*

Since this essay comments at some length on the new atheist movement, I want to call attention to a number of more recent works that present atheism in what seems to me much sounder terms than do the new atheist writings I criticize here.

Especially valuable are George Levine, ed., The Joy of Secularism: 11 Essays for How We Live Now *(Princeton, 2011); Louise M. Antony, ed.,* Philosophers without Gods: Meditations on Atheism and the Secular Life *(New York, 2010); Thomas Nagel,* Secular Philosophy and the Religious Temperament: Essays, 2002–2008 *(New York, 2010); and Philip Kitcher,* Preludes to Pragmatism: Toward a Reconstruction of Philosophy *(New York, 2012).*
　　This essay first appeared in Representations *101 (Winter 2008), 144–154.*

WOULD THE DEMOCRATIC PUBLIC CULTURE OF THE UNITED STATES be well served by a robust, critical discussion of religious ideas? Or do principles of ethical propriety and political prudence encourage us instead to ignore each other's ideas about religion, however silly they may seem?

Two recent developments give point to these questions.

One is a striking increase in the number and intensity of demands for a greater role for religion in public affairs, and for more "flexible" and "realistic" approaches to the constitutional separation of church and state.[1] Faith-based initiatives are widely supported by leaders of both political parties. The very idea of a distinctly secular public sphere is said to entail a bias against religion. Republicans tend to favor more religion in public life than do many leading Democrats, but the latter scramble to assure their constituents that they, too, learned a lot from the nuns when they were in parochial school, or that they still attend services at a church or synagogue. The leaders of the Air Force Academy have not believed it a violation of the church-state separation to place heavy and repeated pressure on cadets and faculty to attend Protestant and Catholic religious services regularly and to decorate the ostensibly secular campus with banners proclaiming the Air Force of the United States to be "Christ's Warriors." Only a lawsuit led the academy's leaders to somewhat modify their practices, as has been pointed out in Ray Suarez's *The Holy Vote.*[2] If religious ideas are going to be more widely accepted as legitimate justifications for public policy, shouldn't those ideas be assessed according the same rules that apply in the public debate of other ideas?

The second development is the sudden appearance of, and extensive public attention given to, what the press likes to call "the new atheism."[3] The books of four polemical atheists—Richard Dawkins, Daniel Dennett, Sam Harris, and Christopher Hitchens—are roundly condemned in one forum after another for their arrogance, ignorance, and sweeping rejection of all religion. Can these writers not distinguish between Methodists and morons? Reviewers and bloggers mock the new atheists for failing to appreciate the intellectual sophistication of the average Episcopalian.[4]

The price of credibility, it seems, is respect for at least some kinds of religion and for a higher standard of civility than other discourses demand. The religion of one's neighbors may be the last stronghold of the old Sunday school maxim, "If you can't say something good about a person, don't say anything at all." Does the buzz-saw now carving up the books written by the new atheists indicate that a vigorous, public debate about religious ideas is a mistake, after all?

Let's begin with what it means to give religious ideas a "pass." I have in mind the *convention of protecting religious ideas from the same kind of critical scrutiny to which we commonly subject ideas about almost everything else.* The new atheists are getting so much attention partly because they are flouting this convention. The convention is deeply rooted in American culture. When Al Gore—one of the most highly educated of liberal democratic politicians, and one whose favorite book is Thomas Kuhn's *Structure of Scientific Revolutions*—claims to resolve life's tough problems by asking "what would Jesus do?" he can count on the respectful silence of those who doubt the guidance actually provided by this principle of applied ethics. Nobody with a modicum of tact asks Gore if he has examined his religious ideas with the same scrutiny he has applied to claims and counterclaims about global warming, or to competing theories of how science makes progress.

The discussion of other topics really is different. If someone says women cannot do first-rate science, or that African Americans are just not as smart as Korean Americans, or that homosexuality is a choice rather than a condition, or that taxation is essentially a form of theft, or that the Americans won World War II with minimal help from the Soviets, it is okay to challenge the speaker with evidence and reasoning. Responding in this argumentative manner is less okay if someone says that his or her support for Israel is based on what God has said in the Bible, or that Jesus Christ will come to earth soon, or that some good thing happened because God answered someone's prayers. Religion, wrote Richard Rorty in a widely quoted essay of 1994, is often a "conversation-stopper."[5] When someone starts going on about "The Rapture," the prescribed behavior is to politely change the subject, or to indulge the speaker as one might a child or an aged relative. In the case of The Rapture, the implications for one's fellow citizens may be uncertain, but to invoke a religious justification for a public policy issue is to discourage an opponent from actually debating it.

This convention of giving religious ideas a pass has impressive foundations, and not only in the virtues of decency and humility. These foundations reside also in a constitutional tradition that does indeed treat religious ideas as a distinct category. These foundations are embedded, further, in a history of religious diversity that renders silence a good way to keep the peace. Protestant ancestors of my own were murdered by Catholic terrorists who were surely convinced that these killings were responsive to God's will. The privatization of religion has been integral to the creation and maintenance of a public sphere in which persons of any and all religious orientations, including nonbelief, can function together.

If religious ideas were genuinely trivial from a civic standpoint, playing no appreciable role in how people dealt with anyone other than themselves and their immediate families and their voluntary associations, religion could be more comfortably ignored. But we are nowadays constantly told that religious ideas are a legitimate and vibrant ground for action in the public square and should not be suppressed. This assertion is frequently bolstered by a historical narrative emphasizing the wholesome effects of religion on American politics. Anyone who worries that religion might be counterprogressive is instantly reminded of the importance of religion to Martin Luther King Jr. and to the role of religious ideas in propelling the civil rights movement. But even when King's supporters among the most liberal of the white Protestants and Catholics are added to his base among the black churches, the total amounts to a small minority of Christians in the United States at that time. Most white Protestants and Catholics were dubious about, if not actually opposed to civil rights agitation prior to about 1964.[6] The most intensely Christian segment of white America during the 1950s and 1960s was the segregationist south. The religion-is-good-for-America narrative proudly invokes the Social Gospel, which largely failed in its effort to advance social and economic equality, but has little to say about the role of religious ideas in bringing about Prohibition, which for more than a decade succeeded. Gaines M. Foster's *Moral Reconstruction* shows the triumph of Prohibition to be the culmination of decades of religiously connected political activity remarkably like that we see around us today.[7]

This popular but seriously imbalanced account of the history of religion-and-politics facilitates today's discourse, in which we are awash with treatises and manifestos claiming that post–World War II interpretations of the church-state separation function to suppress religious faith by preventing its free exercise in the design and execution of public policy. To keep religion out of public life, we are told, is to trivialize religion. How unfair, indeed how absurd it is that the faithful are asked to "check their religion at the door." Among the legions who invoke this phrase is Congressman Mark Souder of Ohio:

> To ask me to check my Christian beliefs at the public door is to ask me to expel the Holy Spirit from my life when I serve as a congressman, and that I will not do. Either I am a Christian or I am not. Either I reflect His glory or I do not.[8]

Yet there is a formidable theoretical tradition that defends the checking of one's religion at the door. The late John Rawls and his followers, including Joshua Cohen and Martha Minow, have argued that participants in a shared democratic polity owe it to one another to conduct the business of that polity within premises that are particular to that polity and not to any of the yet more sectarian persuasions that may be present within it.[9] In this view, checking one's religion at the door, in the sense of declining to use it as a justification for actions in which one asks others of different religious orientations to join, is not a bias, nor an inappropriate restraint on free exercise. Rather, it is a mark of democratic commitment and a sign of solidarity with co-citizens in a diverse society. In this view, if absolutists like Souder are unable to accept a domain in which their religious faith is less all-defining, they should stay out of politics. This is exactly what Souder's Mennonite forebears did: they stayed out of public affairs because, like Souder, they believed "radical discipleship" applied 24/7 in every setting. But today, Souder cries foul if the faithful are discouraged from bringing their unmitigated religious witness into the Congress of the United States.

But some politicians see the appeal of the distinguished tradition of democratic theory represented by Rawls. Barack Obama, who professes Christian faith as fervently as Souder does, has endorsed the Rawlsian view explicitly in speeches widely hailed for the element of religious testimony they embody and defend. Obama does encourage Americans to be up-front about their religious motives. But he offers a qualification not often quoted. Like a good philosopher, he understands the distinction between motivation and warrant:

> Democracy demands that the religiously motivated translate their concerns into universal, rather than religion-specific, values. Democracy requires that their proposals be subject to argument, and amenable to reason. *I may be opposed to abortion for religious reasons, but if I seek to pass a law banning the practice, I cannot simply point to the teachings of my church or evoke God's will. I have to explain why abortion violates some principle that is accessible to people of all faiths, including those with no faith at all. . . .* Politics depends on our ability to persuade each other of common aims based on a common reality. It involves the compromise, the art of what's possible. At some fundamental level, religion does not allow for compromise. It's the art of the impossible. If God has spoken, then followers are expected to live up to God's edicts, regardless of the consequences. To base one's life on such uncompromising commitments may be sublime, but to base our policy making on such commitments would be a dangerous thing.[10]

Obama's example can give courage to those wanting to defend a strong, autonomous sphere of civil government without infringing on the constitutionally protected free exercise of religion. Civic patriotism has been unfashionable on the liberal Left since the late 1960s on account of the efforts made in its name to discourage cultural diversity and to stifle criticism of American foreign and domestic policy. But its renewal in the present context could encourage pride in the church-state separation and celebrate a distinctive civic sphere in which persons of many religious orientations, including persons who count themselves as nonbelievers in any religion, can be full participants in their distinctive capacity as Americans. It might be too crude to brand as "un-American" those who try to bring church and state closer together, but civic patriotism can at once support a secular public sphere and a private religious one.

Yet even if a renewal of civic patriotism were to persuade everyone that a secular public sphere is not in itself a threat to the constitutional right of free exercise of religion, the religious culture of citizens would obviously continue to affect what happened in the secular sphere of public affairs. Religious ideas, even if not put forth as justifications for public policy, do constitute a vital matrix for political culture. Scholars assume this when they study almost any society in the world. Beliefs about the nature of the world and of human beings, whatever the content of such ideas, are understood to be important. Historians and social scientists trying to understand the political and economic order of any society take belief systems into account. Often, these belief systems are religious. Are we going to proceed differently with the United States of our own time? Are basic ideas about the universe assumed to be both constitutive and performative in Victorian England, Nazi Germany, Confucian China, Inca Peru, Maratha India, Soviet Russia, Ancient Athens, Asante Africa, the Crow Nation of nineteenth-century Montana, and Puritan New England but *not* in the United States today? Can we defend a version of American exceptionalism according to which belief systems are functional everywhere else but not here? Do we not all have a stake in what our fellow citizens take to be true about the world?

The religious ideas of masses of Americans have been shielded from the aspects of modern thought that have led so many scientists and social scientists away from religion.[11] Perhaps critical debate would encourage popular faiths more consistent with modern standards of plausibility, more resistant to the manipulation of politicians belonging to any party, and more accepting of the wisdom in the sharp separation between church and state. Where, after all did we get liberal religion? We got it out of orthodox religion. Especially did the great biblical scholars of the eighteenth and nineteenth century provide the cognitive context for a variety of liberalized religious faiths, including the capacity of many Christians to absorb the Darwinian revolution in science. Religious dialogue has been vital to the intellectual and political history of the North Atlantic West for centuries, until twentieth-century secularists complacently assumed religion was on the way out and ceased to engage it critically.

The absence of sustained, public scrutiny of religious ideas in our time has created a vacuum filled with easy God talk. Politicians are not the only ones skilled in this idiom, but President George W. Bush certainly exemplifies it when he assures the world that his policies in Iraq correspond to God's will. How different was the voice of Lincoln, who never joined a church, but whose God talk was anything but easy. Lincoln invoked the deity in a spirit of humility. In his Second Inaugural Address of 1865, Lincoln cautiously alluded to "those divine attributes which the believers in a Living God always ascribe to him," speculated about what such an omniscient God's will might be, and stopped well short of expressing confidence that, as president, he could be sure that God was on his side.

In Lincoln's time, religious ideas were less often given a pass. In much of nineteenth-century America religious ideas were critically debated, sometimes with a touch of ridicule, even as the church-state separation was defended. An example is the antebellum debates over slavery. The bible, proslavery theologians and politicians reasonably argued, had no problem with slavery. These proslavery Christians insisted that abolitionists just did not know their Bible and were projecting their own secular ideas on the sacred text. Leviticus, Exodus, Ephesians, and First Timothy were routinely cited as biblical warrant for the acceptance of slavery, and abolitionists were hard pressed to find scriptural warrant for their side even in the gospels and in the letters of Paul.[12] When proslavery Americans established their own government—the Confederate States of America—they put God right into their constitution, a step that dramatically set their political order apart from that of the United States itself.

But beyond the slavery debates, the nineteenth-century Americans who discussed issues of public policy understood full well that no matter how the church-state separation was construed, the kind of society in which they lived depended in part on the basic view of the world accepted by their fellow citizens. The great feminist Elizabeth Cady Stanton issued what she called *The Woman's Bible* in the 1890s, in which she openly renounced passages of scripture she found offensive to women, and there were a lot of them. Stanton understood, just as the canonrevisers in our English departments of the 1980s understood, that the books people read had something to do with what kind of people they became and what kinds of political culture they would create; Stanton went after the Bible with a vengeance, the New Testament as well as the Old, and scolded the authors of the ancient texts like a confident schoolmistress correcting the spelling mistakes of the class dunce. She ridiculed the male theologians and preachers of her own time who continued to reinforce the scriptures whole, rather than reading them with modern, enlightened understandings of the gender distinction.[13]

Not everyone appreciated this. Stanton's religious writings were felt by many other feminists to be ethically inappropriate and, more important, politically imprudent. Upon her death in 1902 Stanton's memory was largely erased by the American feminist movement and not recovered until the 1960s. Stanton's place in the movement was obscured with a new celebration of the more conventional Susan B. Anthony.

Stanton's contemporary, Robert Ingersoll, the agnostic whose performances as a lyceum speaker made him a household name and a constant foil for preachers, also went after specific religious ideas with a critical sprit. But at least his generation—Ingersoll died in 1900—was familiar with some of the same objections to Christianity that, when raised in our own time by Sam Harris, seem unconscionably rude. Ingersoll had many critics, but Ingersoll and his enemies were at least part of the same conversation, and one in which religious ideas were taken seriously by secular intellectuals as well as by the faithful.

During the twentieth century unbelieving intellectuals too often assumed, complacently, that religion was in the process of dying out and that religious ideas therefore did not need attention. The British philosopher Bertrand Russell's writings of the 1910s and 1920s were among the last to make a big production of attacking Christianity for its intellectual deficiencies, but American secular intellectuals often found Russell's fussing about religion quaintly anachronistic. He displayed the mark of a true Victorian, it was often said in the 1940s and 1950s: Russell still thought that to reject belief in God was an act of great moral courage.[14]

The new atheists echo many of Russell's complaints, but unlike Russell's confident contemporaries they do not take for granted religion's eventual demise. Rather, they treat it as a serious and dangerous enemy of civilization. But if anyone is complacent in the current controversy over the new atheism, it is those who dismiss the writings of Dawkins, Dennett, Harris, and Hitchens too rapidly. The value of bringing evidence and reasoning to a discussion of religious ideas is lost when we jump on the obvious failings of these writers and ignore the power of the basic Enlightenment critique of religious obscurantism that their books embody.

Refuting Sam Harris has become rather like refuting Samuel Huntington: almost any academic can do it, and when you finish you congratulate yourself for your cleverness and move on to something else. But if Huntington is wrong to characterize Mexican Americans as uniquely subversive of the traditional, immigrant-based social order of the United States, the questions he raises about immigration and assimilation and the cultural foundations of democracy are far from silly, and deserve better answers than most of Huntington's critics provide.[15] So, too, with Harris.

Part of the problem is that Harris connects his critique of religion to a naturalistic metaphysics more specific than his mission requires. This portentous turn is also taken by Dennett and Dawkins, whose philosophical reach has struck many informed readers as extending well beyond the grasp of the evolutionary biology on which it is ostensibly based. The biologist H. Allen Orr, who is no apologist for religion, has been particularly convincing in showing the limits of the scientific foundation for the new atheism.[16] But there is more to the problem than simply espousing a metaphysics that even many agnostics and atheists do not feel compelled to accept.

Harris has no sense of history, and no understanding of the traditional role of religious argumentation in promoting liberalized versions of faith. Harris buries his rasping, potentially valuable critique of genuinely obscurantist ideas beneath undiscerning attacks on people he calls "religious moderates." Both *The End of Faith* and *Letter to a Christian Nation* reject the liberal Protestants, liberal Catholics, liberal Muslims, and so on, who could be Harris's strategic allies. Reviewer after reviewer has treated Harris's books as not worth systematic refutation because the author can't tell the difference between Jerry Falwell and Peter Gomes, and can't distinguish between the Muslim fanatics who attacked the World Trade Center and the liberal Muslims written about in Jytte Klausen's *The Islamic Challenge.*[17] Harris accuses religious moderates of serving as covers for more outrageously irrational versions of the faith. Yet these religious moderates are, like him, inheritors of the best features of the Enlightenment, and are thus his natural allies. Harris reveals no understanding of the historical circumstances that have led many highly intelligent and well-educated people to espouse religious faith, or of the range of ideas that have passed as religious. The popular novel by Marilynne Robinson *Gilead* explores a liberal religious culture with strong roots in the United States, yet Harris is altogether oblivious to the character of this culture.[18] Harris's logic is similar to that of the communist international's theory of social fascism as advanced in the early 1930s, when social democrats in Germany, the United States, and other nations were said to be functionally indistinguishable from fascists simply because they had not renounced bourgeois reform in order to side with the communists.

But the social democrats fought back. They did not leave the political arena to the communists and the fascists. What will happen now?

It remains to be seen what kind of political and cultural alliance can develop between (1) secularists who are more patient with religious liberals than the new atheists are and (2) religious liberals themselves. And this is where the issue of giving religious ideas a "pass" has become especially difficult. Political liberals of secular orientation tend to give religious ideas a pass because they hope thereby to achieve issue-specific alliances with faith-affirming Americans on the environment, health care, foreign policy, taxation, and so on.[19] Why mess things up by embarrassing the faithful and demanding that they repudiate more resoundingly their more conservative co-religionists? In the meantime, religious liberals are under constant attack from their conservative coreligionists for being on a slippery slope to secularism and are thus reluctant to break ranks with more conservative believers to an extent that secularists would find productive. Hence these religious liberals, too, prefer to seek issue-specific alliances with secular liberals and leave potentially divisive religious argumentation aside.

This continued avoidance of actual debate about religious issues seems to me viable only if religious liberals and secular liberals can advance a civic patriotism that would celebrate a distinctly secular public sphere along the lines advocated by Rawls and Obama. The need to engage religious ideas diminishes somewhat if those ideas are understood, in keeping with modern church-state separationist doctrine, to be inappropriate justifications for public policy. There is a lot to be said for letting each other alone. But in the absence of such an agreement—repudiating the views of Congressman Souder and comparable defenders of politics as a form of religious witness—the case for a robust, public debate of religious issues seems to me hard to refute. If the new atheists are too sweeping in their rejections, the rest of us need not be.

Notes

This piece has profited from conversations with several colleagues and friends, especially Carol J. Clover, John Connelly, E. J. Dionne, Robert Post, and Alan Wolfe. Several sentences are drawn from my "Among the Believers," *Harper's*, November 2004.

1. A convenient point of access to this discussion is E. J. Dionne Jr., Jean Bethke Elshtain, and Kayla M. Drogosz, eds., *One Electorate Under God? A Dialogue on Religion and American Politics* (Washington, DC, 2004).

2. Ray Suarez, *The Holy Vote: The Politics of Faith in America* (New York, 2006), 73–90.

3. Anthony Gottlieb, "Atheists with Attitude," *New Yorker*, May 21, 2007, is one of the more discerning overviews of "the new atheism." Another is David

Aikman, "The Atheist Onslaught," *Implications,* May 25, 2007, available at http://www.ttf.org/index/ journal/detail/the-atheist-onslaught/. The works most at issue are the following: Richard Dawkins, *The God Delusion* (Boston, 2006); Christopher Hitchens, *God Is Not Great* (New York, 2007); Sam Harris, *The End of Faith: Religion, Terror, and the Future of Reason* (New York, 2005); Sam Harris, *Letter to a Christian Nation* (New York, 2006); Daniel Dennett, *Breaking the Spell: Religion as a Natural Phenomenon* (New York, 2006).

4. A widely discussed example is Terry Eagleton's review of Dawkins: "Lunging, Flailing, Mispunching," *London Review of Books,* October 19, 2006.

5. Richard Rorty, "Religion as Conversation-Stopper," *Common Knowledge* (Spring 1994): 1–6.

6. Historians have recently begun to correct this widespread misunderstanding about the history of religion and politics in mid-twentieth-century America. For an example of the new scholarship on "the theology of segregation," see Jane Dailey, "Sex, Segregation, and the Sacred After *Brown,*" *Journal of American History* (June 2004).

7. Gaines M. Foster, *Moral Reconstruction: Christian Lobbyists and the Federal Legislation of Morality, 1865–1920* (Chapel Hill, NC, 2002).

8. Mark Souder, "A Conservative Christian's View on Public Life," in Dionne, Elshtain, and Drogosz, *One Electorate,* 21.

9. John Rawls, "The Idea of Public Reason Revisited," *University of Chicago Law Review* (Summer 1997): 765–807. See also Martha Minow, "Governing Religion," in Dionne, Elshtain, and Drogosz, *One Electorate,* 144–49, and Joshua Cohen's Tanner Lectures as delivered at the University of California, Berkeley, April 2007.

10. Barack Obama, "Call to Renewal," Keynote Address, June 28, 2006, available at Barack Obama: U.S. Senator for Illinois, http://obama.senate.gov/speech/060628-call_to_renewal/. Emphasis added.

11. Ample evidence shows that, as a general rule, the greater the amount of scientifically warranted knowledge people acquire about the world, the less able they are to accept traditional religious beliefs. There are dramatic exceptions to this general rule: I have not the slightest doubt that some of the most learned and wise people in the world retain religious beliefs of one kind or another. For a helpful summary and analysis of the many studies of religious belief by various occupational and educational groups, especially scientists who have been elected to academies, see Benjamin Beit-Hallahmi, "Atheists: A Psychological Profile," in *The Cambridge Companion to Atheism,* ed. Michael Martin (New York, 2006), 300–318.

12. An excellent intellectual history of the debates over slavery is found in Elizabeth Fox-Genovese and Eugene Genovese, *The Mind of the Master Class: History and Faith in the Southern Slaveholder's Worldview* (New York, 2005), esp. 505–27. The Genoveses demonstrate commandingly that the proslavery writers had superior scriptural warrant for their position that slavery was not a sin, but that the abolitionists were on stronger ground in attacking the specifically racial basis for slavery as it existed in the United States in their time.

13. For an account of the writing and contemporary impact of this important work, rarely discussed today, see Kathi Kern, *Mrs. Stanton's Bible* (Ithaca, 2002).

14. See especially Bertrand Russell, *Why I Am Not a Christian* (London, 1927).

15. Samuel Huntington, *Who Are We? The Challenges to America's National Identity* (New York, 2004).

16. See esp. "A Mission to Convert," *New York Review of Books*, January 11, 2007 (directed primarily at Dawkins), and "A Religion for Darwinians?" *New York Review of Books*, August 16, 2007 (contrasting the approach of the new atheists to the more scientifically and philosophically cautious book of Philip Kitcher, *Living with Darwin: Evolution, Design, and the Future of Faith* [New York, 2007]).

17. Jytte Klausen, *The Islamic Challenge: Politics and Religion in Western Europe* (Oxford, 2005).

18. Marilynne Robinson, *Gilead* (New York, 2004).

19. A comment by Congressman Souder can remind us of the dangers in accepting religious justifications on an issue-specific basis. Souder observes that nobody objects to his using Christian values as a basis for his votes on environmental protection and on the protection of women and children from abuse, but suddenly when he wants to "speak out against homosexual marriages, pornography, abortion, gambling, or evolution across species" on the basis of his religious faith, he is criticized for bringing religion into politics; Souder, "Conservative Christian," 21. Surely, Souder is onto something: if secular liberals refrain from criticizing a theological warrant for policies they embrace, must these secular liberals not also accept the legitimacy of a theological warrant for opposition to same-sex marriage and to the teaching of evolution in public schools?

Reinhold Niebuhr and Protestant Liberalism

REINHOLD NIEBUHR made war safe for American Protestants. He performed other historic functions, too, but this one was central to his becoming a national sage in the early 1940s and it is the key to a sound understanding of the roles his ideas later played, and did not play, in the public life of the United States until, and beyond, his death in 1971. Even in the twenty-first century, debates about his legacy focus on war: Niebuhr's "realism" has been invoked in defense of the wars made by President George W. Bush, and with equal fervor against the hubris and utopian innocence alleged to have driven and sustained those same wars.[1]

This epilogue offers an historical perspective on the career of the most acclaimed intellectual within a distinctive American Protestant generation: the generation that brought the tradition of Protestant liberalism to its greatest moments of public authority, and then presided over that tradition's decline in relation to secular dispositions on the one hand and evangelical sensibilities on the other. Niebuhr's career displays vividly the fissures and fusions that constitute much of Protestant liberalism's struggle to define its own relation to the United States and its various component parts. At issue, often, has been to what extent the faithful should make common cause with, or against, people who do not profess Christianity at all, or who profess the wrong kind. Those fissures and fusions have been propelled by many immediate historical conditions, but also by a variety of often conflicting senses of how Protestant Christianity can best accommodate the Enlightenment. Many of Niebuhr's writings are themselves explicit, and extended efforts to achieve this accommodation by properly acting on the worldly issues of the moment. This preoccupation is especially evident in his wartime classic, *The Children of Light and the Children of Darkness: A Vindication of Democracy and a Critique of Its Traditional Defense*, in which he faulted secular political philosophies for lacking "a Christian view of human nature."[2]

War is indeed the place to begin. Nothing about Reinhold Niebuhr is better known than his critique of pacifism, and nothing is more important to an understanding of his place in history. Although the first major installment of this critique—his volume of 1932, *Moral Man and*

Immoral Society—was very much a "thirties book" and justified violence against the capitalist ruling class, what most catapulted Niebuhr onto the national stage was his vindication of war against the Nazis. This cause was enormously more popular than class struggle within the United States. Niebuhr's earlier critiques of religious pacifism did cut a formidable swath through the pulpits and seminaries, to be sure, but he reached a much larger constituency when he called attention to evils in Europe to which the bulk of Americans were oblivious and when, after the outbreak of war in 1939, he advocated intervention. A skilled polemicist, Niebuhr gained credibility as more and more Americans came around to the view of the administration of President Franklin D. Roosevelt that American interests were at stake in the European conflict. The enterprising Niebuhr founded his own journal in 1940 to combat the resiliently pacifist *The Christian Century*. Niebuhr's *Christianity and Crisis* quickly became an extensively read and discussed forum for the ecumenical Protestant elite, but Niebuhr also spoke in national venues, and by the spring of 1941 his high standing was being hailed by *Time*.[3]

After Pearl Harbor, the claim that American interests were at stake was not such a hard sell. But Niebuhr was the most loquacious and effective voice assuring Protestants that their faith was not in conflict with making war against the Axis powers. There was a huge market for this assurance, which Niebuhr and his admirers proclaimed in the name of "Christian Realism." During the 1920s and 1930s church leaders had preached themselves hoarse explaining to the faithful the iniquity of World War I, and upholding as the model for human conduct Mohandas Gandhi's nonviolent campaign for the independence of India. Niebuhr understood that Gandhi's methods, productive as they were proving to be with British imperial authorities, would have very different results if deployed against the *Wehrmacht*. Enabling churchgoers—and other Americans whose Protestant affiliations were only nominal—to be spiritually at peace with war was not a trivial contribution in a society that was overwhelmingly Protestant and that had just given pacifism the most generous hearing it had ever received in the United States.

It is in this decidedly Protestant context that we can understand the great credit Niebuhr is always given for having emphasized humankind's "sinful" nature. The old Christian doctrine of "original sin" was pivotal in Niebuhr's "Christian Realism." The imperfectability of humankind and the inevitability of some evildoing being bound up with virtuous conduct enabled one to recognize that war might be a good thing, sometimes. Only naïve idealists could take "thou shalt not kill" and "turn the other cheek" literally because such thinking innocently presupposed a world in which God's will could be performed without collateral damage. It may seem odd that Niebuhr so often left the impression that only Christians had avoided a crashingly naïve view of life. Indeed, secular thinkers commonly observe that a number of wise heads, including some among the ancient Greeks, have been sensitive to human imperfections and to the deeply paradoxical, tragic, and ironic dimensions of human experience.[4]

Yet the American 1940s in which Niebuhr came to prominence was a time and place in which the mainstream of ecumenical Protestants inherited an emphasis instead on the positive impact Christians could have on the world if they acted on the ethical prescriptions of Jesus of Nazareth. This "Social Gospel" tradition generated a number of initiatives against racism and labor exploitation in America, and against colonialism abroad. Historians can now recognize the significance of these initiatives without gainsaying Niebuhr's complaint that the Protestants who developed them often exaggerated what could be expected from moral suasion absent a more direct engagement with structures of material power. Niebuhr's attacks on his fellow ecumenical Protestants for not attending enough to humankind's evil nature, then, did address genuine issues within his milieu. Although he often presented his arguments as applying to secular thinkers like John Dewey, the gravamen of his critique was against, and was felt most deeply by, his fellow ecumenical Protestants.[5]

Niebuhr won a number of fans among secular intellectuals of the 1940s, some of whom saw exactly what he saw in the Protestant-saturated life of the period and did not like it any better than he did. The secular thinkers drawn to Niebuhr were often reacting also against a Marxism that many had taken seriously until recently, and which they found deficient in the same senses of tragedy, paradox, and irony that Niebuhr's targeted pacifists lacked. This is the phenomenon that philosopher Morton White disparagingly called "Atheists for Niebuhr," referring to figures like Arthur M. Schlesinger Jr. and Perry Miller, who were glad for Niebuhr's "realistic" influence on public affairs without giving any credibility to the less realistic—from an atheist's perspective—God-and-Jesus talk in which Niebuhr's realism was embedded.[6] Yet we today advance our understanding of Niebuhr and his times if we take account of those secular Americans, like White, who were unimpressed by Niebuhr, or vocally negative toward him. The reactions of Niebuhr's secular critics mark out some of the boundaries of Niebuhr's authority, and prefigure some of the dynamics of his later loss of standing in the 1960s and after.

White himself applied to Niebuhr the standards for epistemological integrity and metaphysical coherence that then prevailed among philosophers. It seemed to White that Niebuhr was offering answers to philosophical questions but not supporting them with philosophical arguments. White accused Niebuhr's secular admirers of intellectual dishonesty, accepting Niebuhr's "political agreement with themselves" while refusing to engage with what Niebuhr presented as the theoretical foundation for that agreement. Moreover, White simply could not abide Niebuhr's cardboard-character representations of secularists. "It is almost ridiculous for Niebuhr to present his own version of the Christian view as the only one to navigate between idiotic optimism and equally idiotic pessimism," White ranted against *The Children of Light and the Children of Darkness*, "as if all rationalists and naturalists said that men were gods, while their extreme opponents maintained that they were devils, and only Niebuhr knew the middle way."[7]

White's annoyance was consistent with complaints of several other philosophers. In 1943 Arthur Murphy devoted ten pages of patient, deliberate argumentation to explaining how Niebuhr's *The Nature and Destiny of Man* was devoid of an elementary understanding of how to apply evidence and reasoning. Similar objections were raised throughout the 1940s in the pages of *The Humanist*, the magazine of the organization of secular humanists. The more widely noticed literary quarterly *Partisan Review* attended to Niebuhr in 1943 in its famous symposium on "The Failure of Nerve." There, a number proudly secular writers associated with the anti-Stalinist left, including the aging Dewey himself, registered their dismay at a turn away from reason-justified social betterment to mystic broodings about God, sin, and the complexities of the soul. Niebuhr and the Catholic philosopher Jacques Maritain, then a much-discussed figure in the New York cultural scene, were prominent targets of these complaints. Sidney Hook was especially impatient with Niebuhr, mocking his doctrine of original sin as a pretentious truism and complaining that Niebuhr ignored "an entire tradition of scientific and naturalistic philosophy" that well understood that "man is a limited creature."[8]

Several of the *Partisan Review*'s regular contributors took up these issues again in the 1950 symposium on "Religion and the Intellectuals." This symposium is sometimes described as more moderate in tone than the one of seven years before, partly because Maritain and the Protestant theologian Paul Tillich were both invited to participate, but the huge document amply records the thread of skepticism to which studies of Niebuhr's career sometimes allude but rarely confront. It was not only professional philosophers like White, Murphy, and Hook who spoke up against Niebuhr; in the 1950 symposium writer Isaac Rosenfeld denounced as "crazy" the view he attributed to "Kierkegaard, Berdyaev, Niebuhr, [and] Maritain" that the essence of humanity lies "outside historical time and the world of nature," dependent upon some notion of "the supernatural." And there, too, art historian Meyer Schapiro asked that standard, scholarly criteria for truth be applied to the claims he and his contemporaries were suddenly being asked to look upon with a respectful straight face: "the existence of a supernatural being, the dependence of morality on such a belief, the various absurd stories, miracles and theological doctrines like original sin . . . the immortality of the soul."[9]

Schapiro, like most of the symposiasts, identified Catholic thinkers as the most outrageous violators of rationality. Neither Schapiro nor any of his fellow skeptics defended the more pacifist-centered style of ecumenical Protestantism against which Niebuhr's style of realism had been most immediately directed. The problem for most of this Europe-preoccupied crowd was just the opposite: Niebuhr with his lingering, provincial fantasies about God and Jesus was not remotely realistic enough. The religious idealism of Niebuhr and Maritain was being taken too seriously by too many people beyond the churches—which is what the *Partisan Review* meant by "intellectuals." Writers William Phillips, James T. Farrell, and Dwight Macdonald all defended the Enlightenment against the libels being thrown at it by contemporary religious thinkers. "When the new religionists dismiss secular thinking as 'village atheism,' they are simply standing on its head the history of modern thought," fumed *Partisan* co-editor Phillips, who credited "the secular curiosity, restlessness and skepticism" of modern urban life for having expanded consciousness "against the provincial obstinacy and depressed faith" all too common in villages.[10]

Writing in the same spirit of incredulity, Princeton philosopher Walter Kaufmann confidently wrote Niebuhr out of learned conversation in his popular book of 1958, *A Critique of Religion and Philosophy.* While Niebuhr was "occasionally hailed as America's greatest thinker," Kaufmann scoffed, "he has not made his mark as a scholar," and his crude apologetics assure his eventual oblivion. After several pages finding that Niebuhr could not reason clearly and could not read scripture except as a mirror of his own ideas, Kaufman curtly dismissed him like a failed undergraduate: "So much for Niebuhr," he said, before moving on to what Kauffmann took to be dozens of more worthy objects of critical reflection.[11]

The point is not that Kaufmann was somehow right and Niebuhr somehow wrong, but that Niebuhr generated a persisting series of skeptical, negative reactions from trained philosophers and from others in the world of learning. The secular critique of Niebuhr is largely ignored in the massive literature we now have on Niebuhr and his career. Richard Fox and others have pointed out that Niebuhr operated more as a preacher than as a philosopher, and some have found Niebuhr's philosophical critics obtuse for not understanding this.[12] There is something to this objection. But Niebuhr did not confine his preacherly denunciations to targets within his faith community. Had he done so, he might not have generated the responses he did from secular philosophers and writers. Niebuhr sometimes called himself a "political philosopher" even while attacking the Enlightenment with fairly blunt instruments.[13] Niebuhr undoubtedly "chose off" John Dewey, as boys say on junior high school playgrounds in an idiom appropriate for Niebuhr's legendary pugnacity. When he did that, the seminarian, whether or not he grasped the meaning of what he had done, was asking for it.

Yet more revealing of the boundaries of the world Niebuhr built for himself are cases of nonengagement on the part of secular thinkers working in a mode that is often compared with Niebuhr's own. Hannah Arendt is frequently grouped with Niebuhr as an "Augustinian" thinker. But nowhere in Arendt's writings about political theory is there any reference to Niebuhr. One widely appreciated book devoted almost entirely to the comparison of Niebuhr and Arendt is Charles T. Matthewes's *Evil in the Augustinian Tradition*. But neither Matthewes nor other scholars have found that Arendt paid any attention whatsoever to her apparent co-traveler in the journey through the dark side of human nature. Arendt lived in New York not far from Niebuhr throughout the 1940s, 1950s, and 1960s. If the two ever met it must have been fleeting because the many socially detailed biographies of these great contemporaries do not record any such contact. Even in Arendt's correspondence, Niebuhr is almost never mentioned. She did write to Karl Jaspers in 1961 dismissing Niebuhr for failing to understand a book by Jaspers that Niebuhr had reviewed in the *New York Times Book Review*.[14]

John Rawls is another pertinent example of a potential interlocutor who was aloof from Niebuhr. Rawls's ideas about justice are often analyzed in relation to Niebuhr's. Interest in any possible connection between the two has intensified in recent years after the rediscovery of Rawls's undergraduate thesis, which turns out to be standard issue ecumenical Protestantism for 1943. Rawls did indeed read Niebuhr when an undergraduate. But he seems to have left that interest firmly behind him from the time he renounced the Christian faith in 1945. Neither in his landmark essay of 1958, "Justice as Fairness," nor at any time in his later writing, does Rawls cite Niebuhr. Some scholars argue that the mature Rawls's ideas show the influence of his ecumenical Protestant background, but it was Kant and Wittgenstein, not Niebuhr, whose arguments Rawls engaged conscientiously and rigorously.[15]

The boundaries of Niebuhr's world are illuminated yet more decisively by his own decision early in 1943 to decline President James B. Conant's offer of a special professorship at Harvard University. Conant knew that Niebuhr would not be acceptable to Harvard's increasingly secular Department of Philosophy and would be easily marginalized if housed at that campus's Divinity School, so he offered Niebuhr a unique professorship reporting only to the university's president. It was an extraordinary opportunity for Niebuhr to press further his engagement with the larger intellectual life of the United States, which is exactly what Conant wanted. Conant, as the chairman of President Roosevelt's National Defense Research Committee that was then overseeing the secret project of building the atomic bomb, was aware of Niebuhr's relevance to the war effort. But Niebuhr decided to remain within what he described to one of his closest friends as the security of Union Seminary's "specifically Christian foundation." At Harvard, Niebuhr explained to his theologian friend William Scarlett, he would be "a slightly queer exponent of the Christian faith among (to use Schleiermacher's phrase) 'its cultured despisers.'" At Union, Niebuhr would never be obliged to face C. I. Lewis and W.V.O. Quine in the elevator. Richard Fox writes discerningly that while Niebuhr "had always been willing to address the cultured despisers," he was "not comfortable about living with them," and "never felt he had as much to learn from them as they did from him."[16]

Rawls was a Protestant by birth, as were several of the others I have mentioned here, but Arendt and most of those I have quoted were Jewish. This demographic fact can focus our attention on how deeply Protestant was the cultural milieu in which Niebuhr became a national sage. Even Conant, who had tried to advance Niebuhr's career in the secular world, was himself was a Unitarian. "When you write as a Christian, which Niebuhr did all his life," notes Alan Wolfe, "you are invariably a particularist." Wolfe made this point in the midst of a largely favourable commentary on one of the many recent books celebrating Niebuhr's contributions to American life, John Patrick Diggins's *Why Niebuhr Now?* Diggins, like so many of Niebuhr's admirers, misses the element of Protestant particularism that Wolfe correctly identifies.[17]

Niebuhr was in no way antisemitic. He enjoyed warm and candid friendships with Felix Frankfurter, Will Herberg, and Lionel and Diana Trilling and many other Jewish intellectuals of his time. He was conspicuous among Protestant clergy in supporting Rabbi Stephen Wise's efforts to call early attention to the massive murder of Jews in Hitler's Germany. He took a more favorable view of Zionism than did a number of ecumenical leaders whose close, missionary-related ties to the Arab peoples rendered them ambivalent about the recognition of Israel in 1948. But Niebuhr's ideas fared much better with religious Jews like Herberg than with secular Jews like Arendt and the celebrated New York writers who made lasting marks on American intellectual life in the pages of the *Partisan Review*.[18] By incorporating Judaism into his formulations, Niebuhr gradually and episodically modified his claim that only "a Christian view of human nature" could serve as a viable foundation for democracy. Religious Jews were recognized in the notion of the "Judeo-Christian tradition," popularized by Herberg and Niebuhr. So, too, were Catholics, and Niebuhr was increasingly outspoken from the mid-1940s onward in his appreciation of Catholics, who were still subject to deep suspicion by the majority of Niebuhr's fellow liberal Protestant leaders until the time of Kennedy's election as President in 1960. But as K. Healan Gaston has reminded us, there was no recognized and appreciated place in this conception of the national community for secular Jews and for other agnostics, atheists, and miscellaneous nonbelievers. Hence it was easy for Herberg, claiming to speak on the basis of Niebuhr's insights, to formulate the concept of a "Judeo-Christian America" in more aggressively religious terms, shutting out secularists with a finality that Niebuhr himself did not.[19]

Niebuhr did speak now and then about the virtues of many religions and of the traditions of the Enlightenment, but repeatedly he came back to the "indispensable resources," as he put it in the climactic passages of *The Children of Light and the Children of Darkness,* to be found in "the profundities of the Christian faith." All the world's peoples must eventually be embraced within a single community, he argued there, but "the task of achieving it must be interpreted from the standpoint of a faith" that understands the role of "Divine Power" in bringing that community to completion. Typically, Niebuhr presented a series of quite general virtues as products of Christianity, without explicitly denying the possibility that these virtues might be cultivated and propagated without Christianity. But even in the absence of such a denial, Niebuhr's message was hard to miss. At the end of *The Irony of American History,* the book of 1952 that later figured large in debates over just how "Niebuhrian" were the wars of President George W. Bush, Niebuhr celebrated a series of insights derived from the Christian faith, in the light of which his book had explicitly addressed American national destiny. He listed the following: "a sense of awe before the vastness of the historical drama" of the times, "a sense of modesty" about the nation's capacities, "a sense of contrition about the common human frailties" behind Soviet demonry and American vanity, and "a sense of gratitude for the divine mercies which are promised to those who humble themselves."[20]

Niebuhr's tendencies toward Christian sectarianism were guarded, but they were substantial enough to have two ironic consequences. These tendencies perpetuated an assumption of the essentially Christian character of the American nation that proved indispensable to the later triumphs of the right-wing evangelicals Niebuhr so much disliked. To be sure, any protean thinker with diverse engagements will inspire a large range of uses, some of which may be contrary to original intent. But for many years Niebuhr's constant theme was the inability of any outlook other than what he ascribed to Christianity—broadly understood, embracing Catholicism for sure and, in a fashion, Judaism—to guide American democracy. Very late in life Niebuhr eased away from this emphasis, and like other ecumenical Protestant leaders of the 1960s, acknowledged more forthrightly the civic equality of Muslims, Buddhists, and nonbelievers. Indeed, he was propelled more strongly in that direction by the spectacle of the hated evangelicals proclaiming the idea of a Christian America in an embarrassingly crude fashion. But by perpetuating the old notion of a Christian America, even when revised as a Judeo-Christian America, Niebuhr and his followers endowed this idea with a legitimacy it would not have otherwise carried when it was picked up by evangelicals from the ideological dustbin into which the ecumenical Protestants had finally tossed it.

A second ironic consequence of Niebuhr's tendencies toward Christian sectarianism is their facilitation of a real measure of secularization. Once the idea of a Christian America had been abandoned by ecumenical Protestant leaders in the 1960s, there was less reason to stay with a faith that had been vindicated so extensively on the basis of its efficacy as an instrument of American democracy. By connecting claims for Christianity's unique value to how it could advance this or that worldly enterprise—be it the sustaining of democracy, or the appreciation of mankind's imperfectability, or the making of a just war—Niebuhr and his allies created an outlook that could then ring hollow when it turned out that so many non-Christians proved able to do the same things equally well, if not better. As the society became less thoroughly Christian, there were more opportunities to recognize the parochialism behind Niebuhr's construction of American democracy and of tragic-ironic sensibilities. But that construction entrapped Niebuhr's writings in an epoch of Protestant cultural hegemony. Niebuhr's successors, living in a more diverse America, had little trouble figuring out that the causes and sensibilities Niebuhr cared about could be easily advanced outside the churches. A sense of contrition? A sense of awe? A capacity for humility? All to the good, and no doubt much needed in larger supply in Washington and beyond, but Christian? Even Judeo-Christian? Hence the great antisecularist ended up enabling the secularization of his own progeny.

Both ironies confirm the wisdom of Martin E. Marty's observation of 2005 that "the culture to which Niebuhr spoke is gone." The words are all the more powerful because they come from one of Niebuhr's most devoted, sincere, and sophisticated admirers. Niebuhr "gained a hearing in the last few decades, or minutes, of an era in which there were coherent audiences and readerships for a religious thinker," continued Marty. It was "certainly the last round for a broad mainstream Protestantism," and anything Niebuhr had to say to "Catholics, Jews, and secular folk" came "out of and through that cohort." The same point was made in 2011 by the most persuasive analyst of Niebuhr's contributions to Protestant theology, Gary Dorrien. The Christian Realism led by Niebuhr "worked for a generation that still lived off the memory of a culturally enfranchised Protestantism," but it had "diminishing returns" even while Niebuhr was still alive. "Mainline Protestantism never outgrew its ethnic families of origin; it even failed to replace itself demographically," Dorrien continued, and it failed to show that "the Christian faith" had a distinct meaning that could not be "translated," as so many eventually came to believe, "into secular terms," thus raising the question, "Why bother with Christianity?"[21]

Dorrien was prompted by a concern for the current prospects of Protestant liberalism. This is one of two engagements that were driving most discussions of Niebuhr by the early years of the twenty-first century. The other engagement has been, of course, the decisions made by the American government, especially in relation to war. Were American leaders following or ignoring Niebuhr's "realism," especially his "Augustinian" counsels about humility, restraint, and the inevitable mixture of good and evil? These debates over whether the foreign policies of the administrations of George W. Bush and Barack Obama were carried out in Niebuhr's spirit have gone forward with a minimum of interest in the preoccupation of the other conversation, the seminary-centered discussion of the destiny of ecumenical Protestantism. But even there Niebuhr's war-related writings about political action in a fallen world were what most gave him a claim on continued attention. For ecumenical Protestant leaders Niebuhr was a massive but enigmatic presence whose assistance by long distance the discussants tried earnestly to mobilize as they faced diminishing membership numbers and a formidable evangelical rival.[22] Each of the two conversations look to Niebuhr to inspire solutions to contemporary challenges.

Perhaps Niebuhr can yet provide the desired inspiration. But what he did for his own generation becomes clearer with the passage of time. Niebuhr was an important member of a cohort of ecumenical Protestant leaders that enabled countless American Protestants to engage, explore, and critically assess the diversity of modern American life.[23] But he was also a bit different.

Niebuhr's exceptional energy, intelligence, polemical skills, and range of public engagements made him distinctive within his cohort. Beyond that, and yet more important, were two features that set him apart: (1) his deep and abiding respect for the perceived imperatives of earthly politics, and (2) the intensity of his polemics against secularism. The two may be related. Perhaps the second made it easier to live with the first? He was indeed more worldly, more secular, than most of the ecumenical Protestant leaders of his generation.

Niebuhr's Christian Realism enhanced the ability of his followers to understand the affairs of the world, and to participate fully in them, but it diminished the capacity of his successors to deploy a distinctly religious justification for progressive political action. In *Moral Man and Immoral Society* Niebuhr had warned against evaluating the actions of the armed proletariat according the Sermon on the Mount. So, too, he revealed later, with the actions of the American government and its military. Niebuhr had many disagreements with federal policy, but always on "realistic" grounds, not because a specific deployment of American power was at odds with what Jesus said his followers should be doing, as might have been argued by the social gospellers and pacifists. Dorrien concludes that Niebuhr "never opposed a real American interest in the name of Christian ethics."

Not all ecumenical Protestants followed Niebuhr's lead, to be sure; some continued in the mode of the old social gospellers to castigate racism and imperialism and other social evils as counter to Christian teachings. Many civil rights workers proclaimed that they were acting in keeping with Christian ethics. Niebuhr was generally sympathetic with them, but his "realism" provided very little religious support. By downplaying the role that Christian ethics might play in public affairs, Niebuhr helped to create, Dorrien argues, "the naked public square into which the Christian Right later rushed with the zeal of the old abolitionists and social gospellers."[24] Politically progressive Protestants found themselves in possession of mostly secular principles to justify their opposition to the Religious Right's construction of a Christian America and their alliance with the Republican party from the era of Ronald Reagan onward. Secular argumentation was fine for those who migrated from the churches over into post-Protestant space. And many sons and daughters of the old Protestant Establishment did just that. For them, there was no problem here. But for those like Dorrien who stayed with the churches and tried to challenge the Religious Right's representations of God's commands for government policy on family life, economic regulation, or foreign affairs, there was a void.

Might Niebuhr's worldly construction of Christianity's role in modern American life have reflected a deeper suspicion than he ever acknowledged of the limits of the Christian project's capability for dealing with conditions of modernity? I raise this question not to pretend to know Niebuhr's ultimate intentions, but to make sure we do not miss how consistent Niebuhr's actions would be with such a feeling. Niebuhr made Christianity relevant to educated Americans amid an increasingly secular environment by developing simultaneously two initiatives that perpetuated Christianity's credibility by sharply limiting it.

One initiative was to present the symbolic capital of Christianity in the form of a "Christian view of human nature" articulated in very general terms, congruent with the secular variations found in the contemporary fiction of Robert Penn Warren and James Gould Cozzens. The second initiative was to renounce the policy-specific application of Christian ethics to the perceived imperatives of politics within democratic constitutional orders, including the imperative to be violent. This combination was ideally suited to a society still under Protestant cultural hegemony but surrounded by threats to it. The first initiative kept Christianity in the action at a time when the intellectual elites of the North Atlantic West threatened Christianity with diminished relevance. The second guarded against the investing of the symbolic capital of Christianity in specific, temporal ventures rendered risky by the potential disconnect between the opinions of ancient Mediterranean preachers and an economically complex, urban, highly industrialized, science-intensive civilization. Was it really so obvious, Niebuhr would have had good reason to wonder, just what Jesus of Nazareth's Sermon on the Mount and the Apostle Paul's letters to the Corinthians and to the Romans meant for the political life of Americans in 1940? 1950? 1960?

It was exactly that uncertainty, after all, that had driven *Moral Man and Immoral Society* back in 1932. Might Niebuhr have always retained, at some level of his being, this suspicion that the Christian project could only do so much for humankind? If he did have this feeling, then the initiatives I have identified might be described as strategies. But even if not designed explicitly enough to be properly called strategies, these initiatives could provide a religious cover for such freethinking doubts—provide, that is, a way of holding onto the faith for a while longer, enabling it to do what good it could, but not actually asking it to do very much. But neither of these two initiatives worked quite as well once Protestant cultural hegemony was gone. The importance of being able to label something you valued as "Christian" diminished for multitudes, especially the more highly educated, and the label, once thus devalued, was all the more easily grabbed up and its meaning defined by groups very different from those whose leadership of the nation Niebuhr had taken for granted. But in his generation Niebuhr's initiatives were exceedingly functional. It is tempting to conclude—although this would take us well beyond the evidence contained in his own utterances—that he understood Christianity to have largely exhausted its ability to serve humankind, and that he did what he could to make his ancestral faith serve as a sturdy conduit to a world that would almost certainly be less Christian than the one into which he was born. Perhaps Niebuhr deserves more respect from secularists than he has been awarded?

Whatever else Niebuhr may or may not have been, he was a great reconciler, another in the imposing tradition of Protestant liberalizers—exemplified by William Ellery Channing, Horace Bushnell, and Walter Rauschenbusch—who have drawn selectively from the cultural inventory of Protestant Christianity in order to speak as directly as they thought possible to the challenges of one's historical moment. But Niebuhr's historical moment turned out to be different from each of theirs in the magnitude and authority not only of religion's cultured despisers, but of those who paid Christianity not even the respect of engaged opposition.

No Protestant intellectual of his time was more proud than Reinhold Niebuhr of his worldly wisdom. It was in that pride that he liked to quote Luke 16:8: "The children of this world are in their generation wiser than the children of light."[25] Niebuhr was a child of this world, and of his generation. But the verse appears, perhaps inconveniently, in Jesus's parable of a dishonest steward whose worldly-wise scheming has led biblical scholars to wonder about the meaning of the parable. Jesus appears to be complimenting the steward's worldly prudence in looking after himself, but commentators are at pains to explain away the text's possible implication that Jesus was endorsing the steward's blatant dishonesty.[26] Just how worldly does this scripture authorize godly men and women to be? The ambiguity is a fitting coda for Niebuhr's relation to the religious resources on which he drew, and for his relation to the mix of goods and evils that his generation produced.

Notes

1. Paul Elie, "A Man for All Reasons," *Atlantic* (November 2007) is an intelligent commentary on the often contradictory uses to which Niebuhr's name was put during the wars of President George W. Bush. Later entries in this animated conversation include David Bromwich, "Self-Deceptions of Empire," *London Review of Books* (October 23, 2008); Brian Urquhart, "What You Can Learn from Reinhold Niebuhr," *New York Review of Books* (March 26, 2009), 22–24; and Andrew J. Bacevich, *The Limits of Power: The End of American Exceptionalism* (New York, 2008). Niebuhr's daughter, Elisabeth Sifton, made an important intervention in these debates in an essay review of Bacevich's book, "A Soldier's Case against Empire," *Raritan* (Spring 2009), 1–13, in which she excoriated, in her father's name, the "harsh amoral unilateralism" of the Bush administration, as built upon "the intense, almost insanely irresponsible attacks that the extreme right wing of the Republican Party" had made against a more reasonable and restrained foreign policy (see esp. 9–10).

2. Reinhold Niebuhr, *The Children of Light and the Children of Darkness: A Vindication of Democracy and a Critique of Its Traditional Defense* (New York, 1944), xv.

3. "Sin Rediscovered," *Time* (March 24, 1941).

4. Niebuhr's peculiarity in this respect has been noted by Richard Fox in what remains, after a quarter-century, the best single book on Niebuhr's thought and career; see Richard Fox, *Reinhold Niebuhr: A Biography* (New York, 1985), 166. A decade later Fox brought out a second edition of this book (Ithaca, 1996) with a lengthy "Afterword" responding generously to criticisms of the first edition, most of which had taken exception to Fox's representation of Niebuhr's personality and family life, and to his relative inattention to the writings of Niebuhr's later years.

5. Niebuhr's struggle with his fellow progressive Protestants has been studied by many historians, but the most cogent account remains Donald Meyer,

The Protestant Search for Political Realism, 1919–1941 (Berkeley, 1960; 2nd rev. ed, Middletown, CT, 1988).

6. Morton White, "Epilogue for 1957: Original Sin, Natural Law, and Politics," within White's *Social Thought in America: The Revolt against Formalism* (Boston, 2nd rev. ed., 1957), 257.

7. White, "Epilogue for 1957," 252, 257.

8. Arthur Murphy, "Coming to Grips with *The Nature and Destiny of Man*," *Journal of Philosophy* LX (April 19, 1943), 458–468; Sidney Hook, "The Failure of Nerve," *Partisan Review* X (January–February 1943), 2–23.

9. Isaac Rosenfield, "Religion and the Intellectuals," *Partisan Review* XVII (March 1950), 244; Meyer Schapiro, "Religion and the Intellectuals," *Partisan Review* XVII (April 1950), 335.

10. William Phillips, "Religion and the Intellectuals," *Partisan Review* XVII (May–June 1950), 482–483.

11. Walter Kaufmann, *A Critique of Religion and Philosophy* (New York, 1958), 302.

12. Fox, *Niebuhr*, throughout. The extensive critical commentaries on Niebuhr offered by Murphy and Kaufmann are not mentioned, for example, in three wide-ranging, generally helpful books in which one might expect to find an analysis of them: Charles C. Brown, *Niebuhr and His Age: Reinhold Niebuhr's Prophetic Role in the Twentieth Century* (Philadelphia, 1992); Daniel F. Rice, *Reinhold Niebuhr and His Circle of Influence* (New York, 2013); and Martin Halliwell, *The Constant Dialogue: Reinhold Niebuhr & American Intellectual Culture* (Lanham, MD, 2005).

13. See, for example, Niebuhr's 1959 "New Forward" to *Children of Light*, viii.

14. Charles T. Matthewes, *Evil in the Augustinian Tradition* (New York, 2001). Arendt to Jaspers, February 5, 1961: Niebuhr showed "not the slightest understanding of the book." *Correspondence: Hannah Arendt and Karl Jaspers, 1926–1969* (New York, 1993), 422. I owe my knowledge of this letter to George Cotkin. Arendt did make brief refence to Niebuhr in a 1944 discussion of Waldo Frank's perspective on Jewish history; see the posthumous volume, Hannah Arendt, *The Jewish Writings* (New York, 2008), 226–227. I owe my knowledge of this reference to K. Healan Gaston.

15. For two well-developed examples of the contemporary effort to interpret Rawls's mature ethical theory in relation to his undergraduate engagement with Niebuhr and other theologians, see Eric Gregory, "Before the Original Position: The Neo-Orthodox Theology of the Young John Rawls," *Journal of Religious Ethics* XXXV (2007), 179–206, and David A. Reidy, "Rawls's Religion and Justice as Fairness," *History of Political Thought* XXXI (2010), 309–343. Neither of these scholars, nor any others known to me, have found evidence that Rawls attended to Niebuhr's writings after Rawls abandoned his religious faith as a combat soldier in World War II. For my certainty that Niebuhr is not mentioned in Rawls's adult correspondence and notes now available in the Harvard University Library, I am indebted to Andrius Galisanka.

16. Fox, *Niebuhr*, 211–212.

17. Alan Wolfe, "Religious Realism," *New Republic*, July 27, 2011.

18. Even Martin Halliwell, in the midst of an ambitious and well-documented case for the intimacy and extended character of Niebuhr's interaction with the leading intellectual currents of his generation, comes up against this reality and

observes that "Niebuhr's life at Union Seminary positioned him apart from the *Partisan Review* circle, with Arthur Schlesinger being his closest point of contact." Halliwell, *Constant Dialogue*, 175. Another scholar, more sensitive than Halliwell to the significance of the Jewish-gentile distinction in New York of the 1940s and 1950s, finds only a small place for Niebuhr in the life of the "New York Intellectuals"; see Alexander Bloom, *Prodigal Sons: The New York Intellectuals & Their World* (New York, 1986), esp. 189–190. In Alan Wald's impressively detailed *The New York Intellectuals: The Rise and Decline of the Anti-Stalinist Left from the 1930s to the 1980s* (Chapel Hill, 1987), Niebuhr figures only as a target for Sidney Hook's attacks. Niebuhr did participate in the 1952 *Partisan Review* symposium, "Our Country and Our Culture."

19. See K. Healan Gaston, "The Cold War Romance of Religious Authenticity: Will Herberg, William F. Buckley, Jr., and the Rise of the New Right," *Journal of American History* (March 2013), and K. Healan Gaston, "'A Bad Kind of Magic': The Niebuhr Brothers, 'Utilitarian Christianity,' and the Defense of Democracy," forthcoming.

20. Niebuhr, *Children of Light*, 188–190; Reinhold Niebuhr, *The Irony of American History* (New York, 1952), 174.

21. Martin E. Marty, "Citing Reinhold," *Christian Century* (October 18, 2005), 71; Gary Dorrien, "Christian Realism: Reinhold Niebuhr's Theology, Ethics, and Politics," in Daniel F. Rice, ed., *Reinhold Niebuhr Revisited: Engagements with an American Original* (Grand Rapids, MI, 2009), 36. For Dorrien's persuasive argument that Niebuhr's contributions to theology should be understood as classically liberal rather than as part of the neo-orthodox revolt against liberalism, see Gary Dorrien, *The Making of American Liberal Theology: Idealism, Realism, & Modernity, 1900–1950* (Louisville, 2003), 435–489. Another theologically sophisticated discussion of Niebuhr's ideas is Robin Lovin, *Reinhold Niebuhr and Christian Realism* (New York, 1995).

22. Rice, *Engagements with an American Original*, is a convenient encapsulation of the early-twenty-first-century debate among Niebuhr's ecumenical Protestant heirs about the present state and future of their tradition. The concluding essay by Mark Hulsether, "After Niebuhr" (338–355) is an especially poignant expression of the volume's combination of reverence for Niebuhr and uncertainty about how best to mobilize his contributions.

23. This is one of the chief conclusions of chapter 2 in this volume.

24. Dorrien, "Christian Realism," 36. For a similar argument that Niebuhr's style of realism "actually inhibited the creation of a popular democratic left" by devaluing the religious resources on which such a left might have drawn, see Eugene McCarraher, *Christian Critics: Religion and the Impasse in Modern American Social Thought* (Ithaca, 2000), 64.

25. This quotation serves as the epigraph for *Children of Light*.

26. See, for example, the honest puzzlement over this passage in the standard commentary on Luke written by Niebuhr's generation of American ecumenical Protestant scholars, *The Interpreter's Bible* (New York, 1952), vol. VIII, 282–284.

Index

83 Tennyth &K

116 MacF....
lightmen